THE SONGS OF
SAPA

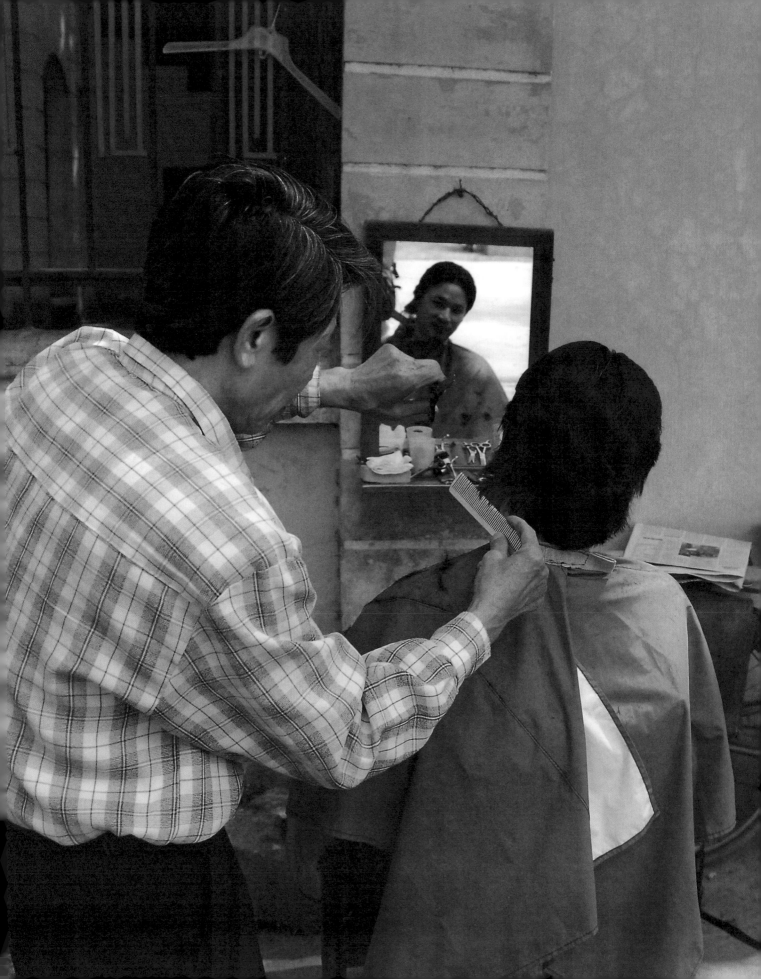

STORIES AND RECIPES FROM VIETNAM

THE SONGS OF SAPA

LUKE NGUYEN
OF RED LANTERN

PHOTOGRAPHY BY ALAN BENSON
AND SUZANNA BOYD

MURDOCH BOOKS

CONTENTS

STORIES AND RECIPES

I have travelled to many countries, but year after year, Vietnam lures me back — I love the vibrant colours of its landscape and the hospitality of its people, and each time I discover more about its diverse regional cuisine.

I begin my journey with my partner Suzanna, in the northern highlands of Sapa. We make our way south to the capital, Hanoi, then further down to the central regions of Hue, Hoi An and the coastal area of Quy Nhon. It is here that Suzanna heads back home, and I continue to travel further south to Saigon, where I meet up with my parents. Together we explore the city where they grew up, visiting family and friends there, as well as in Phan Thiet and the Mekong Delta.

The chapters in this book feature recipes from each region I visited. These are recipes handed down from my mother, father, uncles and aunties; many were inspired from local street food vendors, who cooked for me curbside, or from people who invited me back to their homes for dinner, some even sharing age-old recipes passed down from generation to generation.

Kitchens in Vietnam are small and simple but very efficient. Every kitchen has a wok, a steamer, a stockpot, a mortar and pestle, a heavy cleaver and lots of large soup bowls and clay pots. Before getting started, visit your local Asian market or Chinatown and purchase the basic equipment needed. There, you'll also find all the ingredients that I've used in these recipes.

A typical Vietnamese dinner always consists of many dishes placed in the middle of the table and shared — amazing combinations of meat dishes, seafood dishes, vegetables, salads and simple cleansing soups, all very well balanced and served with jasmine rice.

The recipes in this book are designed to be eaten the Vietnamese way and shared among 4–6 people, with the exception of cakes, desserts and the more substantial broths with noodles, which can be enjoyed as a meal in themselves.

For Vietnamese people, food is our life; we are forever eating, cooking and talking about food. Food is communication — food is culture.

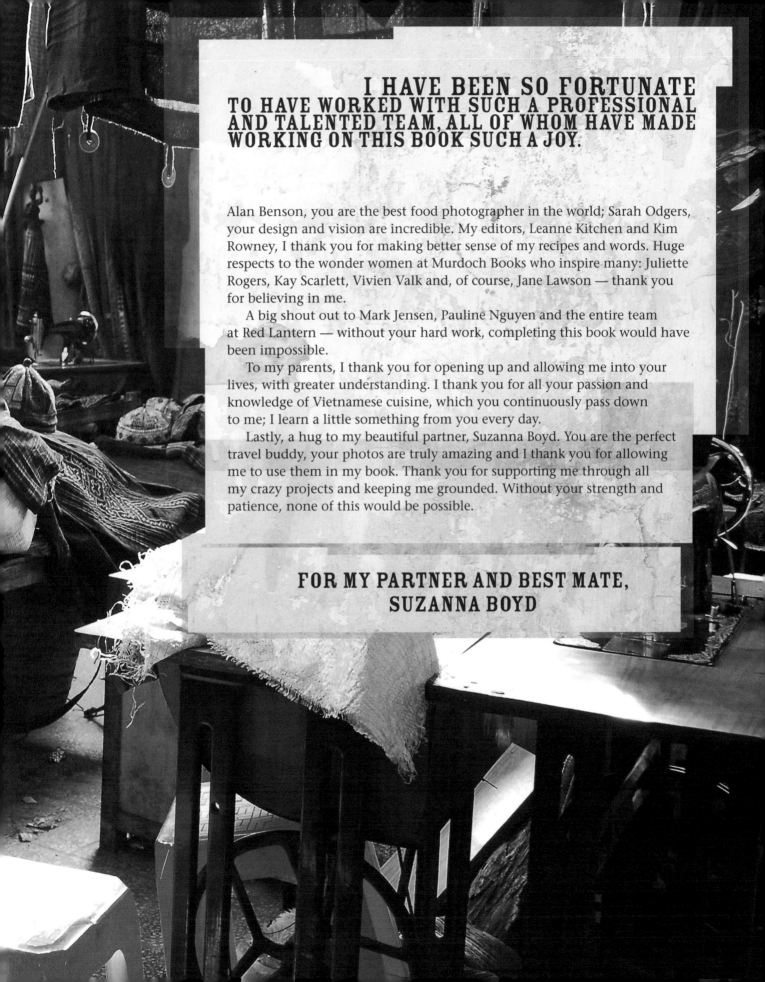

I HAVE BEEN SO FORTUNATE TO HAVE WORKED WITH SUCH A PROFESSIONAL AND TALENTED TEAM, ALL OF WHOM HAVE MADE WORKING ON THIS BOOK SUCH A JOY.

Alan Benson, you are the best food photographer in the world; Sarah Odgers, your design and vision are incredible. My editors, Leanne Kitchen and Kim Rowney, I thank you for making better sense of my recipes and words. Huge respects to the wonder women at Murdoch Books who inspire many: Juliette Rogers, Kay Scarlett, Vivien Valk and, of course, Jane Lawson — thank you for believing in me.

A big shout out to Mark Jensen, Pauline Nguyen and the entire team at Red Lantern — without your hard work, completing this book would have been impossible.

To my parents, I thank you for opening up and allowing me into your lives, with greater understanding. I thank you for all your passion and knowledge of Vietnamese cuisine, which you continuously pass down to me; I learn a little something from you every day.

Lastly, a hug to my beautiful partner, Suzanna Boyd. You are the perfect travel buddy, your photos are truly amazing and I thank you for allowing me to use them in my book. Thank you for supporting me through all my crazy projects and keeping me grounded. Without your strength and patience, none of this would be possible.

FOR MY PARTNER AND BEST MATE, SUZANNA BOYD

THE SONGS OF SAPA

1

MY EYES OPEN TO COMPLETE DARKNESS; SCREECHING VIETNAMESE OPERA IS BLARING FROM THE SPEAKERS ABOVE. WE ARE ON A RICKETY OVERNIGHT TRAIN FROM HANOI TO LAO CAI, BORDERING CHINA, IN NORTHWEST VIETNAM. IT'S DAWN AS THE TRAIN PULLS INTO THE STATION. STILL HALF ASLEEP, SUZANNA AND I SHUFFLE OFF THE TRAIN AND FOLLOW THE CROWD ONTO A MINI VAN, BOUND FOR SAPA.

Fully awake now, I wipe the fogged up window with my sleeve. I can hardly wait for the sun to rise, but for now I allow the mist to tease me with small glimpses of Sapa's breathtaking landscape — sharp, steep mountains painted with luscious green cascading rice terraces, home to the farmers who shepherd their buffaloes across its steep winding roads, and the ethnic hill tribes whose villages dot the valleys and hills. These villages belong to the Hmong and the Dzao, ethnic minorities who live in the verdant valleys and villages that surround Sapa. They have their own native language but most can also speak Vietnamese, French and very good English.

We arrive in town and are instantly mobbed by a large group awaiting our exit from the van, eager to secure our business.

'Hotel sir, madame, hotel cheap, have a look!'

Suze and I split up, we check out a handful of hotels each, break it down to the two we like best, and decide from there. We stay in our room only long enough to dump our backpacks, then head out again, eager to explore Sapa's streets and narrow alleys.

We follow a sign for the market and head down some narrow cobbled stairs. The markets are an essential part of Vietnamese daily life. My mother, along with most women in Vietnam, visit the markets at least once or even twice a day. As do I when I'm in Vietnam.

On my left, an elderly woman sells warm crisp baguettes filled with pâté; pig's ear salad with shaved green papaya, sprinkled with toasted rice powder;

> **❝ I'M SO EXCITED I FEEL LIKE JUMPING UP AND DOWN, BUT I CALM MYSELF, STOP AND SIT DOWN. I CLOSE MY EYES AND LISTEN TO THE SONGS OF THE SAPA MARKET … ❞**

and sizzling rice paper parcels filled with pork, wood ear mushrooms and clear vermicelli noodles. On my right, vendors offer steamed buns, snails dipped in fish sauce, and handmade tofu so freshly pressed there is steam still rising from it. I'm so excited I feel like jumping up and down, but I calm myself, stop and sit down. I close my eyes and listen to the songs of the Sapa market …

Rain splatters on the blue tarpaulin above me, further away ice is bashed with a metal bar into smaller pieces, and cleavers chop through fish onto thick wooden chopping blocks. There is the clatter of bowls, the slurping of slippery noodles and the constant din and loud chatter of people around me.

I open my eyes and my other senses feast on the colourful sights and smells of the market. A lady crouching over a simmering pot of dark master stock removes a wonderfully coloured slow-cooked duck and hooks it up to dry. I see the meat and poultry section, where whole cow heads are on display, their tongues lined up for selection, along with pigs' ears, furry tails and whole legs with hooves intact. The butchers carve the meat with such precision, using the most simple of tools; I envy their skill.

Live chickens are grabbed by their brittle skinny legs and taken out of their tiny cages. A black chicken is being gutted. It is known as 'evil chicken' in Vietnamese because its skin, flesh and bones are jet black. It is said to be better tasting than ordinary chicken, more tender and medicinal. Stalls sag under the weight of mounds of vibrant green herbs, and fruit and vegetables boasting so many colours and varieties, many of them foreign to me; I can't wait to discover them.

I am joined by four hill-tribe people from the Red Dzao, who sit at the table next to me. They are dressed in multiple layers of deep blue, colourful hand-embroidered patterns adorn their sleeves, collar and pants, and a bright red cloth is intricately folded around their heads. They turn my way and greet me with smiles so big and sincere they light up the room, then turn back to their steaming bowls of soup. Weathered faces disappear behind large bowls as they slurp and sip through their noodle soups.

Suze and I move on, squeezing our way through the bustling market. We come across a stall selling tiny live crabs — suddenly a soup comes to mind and I begin to crave *bun rieu*, a crab and tomato soup served with warm vermicelli noodles. I search around, peeking into all the stockpots, hoping to pick up the scent of crab and shrimp paste.

A lady taps me on the shoulder and, to my surprise, asks me in English, 'What are you looking for?'

I reply in Vietnamese, '*Bun rieu* — does anyone make this dish here?' She is equally surprised at my fluent Vietnamese and introduces herself as Dung, and invites Suze and me to take a seat at her stall and drink some hot green tea; it's strong and bitter, just the way I like it. Dung asks us the usual questions: where are we from, where was I born, are we married, do we have kids, but her next question catches me by surprise. 'Have you eaten dog before?'

I shake my head and she tells me that she is shocked by this, especially as I am Vietnamese. She shouts out to the seller near her stall, 'Cut Luke a piece of dog to try.'

I hesitantly wander over to the next stall and the lady there points me towards a large round copper tray; inside it is a dog's head, its mouth wide open with sharp canines showing, and its long, cooked intestines rolled up in a neat spiral. She cuts a piece of intestine for me and stabs it with her sharp blade and directs it towards my mouth. I'm pleasantly surprised as to how aromatic it is, there's hints of cinnamon and mandarin, and its texture is tender, with tiny crunchy bits. I feel quite chuffed with myself; I have finally eaten dog — even though it was only the intestine.

As for my craving for *bun rieu*, Dung offers to prepare the soup for me that evening, ready to eat the next morning for breakfast. In return, Suze and I agree to come to her house when she finishes work to help her with her English lesson. The deal is done and we are to rendezvous at 8 p.m.

It is cold and wet outside the market. The air is covered in such a thick haze that you can barely make out what stands a few metres ahead. Five young children from the Black Hmong tribe appear, selling colourful bracelets for 5,000 Vietnamese dong (VND), about (AUD) 35 cents. As we huddle into our warm jackets, we look at these children wearing short pants and sandals, their face, hands and feet covered in thick dirt. Two girls, about five or six years old, carry small babies more than half their size, strapped to their backs in dusty blankets. This is not an unusual sight — the children of Sapa are expected to look after themselves as well as their younger siblings while their parents tend the rice paddies and make clothes and handicrafts to sell.

I ask them if they have eaten, and they reply softly in Vietnamese, 'We haven't eaten since lunch time yesterday but we aren't hungry.'

With five children in tow, Suze and I head to a nearby soup stand and order three large bowls of *pho*. They demolish the soup within minutes, enjoying every last drop, laughing and giggling after every top up; it is such a joy to watch them. We order another four bowls.

The noodle vendor explains that this is a difficult time for many of the hill tribes. The previous month there had been a cold freeze in Sapa; it fell below zero degrees and there was heavy snowfall. Nearly 4000 buffaloes froze to death, making it difficult for many families to cultivate their rice.

'There is very little rice for them to eat,' she says, then tells us how a young child had died on the back of a scooter, nestled between her mother and father as they rode into town, her parents sadly unaware that the child was not warm enough.

Close to 8 p.m., Suze and I head back down to the market — it's dark and eerily silent, everything is tied down and covered by tarps, the wooden stools and benches are stacked, and rats scurry past our feet — a very different market to that of this morning.

> **" I WONDER THAT IF MY FAMILY HAD NOT ESCAPED THE WAR AND MADE IT TO AUSTRALIA, WHAT WOULD I BE DOING IN VIETNAM. WOULD I BE SELLING NOODLE SOUPS AT THE MARKETS, OR SELLING POSTCARDS ON THE STREETS OR PERHAPS RIDING A CYCLO FOR TOURISTS, OR WOULD I BE BEGGING FOR FOOD AND MONEY LIKE SO MANY IN VIETNAM? "**

Dung arrives with a dimly lit torch and leads us to her house, a five-minute walk away through a maze of narrow cobbled lanes. Her room consists of four grey concrete walls, about 4 metres square. In the room is a bed, a clothes rack and my *bun rieu* soup, simmering on a makeshift coal stove in one corner.

Dung lives in this tiny space with her two sisters. It is where they all sleep, cook and eat. She rolls out a mat for us to sit on.

While Suze and I begin to put sentences together for Dung to practice, Dung asks me question after question, interested in the lives of people from other countries: how many hours do we work a day, how much money do we make, what do our houses look like, how much do they cost, is there any good Vietnamese food where we live?

I wonder that if my family had not escaped the war and made it to Australia, what would I be doing in Vietnam. Would I be selling noodle soups at the markets, or selling postcards on the streets or perhaps riding a cyclo for tourists, or would I be begging for food and money like so many in Vietnam?

We spend the rest of the evening laughing together, bouncing questions off each other, interested in each other's lives and day-to-day routines. Dung tells us she starts work at 5.30 a.m. to set up her soup stall, ready for her first customers, who arrive soon after. By 4 p.m. she has sold out, usually selling about forty bowls of soup and earning about (AUD) $30 for her day's work. She then makes preparations for the next day, firing up her huge stockpot and allowing it to simmer throughout the evening. She's home by 7 p.m. and prepares dinner with her sisters, too exhausted to do much else, and very little time to study English.

The next morning I rise early, keen to get to Dung's stall to try her soup. It tastes wonderful, just like my mother's. I don't need to say anything to Dung; she can see by the look on my face how much I am enjoying it.

Suze and I are taking a short rest in the shade when we notice a young girl standing nearby. She smiles and says hello, and tells us her name is Pen. She is twelve years old and is from the Hmong village in Lao Cai. She speaks a little English, and good Vietnamese. We start to chat and she offers to take us on a walk to see some of the magical gardens of Sapa. As we walk up the steep stairs to the gardens, Pen tells us a story.

'I was at this very place a year ago, when a thirteen-year-old Hmong boy from a nearby village tried to capture me and take me to his home to be his wife. In my culture, this is the way it is done — the men simply grab the girl they want and force them back to the family home. She is introduced to the parents, they all have a happy dinner together and she must spend three days there. If the girl isn't interested in him, she is then free to go home.

'When the boy grabbed my arm, I put up such a fight. I'm too young to get married. He tried to drag me away. I screamed but nobody came to help me; they just stood and watched. So I bit him, then elbowed him in the chest. He fell to the ground, winded, and I ran away.'

Dung has invited Suze, Pen and me to dinner. Keen to get into the kitchen again, I help with the shopping and cooking.

My first choice is to try the wild mushrooms, which are picked from hills high up in the mountains. The mushrooms are strung up by bamboo twine and left to dry, giving them a smoky, earthy flavour. Meanwhile, Suze is eyeing off some wild Sapa honey, so delicately sweet and elegantly fragrant, while Dung buys some buffalo meat, which I had not tried before, along with some fresh bamboo shoots, silken tofu, sweet corn, tomatoes, some live clams and a variety of fresh herbs.

We prepare our meal on the footpath outside Dung's house, with very little light, no chopping board or work bench, simply squatting on the path and cutting everything straight into plastic tubs.

In Dung's room, I light a round block of coal and place it in an earthenware tripod and begin to cook my wok-tossed wild mushrooms with buffalo meat and garlic, while Suze and Pen tear bamboo shoots into fine strips. We cook one dish at a time as Dung only has one pan and one burning coal. Next, a simple corn and tomato stir-fry, then young bamboo shoots tossed with garlic and perilla leaves; silken tofu with a tomato and black pepper sauce; and a delicate clam soup with hints of dill. We sip on chrysanthemum tea, and enjoy the fruits of our labours.

Four people, three different languages, fresh produce and simple, traditional cooking methods — a wonderful dinner that no money can buy.

Later that night we make our way through the streets in the dark, and arrive at a house with a light on. Dung calls out the tofu maker's name, repeating it three times, singing it like a song. A lady opens the door, Dung chats briefly with her, then the lady shakes her head and points further into the darkness. We set off again.

We are wandering around in the dark because I'm keen to meet the man who makes the tofu for the town, and Dung has said she will introduce us … if we can find him.

Dung begins to sing her high-pitched melody again, when into the darkness comes a man with a bright torch, struggling to control his barking dog. He is the tofu maker. He invites us into his home and pours us some tea.

We sit in a musty room where the tofu maker lives with his wife and baby, and his brother. Sandwiched between the two beds and the walls are thirty to forty large green and white dusty mesh sacks filled with soya beans, stacked high to the ceiling.

I explain to him that I had seen his tofu being sold at the markets and that we had just tried some of his delicious tofu for dinner. I tell him how I really wanted to meet him and to learn the process of making fresh tofu.

'Tofu in Australia,' I said, 'is nothing like it is in Vietnam. In Australia, it is made by machines, soaked in water, packed, then sits in refrigerated shelves for a number of days before being consumed.'

He raises his eyebrows. 'In Vietnam, if my tofu arrived at the market and it wasn't piping hot, people simply would not buy it.'

He asks me to come back early the next morning to help him make the tofu. He usually starts work at 1 a.m., but he tells me I can start a bit later — to my relief.

The next morning we make our way back to the tofu maker's house. It's quite early and the air is still crisp when we arrive at his house, perched on top of the hill looking over Cat Cat village, with its spectacular green cascading rice terraces — it feels like we are above the clouds.

The tofu maker is about to begin a new batch. I roll my sleeves up, the humble apprentice, and we begin. First we strain the soya beans, which have been soaking overnight in water. We put them through a rusty crushing machine, which crushes the soya beans, extracting the milk. We repeat the process, then pour the milk into a large stockpot, which comes to the boil over a large coal fire. I cuddle the pot, stirring the silky milk with a monster wooden spoon so the milk doesn't burn, then we strain the milk through a cloth into a big tub. I slowly add some sour soya milk and close the lid, allowing the curdling process to begin. The sour milk is produced by leaving pressed soy liquid unrefrigerated for 24 hours; it works as a natural coagulant, forming curds. We wait ten minutes then add more sour milk, and repeat this process again, the tofu maker tasting the milk each time to decide how much sour milk is needed.

Half an hour later we strain the curdled milk into another tub and the tofu maker works more magic. He places a long cloth over two moulded blocks and transfers the tofu onto the cloth. I can't help but notice how soft and youthful his hands are. He then folds the rest of the cloth over the top, places a heavy block on top and presses down on the tofu with all his weight. The blocks are weighted down, then taken out of the mould. The tofu is carefully unwrapped, cut into lengths and gently stacked onto a round tray, which is then swiftly scootered off to the market for sale, wafts of steam rising from its silky flesh. We continue this process six more times, stopping only when there is no more demand at the market.

For breakfast, he brings us steaming hot mugs of soya bean milk and we eat freshly made, warm silken tofu. I sit in silence, sighing contentedly after every mouthful, looking out of the window into a lush green bamboo forest.

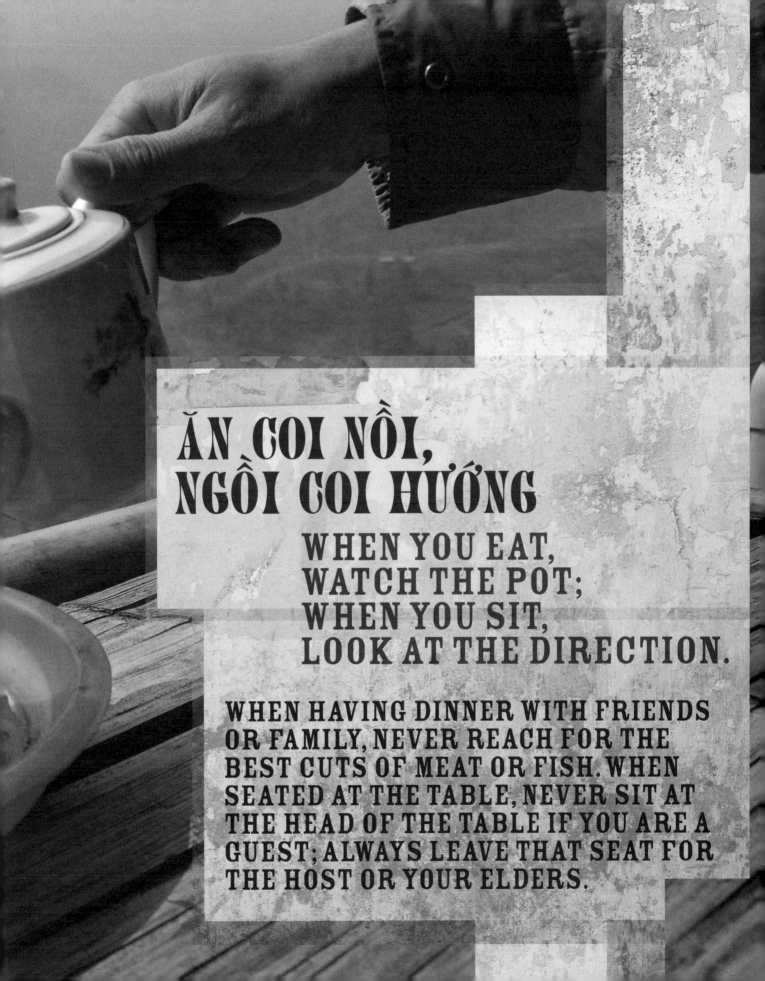

ĂN COI NỒI, NGỒI COI HƯỚNG

WHEN YOU EAT, WATCH THE POT; WHEN YOU SIT, LOOK AT THE DIRECTION.

WHEN HAVING DINNER WITH FRIENDS OR FAMILY, NEVER REACH FOR THE BEST CUTS OF MEAT OR FISH. WHEN SEATED AT THE TABLE, NEVER SIT AT THE HEAD OF THE TABLE IF YOU ARE A GUEST; ALWAYS LEAVE THAT SEAT FOR THE HOST OR YOUR ELDERS.

SILKEN TOFU STEWED WITH SHIITAKE MUSHROOMS
ĐẬU HŨ KHO NẤM

WHEN I THINK OF TOFU I'M REMINDED OF WHEN MY MOTHER WOULD COOK THIS DISH, ON CERTAIN DAYS OF THE LUNAR CALENDAR WHEN WE WERE NOT TO EAT MEAT. NOW I LOOK FORWARD TO IT EVERY MONTH. IF YOU ARE ONE OF THOSE PEOPLE WHO THINK THAT TOFU IS BLAND AND TASTELESS, TRY THIS DISH — IT WILL CONVERT YOU.

250 g (9 oz) silken tofu, drained
vegetable oil, for deep-frying
2 tablespoons sugar
125 ml (4 fl oz/½ cup) light soy sauce
1 teaspoon dark soy sauce
1 tablespoon garlic oil (page 329)
1 tablespoon finely chopped garlic
15 fresh shiitake mushrooms, stems discarded, halved if large
1 bird's eye chilli, sliced, to garnish

Cut the tofu into 3 cm (1¼ inch) cubes and pat dry with paper towel. Pour the oil into a wok or saucepan and heat to 180°C (350°F), or until a cube of bread dropped into the oil browns in 15 seconds. Add the tofu in two batches and deep-fry for about 3 minutes, or until crisp. Remove the tofu with a slotted spoon and drain on paper towel.

In a large bowl, combine the sugar, light and dark soy sauce, garlic oil, half the garlic and ½ teaspoon freshly ground black pepper. Add the shiitake mushrooms and fried tofu and marinate for 15 minutes.

Place all the ingredients in a large saucepan and bring to the boil, then stir gently for 2 minutes. Add 750 ml (26 fl oz/3 cups) of water, bring back to the boil, then reduce the heat and simmer for 15 minutes, or until the liquid has reduced by half. To finish, stir in the remaining garlic and ½ teaspoon freshly ground black pepper. Transfer to a serving bowl, garnish with chilli and serve with jasmine rice.

SERVES 4-6 AS PART OF A SHARED MEAL

PORK SPARERIBS AND PICKLED BAMBOO SOUP
SƯỜN HEO NẤU MĂNG CHUA

BAMBOO IS FOUND IN ABUNDANCE IN VIETNAM. IT IS DISPLAYED AS AN ORNAMENT OR A DECORATIVE PLANT IN HOMES AND GARDENS, IT'S USED AS A BUILDING MATERIAL AND ITS YOUNG SHOOTS ARE USED AS A FOOD SOURCE. IF YOU'RE LUCKY ENOUGH TO FIND FRESH BAMBOO SHOOTS, PEEL OFF THE TOUGH OUTER LAYERS UNTIL YOU ARE LEFT WITH A SOFT INNER CORE. THINLY SLICE AND BOIL IT FOR FIVE MINUTES WITH A TEASPOON OF SUGAR TO ELIMINATE ITS BITTERNESS. IN MOST ASIAN MARKETS, YOU CAN FIND BAMBOO SHOOTS IN TINS OR IN SEALED BAGS SITTING IN WATER. THESE HAVE ALREADY BEEN BOILED, BUT I STILL PARBOIL THEM. THE BAMBOO SHOOTS THAT I USE IN THIS RECIPE HAVE BEEN BOILED BUT THEY'VE ALSO BEEN PICKLED, WHICH BRINGS A SOFT SOUR ELEMENT TO THE DISH.

3 tablespoons fish sauce
300 g (10½ oz) pork spareribs, cut into 2 x 3 cm (¾ x 1¼ inch) pieces
1 teaspoon sugar
450 g (1 lb) pickled (sour) bamboo shoots, washed and drained
2 tablespoons thinly sliced spring onion (scallion)
½ bunch sawtooth herb, leaves sliced
½ bunch rice paddy herb, leaves sliced
1 bird's eye chilli, thinly sliced
fish sauce, for dipping

In a bowl, combine 1 teaspoon salt, ½ teaspoon freshly ground black pepper and 2 tablespoons of the fish sauce. Mix well, then pour over the pork ribs, stirring to coat. Cover and place in the fridge to marinate for 20 minutes.

Put 1.5 litres (52 fl oz/6 cups) of water in a large saucepan and bring to the boil. Add the undrained pork ribs and bring back to the boil, skimming any impurities off the surface, then simmer for 10 minutes. Now stir in the sugar and the remaining fish sauce, then add the bamboo shoots. Return to the boil, then reduce the heat and simmer for a further 15 minutes, or until the pork is tender.

Serve in large soup bowls and garnish with the spring onion, sawtooth herb and rice paddy herb, and sprinkle with a pinch of freshly ground black pepper. Serve with jasmine rice, and a small bowl of sliced chilli and fish sauce for dipping.

SERVES 4-6 AS PART OF A SHARED MEAL

HAIRY MELON WITH DRIED SHRIMP SOUP
CANH BẦU TÔM KHÔ

YOU ARE PROBABLY WONDERING WHAT ON EARTH IS A HAIRY MELON. WELL, THE HAIRY MELON IS IN THE GOURD FAMILY AND IT'S ALSO KNOWN AS A HAIRY GOURD, FUZZY GOURD OR A HAIRY CUCUMBER. IT IS LIGHT GREEN IN COLOUR AND HAS A DOWNY, HAIRY SKIN, WHICH GIVES IT QUITE A FUZZY FEEL. IT HAS A MILDLY SWEET FLAVOUR AND, WHEN COOKED IN SOUP, ITS SOFT TEXTURE MELTS IN YOUR MOUTH. IF YOU CAN'T GET YOUR HANDS ON A HAIRY MELON, YOU CAN SUBSTITUTE IT WITH ZUCCHINI.

Soak the dried shrimp in 125 ml (4 fl oz/$\frac{1}{2}$ cup) of water for 30 minutes. Drain the shrimp, reserving the soaking water. Using a mortar and pestle, pound the shrimp until finely crushed.

Put 1.5 litres (52 fl oz/6 cups) of water and the reserved soaking water in a large saucepan. Add 1 teaspoon salt, $\frac{1}{2}$ teaspoon freshly ground black pepper, the fish sauce and pounded shrimp to the pan. Bring to the boil, skimming any impurities off the surface, then reduce the heat and simmer for 10 minutes. Add the hairy melon, then increase the heat to high and cook for about 10 minutes, or until the melon becomes softened and slightly translucent.

Serve in large soup bowls and garnish with the spring onion and coriander sprigs. Serve with jasmine rice, and a small bowl of sliced chilli and fish sauce for dipping.

SERVES 4-6 AS PART OF A SHARED MEAL

NOTE Vietnamese soups, or broths, are simple to prepare and are usually very light and clear. These soups are not eaten as a meal on their own but are designed to be served with other dishes, to balance out the salty flavours of other foods, and to cleanse the palate.

50 g (1¾ oz/½ cup) dried shrimp
1 tablespoon fish sauce
600 g (1 lb 5 oz) hairy melon, peeled and cut into batons
1 tablespoon sliced spring onion (scallion)
2 coriander (cilantro) sprigs
1 bird's eye chilli, thinly sliced
fish sauce, for dipping

BEEF AND KOHLRABI SALAD
GỎI BÒ SU HÀO

SUZE AND I WERE SITTING AT A STALL IN THE BARBECUE MARKET IN SAPA. WE WERE INVITED BY THE TABLE NEXT TO US TO JOIN THEM; THEY WERE LOCALS FROM HANOI, FEASTING ON TRADITIONAL SAPA DISHES. ONE OF THE DISHES WAS WOK-TOSSED BEEF WITH A STRANGE PALE GREEN VEGETABLE CALLED KOHLRABI. I ASKED ONE OF THE LADIES WHAT THIS SWEET CRUNCHY VEGETABLE WAS. SHE TOOK MY HAND AND WE WENT TO THE MARKETS, WHERE SHE INTRODUCED IT TO ME.

KOHLRABI, MEANING 'CABBAGE TURNIP', IS IN THE SAME FAMILY AS CABBAGE AND BROCCOLI. WHEN I RETURNED TO SYDNEY, I WENT TO THE MARKETS AND FOUND A LOVELY PURPLE VARIETY. I MADE A FEW DISHES WITH IT AND SERVED IT TO MY PARENTS. THEY TOO HAD NEVER EATEN IT, BUT LOVED IT.

In a large bowl, combine the kohlrabi, carrot, vinegar and sugar. Mix well, then cover and place in the fridge to marinate for 1 hour. Remove from the fridge and drain.

Place a frying pan over high heat, add the oil and fry the garlic until fragrant. Add the beef, season with 1/2 teaspoon freshly ground black pepper, and stir-fry for no longer than 3 minutes. Remove the beef from the pan and set aside.

In a serving bowl, combine the kohlrabi, carrot, Vietnamese mint, Asian basil, perilla, fried garlic and beef. Dress with Aunty Nine's salad dressing and garnish with the peanuts and fried shallots.

SERVES 4-6 AS PART OF A SHARED MEAL

500 g (1 lb 2 oz) kohlrabi, peeled and julienned
1 carrot, peeled and julienned
100 ml (3½ fl oz) white vinegar
100 g (3½ oz) caster (superfine) sugar
2 tablespoons vegetable oil
2 garlic cloves, finely chopped
350 g (12 oz) beef eye fillet, trimmed and sliced into strips
1 handful Vietnamese mint leaves
1 handful Asian basil leaves
1 handful perilla leaves
1 tablespoon fried garlic (page 329)
4 tablespoons Aunty Nine's salad dressing (page 330)
2 tablespoons roasted peanuts, chopped (page 328)
2 tablespoons fried red Asian shallots (page 329)

CRISP SILKEN TOFU IN A TOMATO AND BLACK PEPPER SAUCE
TÀU HŨ SỐT CÀ CHUA

IT'S FIVE O'CLOCK AND DUNG HAS SOLD OUT OF NOODLE SOUP AT HER MARKET STALL. WE SIT ON SMALL STOOLS AROUND A HOT PAN SIZZLING WITH PORK FAT, FUELLED BY BURNING COAL. WE THROW SILKEN TOFU INTO THE PAN TO CRISP IT UP. IT LOOKS EXTREMELY HIGH IN SATURATED FAT, BUT IT TASTES SO GOOD.

500 g (1 lb 2 oz) silken tofu, drained
200 ml (7 fl oz) vegetable oil
1 tablespoon finely chopped garlic
1 tablespoon finely chopped red Asian shallots
1 bird's eye chilli, thinly sliced
4 ripe tomatoes, roughly chopped
2 teaspoons sugar
2 tablespoons fish sauce
3 spring onions (scallions), cut into 5 cm (2 inch) lengths
2 coriander (cilantro) sprigs, to garnish

Cut the tofu into 3 cm (1¼ inch) cubes and pat dry with paper towel. Pour the oil into a wok and heat to 180°C (350°F), or until a cube of bread dropped into the oil browns in 15 seconds. Add the tofu in two batches and deep-fry for about 3 minutes, or until crisp. Remove the tofu with a slotted spoon and transfer to paper towel to drain.

Drain off the oil, leaving about 1 tablespoon of oil in the wok. Return the wok to medium heat and add the garlic, shallots and chilli, and stir-fry for 1 minute, or until fragrant. Add the tomatoes, 1/2 teaspoon salt, the sugar and fish sauce, then cook for a further 5 minutes, stirring, until the tomatoes start to soften and break down.

Add 100 ml (3½ fl oz) of water to the wok, bring to the boil, then reduce the heat to a low simmer for 10 minutes. Add the crisp tofu, spring onions and 1 teaspoon freshly ground black pepper, tossing gently to combine, and simmer for no longer than 1 minute, as you want to keep the crisp texture of the tofu. Garnish with coriander sprigs and serve with jasmine rice.

SERVES 4-6 AS PART OF A SHARED MEAL

HMONG CHARGRILLED BLACK CHICKEN
GÀ ÁC NƯỚNG HMONG

BLACK CHICKENS ARE VERY POPULAR IN ASIA, PARTICULARLY IN CHINA AND VIETNAM, WHERE THEY ARE CALLED *GA AC*, MEANING 'EVIL CHICKEN'. THEY ARE INDEED SCARY-LOOKING SCRAWNY THINGS, WITH BLUE-BLACK SKIN, JET BLACK BONES AND FIVE TOES INSTEAD OF FOUR — PURE EVIL! YOU CAN BUY THEM AT YOUR LOCAL CHINATOWN.

WHILE WE WERE AT THE MARKETS WE MET A LADY SELLING WILD SAPA HONEY. SHE POURED SOME INTO A TINY TEACUP FOR US. WE WERE AMAZED AT HOW LIGHT AND DELICATE THE HONEY WAS; I COULD HAVE DRUNK IT STRAIGHT FROM THE BOTTLE. WE BOUGHT TWO BOTTLES AND KEPT THEM IN OUR BAGS, AND DIPPED CRISP BAGUETTES INTO THE HONEY AS A SNACK.

In a large bowl, combine all the ingredients for the marinade. Season with 1 teaspoon each of salt and freshly ground black pepper, and mix together well. Add the chicken, rubbing the marinade over and under its skin. Cover the bowl and place in the fridge to marinate for 2 hours, or overnight for a better flavour.

Heat a barbecue grill to medium–high. Add the chicken and cook for 6 minutes on each side. Once cooked, place the chicken on a cutting board, skin side up, and chop the chicken into a total of eight pieces with a heavy cleaver. Place the chicken on a platter and serve with jasmine rice.

SERVES 4-6 AS PART OF A SHARED MEAL

NOTE This makes enough marinade for two small black chickens or one large ordinary chicken.

1 small black chicken, legs
    separated from the breast

MARINADE
4 red Asian shallots, finely chopped
1 lemongrass stem, white part
    only, finely chopped
3 tablespoons fish sauce
2 teaspoons chilli powder
1 tablespoon toasted sesame
    seeds
4 kaffir lime leaves, thinly sliced
3 tablespoons Sapa honey
    (or regular honey)
50 g (1¾ oz) galangal, peeled
    and pounded to a paste using
    a mortar and pestle

CHARGRILLED GOAT IN WHITE BEAN CURD PASTE
DÊ NƯỚNG CHAO

WHEN MY FAMILY ARRIVED IN AUSTRALIA, WE HAD VERY LITTLE. MY FIRST MEMORIES OF OUR FAMILY MEALS WERE OF STEAMED RICE AND PRESERVED BEAN CURD SERVED WITH CUCUMBER. WE COULDN'T AFFORD MEAT OR SEAFOOD, AND A SMALL JAR OF THIS BEAN CURD WENT A LONG WAY — IT FED THE WHOLE FAMILY FOR WEEKS. PRESERVED BEAN CURD HAS A BIG, BOLD FLAVOUR AND CAN BE USED FOR MARINADES, IN STIR-FRIES WITH GREEN VEGETABLES, OR USED TO MAKE A DIPPING SAUCE.

GOAT MEAT IS WIDELY EATEN IN VIETNAM, AND THERE ARE MANY RESTAURANTS THAT SPECIALISE IN GOAT AND SERVE IT SEVEN DIFFERENT WAYS, 'DE 7 MON'. GOATS ARE PRIZED FOR THEIR TEXTURE, DEEP FLAVOUR AND LITTLE FAT CONTENT. TO FIND GOAT MEAT, GO TO YOUR ASIAN OR HALAL BUTCHER.

50 g (1¾ oz) preserved white bean curd
1 tablespoon sugar
1 tablespoon lemon juice
2 teaspoons hot paprika
3 tablespoons shaoxing rice wine
1 teaspoon sesame oil
2 teaspoons fish sauce
2 teaspoons honey
4 garlic cloves, crushed
1 lemongrass stem, white part only, finely chopped
10 cm (4 inch) piece of ginger, peeled and pounded using a mortar and pestle
2 tablespoons vegetable oil
500 g (1 lb 2 oz) boneless baby goat leg, thinly sliced
200 g (7 oz) okra, trimmed and halved lengthways
250 ml (9 fl oz/1 cup) preserved bean curd dipping sauce (page 332)
baguette, to serve

Soak 12 bamboo skewers in cold water for 30 minutes to prevent them from burning.

In a small bowl, mash the preserved bean curd with a fork, then add the sugar and lemon juice. Mix well to dissolve the sugar, then taste a little to see if there is a good balance of sweet and sour flavours, adding a little extra sugar or lemon juice if necessary. Set aside.

In a large bowl, combine the paprika, rice wine, sesame oil, fish sauce, honey and ½ teaspoon salt. Add the garlic, lemongrass, ginger, vegetable oil and bean curd mixture and stir well to combine. Add the goat meat and stir to coat well in the marinade. Cover the bowl and place in the fridge to marinate for 2 hours.

Thread the goat meat onto the bamboo skewers evenly. Heat a barbecue grill or chargrill pan to high and cook the undrained goat meat skewers for 3 minutes on each side, or until browned and cooked through. Chargrill the okra for 2 minutes on each side. Place the skewers and okra on a serving platter. Dip the goat meat and okra into the preserved bean curd dipping sauce and serve with a crisp, hot baguette.

MAKES 12 SKEWERS

STIR-FRIED GINGER CHICKEN
GÀ XÀO GỪNG

THE CHICKEN THIGH FILLET IS COMMONLY USED IN VIETNAMESE COOKING, AS IT IS INEXPENSIVE AND PERFECT FOR GRILLING OR FRYING — IT ABSORBS FLAVOURS AND REMAINS TENDER AND SUCCULENT THROUGHOUT THE COOKING PROCESS.

In a large bowl, combine the soy sauce, oyster sauce, 2 tablespoons of the fish sauce and 1 tablespoon of the brown sugar. Mix well, then add the chicken. Cover and place in the fridge to marinate for 20 minutes.

In a small bowl, combine 4 tablespoons of water with the remaining fish sauce and brown sugar. Stir to dissolve the sugar, and set aside.

Place a wok on the stove to heat up, then add the oil and ginger and stir-fry over medium heat until fragrant. Turn the heat up high, then add the chicken to the wok, tossing the chicken to seal all sides. Add the water and sugar mixture, stir for 2 minutes, then reduce the heat to medium. Add the garlic, cover the wok, and cook for a further 3 minutes.

Remove the lid and increase the heat to high to reduce the sauce by half, then stir in the sesame oil. Transfer to a serving plate and garnish with coriander and sesame seeds, and serve with jasmine rice.

SERVES 4-6 AS PART OF A SHARED MEAL

¼ teaspoon dark soy sauce

2 teaspoons oyster sauce

4 tablespoons fish sauce

2 tablespoons soft brown sugar

500 g (1 lb 2 oz) boneless, skinless chicken thighs or chicken drumsticks, cut into 2 x 3 cm (¾ x 1¼ inch) pieces

2 tablespoons vegetable oil

10 cm (4 inch) piece of ginger, peeled and julienned

4 garlic cloves, finely chopped

1 teaspoon sesame oil

1 small handful coriander (cilantro) leaves

1 tablespoon toasted sesame seeds

HANOI
ELEGANCE

2

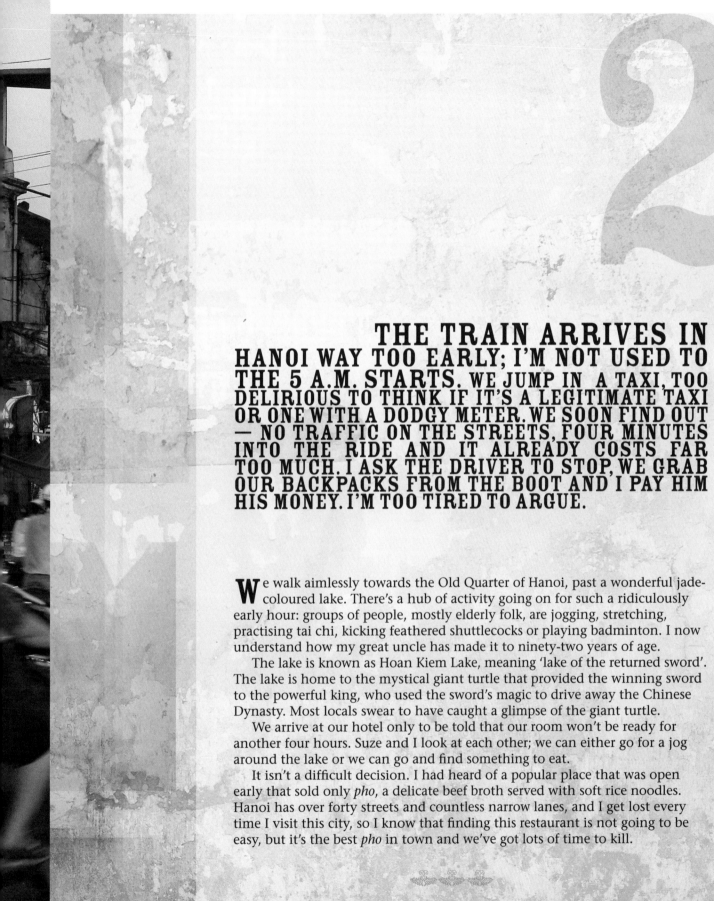

THE TRAIN ARRIVES IN HANOI WAY TOO EARLY; I'M NOT USED TO THE 5 A.M. STARTS. WE JUMP IN A TAXI, TOO DELIRIOUS TO THINK IF IT'S A LEGITIMATE TAXI OR ONE WITH A DODGY METER. WE SOON FIND OUT — NO TRAFFIC ON THE STREETS, FOUR MINUTES INTO THE RIDE AND IT ALREADY COSTS FAR TOO MUCH. I ASK THE DRIVER TO STOP, WE GRAB OUR BACKPACKS FROM THE BOOT AND I PAY HIM HIS MONEY. I'M TOO TIRED TO ARGUE.

We walk aimlessly towards the Old Quarter of Hanoi, past a wonderful jade-coloured lake. There's a hub of activity going on for such a ridiculously early hour: groups of people, mostly elderly folk, are jogging, stretching, practising tai chi, kicking feathered shuttlecocks or playing badminton. I now understand how my great uncle has made it to ninety-two years of age.

The lake is known as Hoan Kiem Lake, meaning 'lake of the returned sword'. The lake is home to the mystical giant turtle that provided the winning sword to the powerful king, who used the sword's magic to drive away the Chinese Dynasty. Most locals swear to have caught a glimpse of the giant turtle.

We arrive at our hotel only to be told that our room won't be ready for another four hours. Suze and I look at each other; we can either go for a jog around the lake or we can go and find something to eat.

It isn't a difficult decision. I had heard of a popular place that was open early that sold only *pho*, a delicate beef broth served with soft rice noodles. Hanoi has over forty streets and countless narrow lanes, and I get lost every time I visit this city, so I know that finding this restaurant is not going to be easy, but it's the best *pho* in town and we've got lots of time to kill.

Forty-five minutes later we finally find the right street and, judging by the crowd, it isn't hard to see which restaurant it is. A husband and wife team are working with their two young boys. They have a noodle stand towards the front of the shop, and beside them sits a simmering stockpot, with chunks of onion and garlic floating on top, fragrant with ginger and cassia bark. We join the long queue curling out of the restaurant doors.

I feel nervous about ordering. I know that when I order I have to be brisk, I have to know exactly what I want and I probably need to have the exact amount of money too. I notice an oily handwritten sign with the prices on it: *pho* with brisket and raw sirloin, VND 30,000 (AUD $2.50).

66 WITH HER HEAD DOWN, SHE RAISES ONLY THE BALLS OF HER EYES AT ME, CLEARLY ASKING, 'ARE YOU GOING TO ORDER OR JUST STAND THERE?' I QUICKLY ORDER TWO BOWLS OF SOUP AND GIVE HER MY MONEY. THERE IS NO PLEASE OR THANK YOU, AND DEFINITELY NO SMILE. 99

I wait in line; I'm pushed and shoved. I extend my elbows out and gradually muscle my way to the front — I'm in the midst of a *pho* frenzy. The wife stands on the left side of the noodle stand, holding a rusted cleaver, skilfully slicing through the juicy brisket. With her head down, she raises only the balls of her eyes at me, clearly asking, 'Are you going to order or just stand there?' I quickly order two bowls of soup and give her my money. There is no please or thank you, and definitely no smile.

Her son throws a handful of rice noodles into each bowl, lays cooked brisket and raw sirloin slices on top, then passes the bowls to his father, who pours a giant ladle of steaming broth into the bowls, filling them to the rim. He sprinkles spring onion over the top and hands them to me, with a jerk of his head to his left, meaning, 'Move on!'

We secure a spot at a low wooden communal table, dressed only with plates of fresh chilli and lime. There's no chilli paste, no hoisin sauce, no fish sauce, no sugar, no bean sprouts, no basil or sawtooth herb — no accompaniments — just a clean bowl of fragrant beef broth, uncomplicated and delicious.

My family in Saigon tell me that food in Hanoi is bland, tasteless and boring, whereas food in Saigon is much more exciting, creative and flavoursome. Locals in Hanoi tend to differ, saying that food in Saigon is way too complex and uses far too much sugar, the flavours being too sweet, too spicy and too bold for their palates. I have learned to appreciate the subtlety of Hanoi food; it is delicate, simple and clean, and allows the natural flavours of the produce and the freshness of the ingredients to really shine in the dish. But I am yet to convince my family in Saigon on this theory.

As we finish our *pho*, son number two collects our bowls. We quickly leave, freeing up our chairs for the next customers, and make our way to the closest

coffee stand. We come across some red plastic tables and chairs lined up against a textured bright green wall — a kerbside café with character. We order *cafe sua chua*, coffee with Vietnamese yoghurt and ice, a drink that can only be found in Hanoi. Across the road there are several street stalls serving *nem*, a Hanoi-style *cha gio* (as we know it in the south) — crisp parcels filled with glass noodles, wood ear mushrooms, crab and pork. Others sell *banh cay*, a spicy cassava snack, served in folded newspaper. A *bun cha* lady cooks her round pork patties on a small grill, heated by only a handful of hot coal. She waves a bamboo fan over the coals to turn up the heat.

Gangs of riders on scooters pull over, opting either to sit on tiny stools to eat or simply squat on the side of the street. This is one of the things that I love about Vietnam: on every street corner there is food and at every street stall there are locals snacking, at all times of the day.

Suddenly there is a loud scream and all the street-stall holders frantically grab their tables, chairs and cooking equipment. As they try to get away, they are chased by police, who confiscate anything they can get their hands on, throwing it in the back of the police truck. Some of the ladies cry, stubbornly stamping their feet, waving their arms, arguing and pleading with the officers. 'We're only trying to earn a living here, we're not hurting anyone, we're only selling food! How can we survive when you keep taking our livelihood away? How are we going to feed our families?'

The officers ignore them, yanking equipment out of their hands, yelling back, 'How many times have we come around and taken everything, given you fines and told you that you can't do business here. But you don't listen; as soon as we leave you come back again!'

The coffee lady explains to us that it's against the law for the stalls to operate on the street. You either have to have a permit or you need your own shop front; you can sell goods in your home if you like, but not on the streets. I find it hard to comprehend; there are street stalls everywhere, and each and every one of them has to keep an eye out for police every minute of the day. This explains why all these stalls are either on wheels, balanced on bamboo poles or have light equipment that can be easily folded up and transported in a flash.

We drink our very strong coffee and decide to book a trip to Ha Long Bay. As we walk through the city we take note of its charms and of the strong influence that the French have had here — the bakeries, pâtisseries, and the architecture of its hotels, cafés and restaurants. We walk past men wearing berets, stroking their long grey beards, speaking French to each other.

We buy our tickets to Ha Long in the travel agency. A young lady there notices me booking my ticket in Vietnamese, and asks me in broken English if I could help her buy a return bus ticket to Hue. I'm surprised to hear that she can't speak Vietnamese as she looks like a local. She tells us she is from France and that her name is Mai.

MAI'S STORY

'I was born in Hue in central Vietnam. I have three brothers: two are older and one younger. When I was five years old, my parents took me to the local monastery and left me there.

'I haven't seen my parents or my brothers since that day. I'm not sure why I was given away; maybe they just couldn't afford to raise me or maybe it was because I was a girl.

'Two years later a French couple came to visit the monastery. I met them briefly, then months later they adopted me and took me to France. I now have an older sister and a younger brother, whom I love dearly. Each year my adopted parents send money to the monastery to give to my family in Hue. They don't have to, of course, they just want to.

'When I turned eighteen, I felt it was time to get in contact with my biological parents and learn more about my heritage — I feel I am 100 per cent French and not Vietnamese in the slightest, but I was curious to meet them. I found an interpreter and called my family in Hue. They were all well, but I learned that the money sent to the monastery had never made it to my family, not one single payment.

'So I'm in Vietnam to see them for the first time since I was a child. I have no memory of Vietnam, my family in Hue or even the monastery. I don't remember a single thing, and being in Vietnam hasn't triggered any memories yet. Maybe I've subconsciously blocked all of it out of my mind. I'm hoping that meeting my family will allow my emotions and memories to come back, and I want to see that my family are healthy and not in need for anything.'

I was intrigued and moved by Mai's story, and I began to think about my own family and my own identity. I wasn't born in Vietnam, but in Thailand, after my parents escaped Vietnam by boat. I've lived in Australia practically all my life, but I speak fluent Vietnamese and have such a strong attachment to Vietnam, its people, its cuisine and culture.

I can really see how growing up in Cabramatta and living among the largest Vietnamese community in Australia was quite a unique experience. For my parents, I guess it was almost like living in Saigon. As a child, I would receive heavy knocks to the head from my father every time I spoke English to my siblings. 'Speak Vietnamese! You are Vietnamese! In this house you speak ONLY Vietnamese!'

It is only now as an adult that I can appreciate my father's strict ways. I can communicate with the locals when I travel in Vietnam, and it is such a unique experience to be able to talk freely with them and hear their stories.

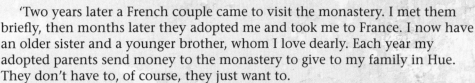

A group of funky Japanese travellers sitting at the restaurant table next to me offer me a container of what looks like slices of roasted pork.

'Woof, woof,' they say, cheeky grins on their faces. The skin looks crisp and thin, with no fat. I take a bite and enjoy every crunch, its texture, its smoky flavour and tenderness; its meat is superior even to that of suckling pig. Delighted that I love it so much, they take a photo with me, then give me the whole container as a gift.

Dog meat is a speciality of Hanoi. Dog restaurants are everywhere in the city, and, like goat meat, dog meat can be prepared in seven different ways. Locals started to eat dog when they had nothing else to eat during the many years of war.

Since then, eating dog has become quite popular and is believed to make you strong and bring you good luck. But it is not available on the first three days of the lunar calendar, for eating dog on these days will bring you bad luck. It's an expensive meat, so don't worry that you'll be served dog meat if you order a pork dish.

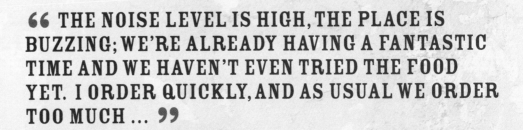

" THE NOISE LEVEL IS HIGH, THE PLACE IS BUZZING; WE'RE ALREADY HAVING A FANTASTIC TIME AND WE HAVEN'T EVEN TRIED THE FOOD YET. I ORDER QUICKLY, AND AS USUAL WE ORDER TOO MUCH ... "

That evening, our search to find some of Hanoi's culinary specialities ended in a place called 'Quan An Ngon', a restaurant that offers all of Hanoi's regional dishes, under the one roof. A brilliant concept, this takes the best of Hanoi's street-food vendors and places them in a beautiful courtyard setting. Each cooks their own specialities at their own stations, for the one restaurant, and the dishes are all offered on the one menu.

We arrive at the restaurant at 6 p.m., but already there is a long wait. The restaurant is set in a two-story French colonial building with balconies on all sides, and the courtyard eating area is shaded by beautiful old trees.

Around the perimeter of the courtyard are individual cooking stations, each with ladies cooking their own Hanoi speciality. The energy of the place is contagious. Mists of water spray out from fans above, keeping us cool, while smoke from the grills fills the air. The noise level is high, the place is buzzing; we're already having a fantastic time and we haven't even tried the food yet.

I order quickly, and as usual we order too much — *banh tom* (fried prawn cakes), *bun thang* (chicken and egg vermicelli soup), *mien cua* (mud crab broth), *chim cut chien* (crisp baby quail), *muc nuong* (chargrilled squid), *goi ngo sen* (lotus root salad) — yet we still find room to finish with *che dau van* (sweet haricot pudding). It was a perfect introduction to regional Hanoi cuisine and a very memorable experience.

A new day and with it a new culinary challenge: today we want to find the city's best *banh cuon nong*, steamed rice noodle sheets rolled and filled with pork and wood ear mushrooms.

A tiny shop not far from the lake begins its early morning trade. Today the young daughter is heading the pots as her mother mixes the batter. The girl sits on an ankle-high plastic stool in front of a large steaming pot of water, with muslin cloth tightened across the top, and tied around the pot. Beside her sits a red bucket filled with a runny batter of rice flour and water. She dunks a bamboo ladle into the bucket and pours the batter onto the cloth over the steaming pot. I watch her graceful movements; each sheet is made to order, and you can see by her speed and accuracy that she has been doing this for many years.

It's only 6.30 a.m. and already the place is full. I ask her how many buckets of batter she goes through each day.

'I have no idea, I start at 6 a.m. and finish at 9 p.m., and my mum just keeps making more batter until we close. We never keep count of how many serves or buckets we go through. We do this every day of the week.'

She uses a long flat wooden stick to delicately lift the thin steamed sheet of rice noodle onto an oiled tray, then spreads a handful of pork and mushroom filling over the rice noodle sheet, and rolls it up. Fresh mint is scattered over the soft white noodles, along with slices of pork terrine. It is then dipped in a warm, sweet fish sauce. This was to become one of Suze's favourite Vietnamese dishes — it's so light, fresh and textural.

After a four-hour drive, we arrive at Ha Long City. The city itself looks more like an industrial, commercial town with tall buildings and tasteless hotels — it's Ha Long Bay that all the tourists want to see.

We step out of the bus and are ushered onto our wooden junk, a replica of junks that used to sail between Singapore and China hundreds of years ago, with wooden carvings of dragons stretching down the handrails, antique furniture throughout the cabins, each with a window that opens out onto a balcony. There are more than 300 boats and junks that cruise Ha Long Bay each day, and more than 2 million people visit every year.

As our junk sets sail, we escape from the others to a quiet spot on the sundeck, with a '333' beer in hand. We watch as other junks laden with tourists sail off; one by one they vanish into the mist until we find ourselves alone, lost in the mystical bay of turquoise waters and spectacular limestone karsts, carpeted in trees. My mind begins to drift and images of old Vietnamese folktales fill my imagination — powerful dragons fly past, perching themselves on top of the limestone formations, firing jewels of jade from their mouths, protecting this beautiful bay from evil.

My reverie is interrupted by the sight of a small floating fishing village. I race downstairs to take a closer look. I yell out, 'xin chao', hello, to a lady and her young boy, who wave back and ask if I want to buy some live seafood. They both get into their canoe and row towards me. 'Climb down, we'll take you to our home,' they say. I ask the junk to stop, then I carefully manoeuvre my way into the canoe. The boy, no more than five years old, sits in between his mother's legs and rows us towards his village.

There are several homes, made from bamboo and wood, most of them painted pastel green, tied and balanced on empty floating blue plastic barrels. Each has a TV aerial and a small area out front, with just enough space to hang a hammock. All the homes have enclosed areas beside or underneath where the live seafood is kept, which can be fished out as needed, weighed and sold. The skipper from the junk calls out, 'Choose what you want and we'll cook it for you.' I pick out a cuttlefish, some prawns, a whole fish and some mussels.

What a place to live, so quiet and tranquil. I'm curious about their lifestyle and ask the woman how she fills her day.

'My husband leaves on his fishing boat in the early morning and is gone until late afternoon,' she says. 'I feed the fish and my dog, then take my son to his floating school. I come back and sell our catch to other floating villagers or to tourist boats like yours. When my husband returns home, I prepare dinner, then I might go next door to the café and sing karaoke.'

We chat some more while she rows me back to the junk. I sit, happily clutching my bag of fresh seafood, wondering how we'll cook it — perhaps chargrilled, with a dipping sauce of sea salt, pepper, chilli and lime?

SPICY CASSAVA BITES
BÁNH CAY

LOST IN ONE OF THE MANY NARROW STREETS OF HANOI, I CAME ACROSS AN ELDERLY LADY
DEEP-FRYING THESE SPICY CASSAVA BITES IN AN OLD WOK, WHICH SHE THEN SERVED IN
HAND-FOLDED CONES OF NEWSPAPER. I HADN'T SEEN THESE SNACKS SINCE MY VERY FIRST VISIT.
I ASKED HER HOW THEY WERE MADE. SHE POINTED ME UP THE STAIRS AND TOLD ME TO GO UP AND HAVE A
LOOK. I WALKED UP THE CREAKY WOODEN STAIRS TO HER LIVING ROOM, WHERE HER SON WAS PREPARING
TRAY UPON TRAY OF THEM. HE WELCOMED ME IN AND WE MADE THE NEXT BATCH TOGETHER.

FRESH CASSAVA IS AVAILABLE IN MOST ASIAN MARKETS. IF IT IS OUT OF SEASON, BUY FROZEN CASSAVA,
WHICH WILL HAVE BEEN ALREADY PEELED.

1 kg (2 lb 4 oz) small fresh cassava,
    or use frozen
2 teaspoons ground turmeric,
    dissolved in 1 tablespoon
    of hot water
2 bird's eye chillies, finely chopped
1 tablespoon chilli flakes
100 g (3½ oz/⅔ cup) plain
    (all-purpose) flour
4 spring onions (scallions), sliced
4 tablespoons coconut milk
1 tablespoon sugar
vegetable oil, for deep-frying
chilli sauce, for dipping

Peel the cassava and soak it in water for 2 hours. Wash again and dry with
paper towel. Grate the cassava into a bowl using a fine cheese grater. If
using frozen cassava, the skin has already been removed, so finely grate
it into a bowl. Transfer the grated cassava to a piece of muslin, wrap it up
to enclose the cassava, and squeeze out the liquid.

Transfer the cassava to a bowl. Now add the turmeric and water, chilli,
chilli flakes, flour, spring onions, coconut milk, sugar and 1 teaspoon each
of salt and freshly ground black pepper. Mix well, then set aside.

Pour the oil into a wok and heat to 180°C (350°F), or until a cube of
bread dropped into the oil browns in 15 seconds. Take a heaped teaspoon
of the cassava mixture and use another teaspoon to shape the mixture into
quenelles (small oval-shaped mounds). Working in batches, carefully drop
them into the hot oil and deep-fry for 5 minutes, or until light brown.
Scoop out the cassava bites with a slotted spoon and place on paper towel
to drain. Serve as a light snack with the chilli sauce.

MAKES ABOUT 50

HANOI BEEF NOODLE SOUP
PHỞ BÒ HÀ NỘI

IN MY PREVIOUS COOKBOOK, *SECRETS OF THE RED LANTERN*, I SHARED A *PHO* RECIPE FROM SAIGON, WHICH WAS PASSED DOWN THROUGH THE NGUYEN FAMILY. THIS RECIPE, HOWEVER, STAYS TRUE TO THE HANOIAN STYLE: SIMPLE, CLEAN AND UNCOMPLICATED. I USE OXTAIL HERE AS I FIND IT RELEASES DEEPER FLAVOURS THAN THE ORDINARY SHIN BONE, AND IT TENDS TO BE MORE SUITABLE FOR SLOW COOKING IN STOCKS. I ALSO USE CASSIA BARK. IT'S IN THE SAME FAMILY AS CINNAMON AND IS SMALLER IN SIZE BUT GIVES OUT A MORE INTENSE FLAVOUR, WITH ADDED HEAT.

THIS RECIPE SERVES EIGHT, BUT YOU CAN PORTION THE STOCK INTO SEVERAL CONTAINERS AND FREEZE THEM FOR UP TO ONE MONTH. I HIGHLY RECOMMEND HAVING A BOWL OF *PHO* FOR BREAKFAST.

In a large pot, submerge the oxtail in cold water, add 3 tablespoons of the salt and set aside to soak for 1 hour, then drain.

To make the spice pouch, dry-roast each ingredient separately in a frying pan over medium heat until fragrant. Cool, then coarsely grind using a mortar and pestle or small spice grinder. Wrap the ground spices in a piece of muslin and tie up tightly in a knot. Set aside.

Heat a barbecue grill or chargrill pan to medium–high and cook the unpeeled garlic bulb, onions and ginger for 15–20 minutes, turning them, until all sides are blackened. When cool enough to handle, peel the blackened skins and discard them, then roughly chop. By chargrilling them first, the garlic, onion and ginger become sweet and fragrant, releasing more flavour into the stock.

Put the oxtail, brisket and 6 litres (200 fl oz/24 cups) of cold water in a stockpot and bring to the boil. While the stock is boiling, constantly skim any impurities off the surface for 15 minutes (this will ensure a clean, clear broth), then reduce the heat to a low simmer. Add the fish sauce, remaining 1 tablespoon of salt, the rock sugar, chopped garlic, onion and ginger, and the spice pouch. Cover and simmer for 3 hours, or until the stock has reduced to almost half.

Strain the stock through a piece of muslin. Remove the brisket, set aside to cool, then thinly slice.

Blanch each 200 g (7 oz) portion of rice noodles in boiling water for 20 seconds. Drain, then transfer the noodles to a large soup bowl. Repeat for the remaining portions. Place three or four slices of brisket on top of the noodles, followed by three or four pieces of raw sirloin. Pour over the hot stock to cover the noodles and beef. Garnish each bowl of soup with some spring onion, a pinch of freshly ground black pepper and a coriander sprig. At the table, add sliced chilli and a squeeze of lime.

SERVES 8

2 kg (4 lb 8 oz) oxtail (ask your butcher to chop it into 3 cm/ 1¼ inch pieces)
4 tablespoons salt
1 unpeeled garlic bulb
4 large unpeeled onions
150 g (5½ oz) unpeeled ginger
2 kg (4 lb 8 oz) beef brisket
185 ml (6 fl oz/¾ cup) fish sauce
80 g (2¾ oz) rock sugar
1.6 kg (3 lb 8 oz) fresh rice noodles (about 200 g/7 oz per person)
400 g (14 oz) beef sirloin, trimmed and thinly sliced
4 spring onions (scallions), sliced
coriander (cilantro) sprigs, to garnish
2 bird's eye chillies, sliced
1 lime, cut into wedges

SPICE POUCH
8 whole cloves
5 whole star anise
2 cassia bark, about 10 cm (4 inch) in length
1 tablespoon black peppercorns

BEEF AND AMARANTH STEM SOUP
CANH RAU DỀN NẤU THỊT BÒ

IF YOU WANT TO FIND AMARANTH STEMS AT YOUR LOCAL MARKET, YOU SHOULD KNOW THAT THEY ARE ALSO KNOWN AS CHINESE SPINACH, AFRICAN SPINACH OR INDIAN SPINACH — THE VIETNAMESE DON'T CLAIM IT TO BE THEIRS. THERE ARE MANY VARIETIES OF AMARANTH, BUT GO FOR THE THICK-STEMMED ONES WITH RED AND GREEN LEAVES. THE STEMS TASTE SIMILAR TO ARTICHOKE, WHILE THE LEAVES TASTE LIKE SPINACH.

350 g (12 oz) beef eye fillet, trimmed and thinly sliced
2 tablespoons vegetable oil
2 garlic cloves, finely chopped
2 tablespoons fish sauce
1 teaspoon sugar
100 g (3½ oz) silken tofu, cut into 1 cm (½ inch) cubes
1 bunch amaranth, washed and torn into 4 cm (1½ inch) pieces
2 tablespoons sliced spring onion (scallion), white part only
1 small handful coriander (cilantro) leaves
1 bird's eye chilli, thinly sliced
fish sauce, for dipping

Season the beef with ½ teaspoon each of salt and freshly ground black pepper. Heat the oil in a heavy-based frying pan over medium heat, add the garlic and lightly brown, then add the beef and stir-fry for 3 minutes. Remove the beef from the pan and set it aside.

Fill a large saucepan with 1.5 litres (52 fl oz/6 cups) of water and bring to the boil. Add the fish sauce, sugar and tofu and simmer for 5 minutes. Now add the beef and amaranth, and return to the boil. Remove from the heat and transfer to large soup bowls.

Garnish with the spring onion and coriander. Serve with jasmine rice, and a small bowl of sliced chilli and fish sauce for dipping.

SERVES 4-6 AS PART OF A SHARED MEAL

CARAMELISED ROASTED PORK BELLY WITH PICKLED MUSTARD GREENS
HEO QUAY KHO DƯA CẢI

WHENEVER I MAKE ROAST PORK I ALWAYS MAKE MORE THAN ENOUGH SO I CAN THEN USE IT THE NEXT DAY TO MAKE THIS DISH. I LEARNT THIS FROM MY GRANDMOTHER, WHO NEVER WASTED A THING. IF YOU DON'T HAVE ANY LEFTOVER PORK AND YOU DON'T FEEL LIKE MAKING IT YOURSELF, YOU CAN BUY PIECES OF ROAST PORK FROM ASIAN BARBECUE SHOPS. FOR THE PICKLED MUSTARD GREENS, TURN TO PAGE 335 FOR A RECIPE OR YOU CAN FIND THESE READY-MADE IN ASIAN MARKETS.

Wash the mustard greens well, drain and then slice into 1 cm (½ inch) pieces. Set aside.

Heat a large saucepan over medium heat, add the oil and stir-fry the mustard greens and spring onions with the sugar for 3 minutes. Add the pork, fish sauce, soy sauce, 1 teaspoon freshly ground black pepper and 250 ml (9 fl oz/1 cup) of water. Bring to the boil, then reduce the heat to low and simmer for 30 minutes, or until the sauce thickens. Garnish with the chilli and serve with jasmine rice.

SERVES 4-6 AS PART OF A SHARED MEAL

500 g (1 lb 2 oz) pickled mustard greens (page 335)
2 tablespoons vegetable oil
5 spring onions (scallions), white part only, cut in half crossways
2 tablespoons sugar
500 g (1 lb 2 oz) cold roast pork belly (page 255), sliced into 3 x 5 cm (1¼ x 2 inch) pieces
1 tablespoon fish sauce
½ teaspoon dark soy sauce
2 bird's eye chillies, sliced

HANOI PORK AND VERMICELLI NOODLE SOUP
BÚN MỘC HÀ NỘI

THIS NOODLE SOUP ORIGINATED IN HANOI BUT I HAVE SEEN DIFFERENT VERSIONS OF IT IN SAIGON. THIS RECIPE IS MY BLEND OF THE TWO REGIONS AND IS VERY SIMPLE TO PREPARE. YOU CAN BUY THE PORK PASTE (*GIO SONG*) FROM AN ASIAN BUTCHER AND THE FRIED PORK TERRINE (*CHA QUE*) FROM AN ASIAN FOOD MARKET. IT'S A GOOD IDEA TO WRITE DOWN THE VIETNAMESE NAMES AND BRING THE LIST WITH YOU IN CASE THEY DON'T SPEAK ENGLISH. WHILE YOU'RE THERE, BUY A JAR OF SHRIMP PASTE — IT'S ESSENTIAL TO THE FLAVOUR OF THE SOUP.

3 dried wood ear mushrooms
250 g (9 oz) dried rice vermicelli noodles
200 g (7 oz) pork paste (*gio song*)
250 ml (9 fl oz/1 cup) vegetable oil
2 litres (70 fl oz/8 cups) chicken stock (page 328)
3 tablespoons fish sauce
2 teaspoons sugar
100 g (3½ oz) pork terrine (page 336), sliced into batons
100 g (3½ oz) fried pork terrine (*cha que*), thinly sliced

TO SERVE
2 teaspoons garlic oil (page 329)
2 tablespoons sliced spring onion (scallion), green part only
3 tablespoons fried red Asian shallots (page 329)
1 large handful coriander (cilantro) leaves
1 large handful mint leaves
1 large handful Vietnamese mint leaves
90 g (3¼ oz/1 cup) bean sprouts
shrimp paste, to taste (optional)
1 bird's eye chilli, thinly sliced
fish sauce, for dipping

Put the mushrooms in a bowl, cover with water and soak for 20 minutes, then drain and thinly slice. Put the rice vermicelli in a saucepan of boiling water and bring back to the boil. Cook for 5 minutes, then turn off the heat and leave in the water for 5 minutes. Drain the noodles, rinse under cold water, and set aside.

In a bowl, combine the pork paste and mushrooms, then using your hands knead well. Divide into two portions and set aside.

Heat the oil in a saucepan over medium heat. Form half the pork paste into small balls using oiled hands, then carefully drop the pork balls into the oil. Fry for 2 minutes, turning in the oil until browned, then remove from the pan with a slotted spoon and transfer to paper towel to drain. Set aside.

Bring the chicken stock to the boil in a large saucepan, add the fish sauce, sugar, 2 teaspoons salt and 1 teaspoon freshly ground black pepper. Stir to combine, then reduce the heat to a low simmer. Shape the remaining pork paste into small balls and drop them into the simmering stock. When they rise to the surface they are cooked, so remove with a slotted spoon and set them aside.

Divide the vermicelli among serving bowls. On top of the vermicelli, arrange even amounts of pork terrine, fried pork terrine and the fried and poached pork balls. Pour over the stock to cover all the ingredients. Drizzle each bowl with some garlic oil and garnish with spring onions, fried shallots and coriander. Serve with a separate platter of fresh mint, Vietnamese mint and bean sprouts, to add to the soup as desired.

For a more intense flavour, add about ¼ teaspoon of shrimp paste to each bowl, stirring to dissolve the paste. Serve with a small bowl of sliced chilli and fish sauce for dipping.

SERVES 4-6

CHARGRILLED PORK PATTIES WITH VERMICELLI SALAD
BÚN CHẢ

WALKING THROUGH THE STREETS OF HANOI YOU ARE OFTEN ENGULFED IN A THICK CLOUD OF SMOKE FROM BURNING COAL AS IT CHARS PORK PATTIES. THE FRAGRANT SMOKE GRABS YOU, PULLING YOU IN AS YOU WALK PAST. EVEN WHEN I'M NOT HUNGRY, I FIND IT HARD TO RESIST THEM. THERE ARE ONLY ONE OR TWO *BUN CHA* STALLS THAT LOCALS TELL YOU TO GO TO IN HANOI, BUT I'VE EATEN AT OVER FIFTEEN STALLS AND HAVE NOT BEEN DISAPPOINTED WITH ANY. IN HANOI, *BUN CHA* IS USUALLY SERVED WITH *NEM RAN* (ON THE NEXT PAGE), SO TRY SERVING THEM TOGETHER.

In a large bowl, combine the pork, fish sauce, spring onions, garlic chives, soy sauce, egg, shallots, garlic and 1 teaspoon freshly ground black pepper. Mix well, then cover and place in the fridge to marinate for 2 hours, or overnight for a better flavour.

Meanwhile, put the rice vermicelli in a saucepan of boiling water and bring back to the boil. Cook for 5 minutes, then turn off the heat and leave in the water for 5 minutes. Drain the noodles, rinse under cold water, and set aside.

Form the pork mixture into small balls with oiled hands, then gently press down on each ball to form patties, about 5 cm (2 inches) in diameter and 1 cm (1/2 inch) thick.

Heat a barbecue grill or chargrill pan to medium–high and cook the patties for 4 minutes on each side, or until brown. Place the pork patties on one platter, the vermicelli on another, and the bean sprouts and herbs on a third platter.

In a small saucepan, heat the dipping fish sauce and bring to just before boiling point, then transfer to 4–6 small bowls. Each guest should have their own dipping bowl, with all the ingredients in the middle of the table. Take a mixture of meat, vermicelli, bean sprouts and herbs and dip into the warm fish sauce with every mouthful.

SERVES 4-6 AS PART OF A SHARED MEAL

500 g (1 lb 2 oz) minced pork
2 tablespoons fish sauce
5 spring onions (scallions), thinly sliced
50 g (1¾ oz/1 bunch) garlic chives, roughly chopped
2 teaspoons dark soy sauce
1 egg, lightly beaten
3 tablespoons finely chopped red Asian shallots
2 tablespoons finely chopped garlic
500 g (1 lb 2 oz) dried rice vermicelli noodles
180 g (6 oz/2 cups) bean sprouts
1 bunch perilla, leaves picked
1 bunch Asian basil, leaves picked
1 bunch Vietnamese mint, leaves picked
1 bunch mint, leaves picked
750 ml (26 fl oz/3 cups) dipping fish sauce (page 331)

HANOI CRISP PARCELS
NEM RÁN HÀ NỘI

IN THE SOUTH WE CALL THESE CRISP PARCELS *CHA GIO*, AND IN THE NORTH THEY ARE CALLED *NEM RAN* AND ARE ROLLED MUCH LARGER. THESE CRISP PARCELS ARE TRADITIONALLY SERVED TOGETHER WITH *BUN CHA*, CHARGRILLED PORK PATTIES (PAGE 59).

40 g (1½ oz) dried wood ear mushrooms

40 g (1½ oz) dried bean thread (glass) vermicelli noodles

200 g (7 oz) raw small tiger prawns (shrimp), peeled and deveined, roughly chopped

200 g (7 oz) minced pork

200 g (7 oz) crabmeat (from your fishmonger)

½ onion, finely diced

1 tablespoon fish sauce

1 tablespoon caster (superfine) sugar

2 teaspoons ground white pepper

20 dried round rice paper wrappers (20 cm/8 inch diameter)

1 egg white, lightly beaten

vegetable oil, for deep-frying

TO SERVE

1 iceberg lettuce, leaves separated

1 large handful perilla leaves

1 large handful mint leaves

1 large handful Vietnamese mint leaves

250 ml (9 fl oz/1 cup) dipping fish sauce (page 331)

Put the mushrooms in a bowl, cover with water and soak for 20 minutes, then drain and thinly slice. Soak the bean thread vermicelli in water for 20 minutes, then drain and use kitchen scissors to cut into 4 cm (1½ inch) lengths. Meanwhile, pound the prawns to a paste using a mortar and pestle.

In a large bowl, combine the mushrooms, vermicelli, prawn meat, pork, crabmeat, onion, fish sauce, sugar, white pepper and 2 teaspoons salt. Knead the mixture in the bowl for 10 minutes, or until your arms get tired.

Working with one rice paper wrapper at a time, briefly dip the rice paper in a large bowl of warm water until just softened, then lay it flat on the work surface. Take 1½ heaped tablespoons of the prawn and pork mixture and place it on the bottom edge of the rice paper. Fold the two adjacent sides, one on top of the other, into the centre. Roll up to form a nice firm roll, and secure with a dab of egg white. Repeat until you have filled all the rice paper wrappers.

Pour the oil into a wok and heat to 180°C (350°F), or until a cube of bread dropped into the oil browns in 15 seconds. Deep-fry the parcels in three batches for 6 minutes, or until lightly browned and crisp. Remove and drain on paper towel. Wrap the crisp parcels in a lettuce leaf, adding some herbs, and serve with the dipping fish sauce.

SERVES 4-6 AS PART OF A SHARED MEAL

MUD CRAB SOUP WITH GLASS NOODLES
MIẾN CUA BỂ

IT'S MY FIFTH DAY STAYING AT THIS MINI HOTEL IN THE DARK LANES OF HANOI. I'M HUNGRY SO I MAKE MY WAY DOWN THE EIGHT FLIGHTS OF STAIRS TO GO AND SEARCH FOR SOMETHING TO EAT. THE FRONT DESK PERSON, PROBABLY NO OLDER THAN FIFTEEN, SAYS, 'MR NGUYEN, I'VE JUST COOKED DINNER; DO YOU WANT TO JOIN ME?' HE HAD PREPARED THE MOST AMAZING, DELICATE CRAB SOUP, AND I REMEMBER IT BEING SO CLEAR AND CLEAN, THE CRAB COOKED TO PERFECTION. THIS IS HIS RECIPE — IT'S FAIRLY EASY AND STRAIGHTFORWARD.

To prepare your crab humanely, put it in the freezer for 1 hour to put it to sleep. Remove the upper shell of the crab, pick off the gills, which look like little fingers, and discard them. Clean the crab under running water and drain. Place the crab on its stomach and chop the crab in half lengthways with a heavy cleaver, then chop in half again to give 4 pieces. Set aside.

Soak the bean thread vermicelli in water for 20 minutes. Drain the vermicelli and use kitchen scissors to cut into 4 cm (1½ inch) lengths.

Put the chicken stock in a large saucepan and bring to the boil. Add the crab, then reduce the heat to medium and simmer for 20 minutes. Remove the crab and allow to cool.

Pour the stock through a fine strainer into a clean saucepan. Place the pan over high heat and add the fish sauce and sugar. Reduce the heat and simmer for 5 minutes.

Meanwhile, remove the crabmeat from its shell and set aside, leaving the claws intact to use as garnish. Divide the vermicelli among large serving bowls and arrange some crabmeat on top, garnishing a few of the bowls with the reserved crab claws. Pour the stock over the vermicelli and crab. Garnish with the spring onions, garlic chives and Vietnamese mint, adding a pinch of freshly ground black pepper to each bowl.

SERVES 4-6 AS PART OF A SHARED MEAL

1 kg (2 lb 4 oz) live mud crab or blue swimmer crab
300 g (10½ oz) dried bean thread (glass) vermicelli noodles
1.25 litres (44 fl oz/5 cups) chicken stock (page 328)
3 tablespoons fish sauce
2 teaspoons sugar
4 spring onions (scallions), thinly sliced
5 garlic chives, cut into 3 cm (1¼ inch) lengths
½ bunch Vietnamese mint, leaves picked

HANOI CHICKEN AND VERMICELLI NOODLE SOUP
BÚN THANG HÀ NỘI

THIS VERMICELLI SOUP IS AS POPULAR AS *PHO* IN THE STREETS OF HANOI AND, LIKE *PHO*, IT CAN BE EATEN FOR BREAKFAST, LUNCH OR DINNER. I HAVE NEVER FOUND THIS DISH ANYWHERE ELSE IN VIETNAM, SO BE SURE TO TRY A BOWL OF THE LOCAL SPECIALITY IF YOU EVER FIND YOURSELF IN HANOI. IF YOU DECIDE TO MAKE IT AT HOME, PLEASE ADD THE SHRIMP PASTE. I KNOW THAT SHRIMP PASTE CAN BE TOO INTENSE FOR SOME PEOPLE'S PALATES (AND NOSES), BUT I ASSURE YOU THAT WHEN DISSOLVED INTO THE BROTH, YOU WON'T BE ABLE TO SMELL IT, AND IT WILL TRULY ADD ANOTHER DIMENSION TO YOUR SOUP.

2 litres (70 fl oz/8 cups) chicken stock (page 328)
2 teaspoons sugar
3 tablespoons fish sauce
2 teaspoons garlic oil (page 329)
100 g (3½ oz) boneless, skinless chicken breast
100 g (3½ oz) pork fillet, trimmed
250 g (9 oz) dried rice vermicelli noodles
2 eggs, lightly beaten
2 tablespoons vegetable oil
100 g (3½ oz) pork terrine (page 336), sliced into thin strips (optional)
2 tablespoons sliced spring onion (scallion)
1 large handful coriander (cilantro) leaves
1 large handful mint leaves
1 large handful Vietnamese mint leaves
90 g (3¼ oz/1 cup) bean sprouts
shrimp paste, to taste (optional)
1 bird's eye chilli, thinly sliced
fish sauce, for dipping

In a large saucepan, combine the chicken stock, sugar, fish sauce, garlic oil and 2 teaspoons salt. Bring to the boil, then add the chicken and pork. Reduce the heat to low and cook for 20 minutes. Remove the chicken and pork, cool, then cut into 1 cm (½ inch) slices. Reserve the chicken stock.

Put the rice vermicelli in a saucepan of boiling water and bring back to the boil. Cook for 5 minutes, then turn off the heat and leave in the water for 5 minutes. Drain the noodles, rinse under cold water, and set aside.

Place a non-stick frying pan over medium–low heat. Combine the eggs and ½ teaspoon of the oil in a bowl, then pour about a quarter of the beaten egg into the pan to form a thin layer over the base. Cook for 1 minute, or until the egg sheet will slide off the pan, then turn it over and cook for a further 30 seconds. Remove and place on a chopping board. Repeat this process until all the egg mixture is cooked; you should end up with three or four egg sheets. Stack the egg sheets on top of each other as they are cooked, then roll them together into a tight roll and slice thinly.

Divide the vermicelli among serving bowls. On top of the vermicelli, arrange even amounts of pork terrine (if using), followed by egg strips, then the chicken and pork. Pour enough hot stock into each bowl to cover the noodles. Garnish with spring onions and coriander, adding a pinch of freshly ground black pepper to each bowl.

Serve with a platter of mint, Vietnamese mint and bean sprouts, to add to the soup as desired. For a more intense flavour, add about ¼ teaspoon of shrimp paste to each bowl, stirring to dissolve the paste. Serve with a small bowl of sliced chilli and fish sauce for dipping.

SERVES 4-6

STEAMED RICE NOODLES FILLED WITH PORK AND WOOD EAR MUSHROOMS
BÁNH CUỐN

THESE NOODLES ARE MADE WITH A BATTER OF RICE AND TAPIOCA FLOURS. TAPIOCA FLOUR MAY ALSO BE LABELLED AS TAPIOCA STARCH — BOTH FLOURS ARE GLUTEN- AND GRAIN-FREE.

WHEN I WAS A CHILD, MY AUNTY FIVE WOULD MAKE THIS DISH EVERY SIX MONTHS. FAMILY WOULD TRAVEL FROM ALL OVER SYDNEY TO EAT HER *BANH CUON*. I CAN REMEMBER STANDING ON A MILK CRATE WATCHING HER PREPARE HER DELICATE RICE NOODLE SHEETS. IN HANOI THE NOODLES ARE MADE OVER A POT OF RAPIDLY BOILING WATER, WITH A PIECE OF CLOTH TIED ACROSS THE TOP. A THIN LAYER OF BATTER IS POURED ONTO THE CLOTH AND STEAMED, CREATING THE RICE NOODLE SHEETS. FOR THE HOME COOK, AUNTY FIVE'S TECHNIQUE IS LESS COMPLEX. THIS RECIPE AND COOKING TECHNIQUE BELONG TO HER.

Put the mushrooms in a bowl, cover with water and soak for 20 minutes, then drain and thinly slice. Return the mushrooms to the bowl and combine with the fish sauce.

To make the batter, combine the rice flour, tapioca flour and 1/2 teaspoon salt with 750 ml (26 fl oz/3 cups) of cold water. Whisk well, until a smooth batter forms.

Heat a non-stick frying pan over medium heat, add 2 tablespoons of the oil and fry the garlic and shallots until fragrant. Add the mushrooms, pork, sugar and a pinch of salt and freshly ground black pepper, and stir-fry for 4 minutes. Transfer to a bowl and set aside.

Brush a round tray with oil and place beside the stove. Heat a large non-stick frying pan over medium heat, and add enough oil to coat the base of the pan. Pour a small ladleful (2–3 tablespoons) of the batter into the pan, turning the pan in a circular motion to cover the base with a thin layer of batter. Cover the pan with a lid and cook for 30 seconds. Remove the lid and slide the thin noodle sheet onto your oiled tray. Spoon 1 tablespoon of pork mixture onto the noodle sheet, fold two sides in, then fold over to form a roll. Transfer to a plate. Repeat this process using the remaining batter and pork mixture, adding oil to the pan as necessary.

Top the rolls with the pork terrine (if using), cucumber, perilla, mint, Vietnamese mint, bean sprouts and fried shallots. Dress with the dipping fish sauce and garnish with sliced chilli.

SERVES 4-6 AS PART OF A SHARED MEAL

4 dried wood ear mushrooms
1 teaspoon fish sauce
125 g (4 1/2 oz/1 cup) rice flour
125 g (4 1/2 oz/1 cup) tapioca flour
about 125 ml (4 fl oz/1/2 cup) vegetable oil
4 garlic cloves, finely chopped
4 red Asian shallots, finely chopped
300 g (10 1/2 oz) minced pork
1/2 teaspoon sugar

TO SERVE
500 g (1 lb 2 oz) pork terrine (page 336), sliced into thin strips (optional)
2 Lebanese (short) cucumbers, sliced into batons
1 bunch perilla, leaves picked
1 bunch mint, leaves picked
1 bunch Vietnamese mint, leaves picked
300 g (10 1/2 oz) bean sprouts
50 g (1 3/4 oz/1/2 cup) fried red Asian shallots (page 329)
250 ml (9 fl oz/1 cup) dipping fish sauce (page 331)
2 bird's eye chillies, sliced

CHARGRILLED LEMONGRASS BEEF
BÒ NƯỚNG XẢ

THERE ARE MANY VARIATIONS OF THIS DISH FOUND THROUGHOUT VIETNAM BUT I FIND THIS ONE THE EASIEST TO PREPARE. MAKE SURE YOU BUY THE VIETNAMESE-STYLE BAGUETTES, WHICH ARE MUCH SMALLER THAN THE FRENCH TYPE.

10 spring onions (scallions), white part only, sliced

2 lemongrass stems, white part only, finely chopped

2 garlic cloves, finely chopped

600 g (1 lb 5 oz) minced beef

1 teaspoon shrimp paste

1 tablespoon fish sauce

1 tablespoon light soy sauce

1 teaspoon sesame oil

1 tablespoon soft brown sugar

2 tablespoons toasted sesame seeds

2 tablespoons vegetable oil

4 small baguettes or small Vietnamese bread rolls, warmed

250 ml (9 fl oz/1 cup) hoisin dipping sauce (page 330)

Put the spring onions, lemongrass, garlic and a pinch of salt and freshly ground black pepper in a mortar, and pound to a fine paste. Alternatively, use a food processor to make the paste.

Transfer the paste to a large bowl and add the beef, shrimp paste, fish sauce, soy sauce, sesame oil, brown sugar and sesame seeds. Mix well, then cover and refrigerate for 1 hour for the flavours to develop.

Meanwhile, soak 12 bamboo skewers in cold water for 30 minutes to prevent them burning.

With wet hands, divide the beef mixture into 24 portions and roll each portion into a sausage shape, about 4 cm (1½ inches) long. Thread 2 beef sausages onto each bamboo skewer and brush with a little oil.

Heat a barbecue grill or chargrill pan to medium and cook the beef skewers for 6 minutes, turning every few minutes, until cooked. Serve with warm baguettes and hoisin dipping sauce.

MAKES 12 SKEWERS

CHICKEN CHARGRILLED WITH FIVE-SPICE AND TURMERIC
GÀ NƯỚNG NGŨ VỊ HƯƠNG

I SIT AMONGST A CROWD OF LOCALS ON A BUSY STREET CORNER NEAR THE HOAN KIEM LAKE. THE STREET STALL HAS A TABLE COVERED WITH VARIETIES OF PREPARED SKEWERS — PRAWNS, SCALLOPS, MUSHROOMS, ASPARAGUS, BEEF, EGGPLANT AND THIS FIVE-SPICE TURMERIC CHICKEN. YOU POINT AT WHAT YOU WANT AND THEY COOK IT ON THE SPOT.

1 onion, diced
3 garlic cloves, peeled and pounded using a mortar and pestle
2 kaffir lime leaves, thinly sliced
1 teaspoon five-spice
½ teaspoon ground turmeric
½ teaspoon hot paprika
2 teaspoons sugar
1 tablespoon fish sauce
1 tablespoon light soy sauce
2 teaspoons coconut milk
500 g (1 lb 2 oz) boneless, skinless chicken thighs, cut into 3 x 5 cm (1¼ x 2 inch) pieces
1 tablespoon vegetable oil

In a bowl, combine the onion, garlic, lime leaves, five-spice, turmeric, paprika, sugar, fish sauce, soy sauce and coconut milk. Mix well, then add the chicken, stirring to coat it in the marinade. Stir in the oil, then cover the bowl and place in the fridge to marinate for 2 hours, or overnight for a better flavour.

Soak 12 bamboo skewers in cold water for 30 minutes to prevent them burning. Thread the chicken onto the skewers and cook on a hot barbecue grill or chargrill pan for 5 minutes on each side, or until browned. Serve with jasmine rice.

MAKES 12 SKEWERS

HARICOT BEAN PUDDING
CHÈ ĐẬU VÁN

CHE ARE SWEET DESSERTS MADE FROM VARIOUS COMBINATIONS OF TAPIOCA PEARLS, BEANS, PANDAN LEAF, JELLIES, CONDENSED MILK AND SHAVED ICE. VIETNAMESE PEOPLE LOVE SWEET FLAVOURS, BUT THEY RARELY FINISH A MEAL WITH A SWEET DESSERT, INSTEAD PREFERRING TO EAT SOME FRESH FRUIT TO CLEANSE THE PALATE AND HELP WITH DIGESTION. IN VIETNAM, *CHE* ARE EATEN AS A SWEET SNACK, AND *CHE* STALLS ARE FOUND ON MOST STREET CORNERS.

I'VE USED HARICOT BEANS HERE, ALSO KNOWN AS BOSTON OR NAVY BEANS. WHEN PREPARING THIS DESSERT, DO AS THE VIETNAMESE DO AND GET THE WHOLE FAMILY INVOLVED — IT WILL CUT DOWN YOUR PREP TIME, AS THE BEANS MAY TAKE A WHILE TO PEEL. YOU MAY ALSO FIND THE CONSISTENCY OF THE DESSERT QUITE UNUSUAL — IT SHOULD BE QUITE THICK AND STICKY — PROBABLY A TEXTURE THAT YOU'RE NOT USED TO.

Soak the haricot beans in 1 litre (35 fl oz/4 cups) of hot water from the tap for 2 hours. Drain, then peel the beans and discard the skins. Combine the beans with 750 ml (26 fl oz/3 cups) of water in a saucepan and bring to the boil. Reduce the heat to low and simmer for 1 hour, or until the beans are soft, then drain.

In the same saucepan, combine 625 ml (21 fl oz/2½ cups) of water with the sugar and pandan leaves. Stir over medium heat until the sugar has dissolved.

In a bowl, combine the tapioca flour with 2 tablespoons of water and slowly stir it into the liquid in the saucepan. The sugar syrup should start to become sticky and clear. Add the haricot beans and stir for a further 2 minutes. Take the pan off the heat and discard the pandan leaves. Divide among small serving bowls and drizzle about 2 tablespoons of sweet coconut milk over each bowl.

SERVES 6

300 g (10½ oz/1½ cups) dried haricot beans
220 g (7¾ oz/1 cup) sugar
2 pandan leaves, bruised and knotted
50 g (1¾ oz) tapioca flour
250 ml (9 fl oz/1 cup) sweet coconut milk (page 337)

IMPERIAL HUE
3

ARRIVING IN HUE FEELS AS IF I'M ARRIVING IN A DIFFERENT ASIAN COUNTRY ALTOGETHER. I ASK A LOCAL FOR DIRECTIONS AND I CAN'T UNDERSTAND A WORD HE IS SAYING. HE ISN'T SPEAKING A DIFFERENT DIALECT, BUT IT SOUNDS AS THOUGH ALL THE TONES AND ACCENTS ARE CONFUSED. I SUDDENLY FEEL LIKE A REAL TOURIST. WE HIRE TWO BICYCLES AND PEDDLE AROUND THE CITY, MAP IN HAND.

We don't get too far before I see a handwritten sign on a fence, '*bun bo Hue*' — a regional noodle soup of Hue and one that my mother makes on special occasions. It has the same origins as *pho*, but with added chilli, shrimp paste and lemongrass, with rice noodles that look like spaghetti. My mother's version, which I included in my first cookbook, has added pig trotters and blood jelly. I'm curious to find out if this soup is authentic to Hue or if it's another complex version of the south.

We lean our bikes against the fence and wander in; we feel as if we're trespassing in someone's backyard. A man tends to his roosters while his wife, who sits under the shade of a tamarind tree, seasons and sips from her large pot of aromatic broth.

We sit down at one of the tables and enjoy the sights and colours around us: walls coloured in varying shades of sky blue; French windows painted vibrant green; and our little plastic maroon table, laden with small bowls — in colours of red, lime and purple — filled with shaved banana blossom, bean sprouts, mint, lime, chilli, chilli and more chilli. We have moved on from the delicate flavours of Hanoi and into the sharper flavours of central Vietnam.

The wife brings steaming bowls of soup to our table and I crunch through cartilage and sprouts, all the elements of Vietnamese cuisine tickling my palate: the saltiness of shrimp paste and fish sauce balanced with citrusy lime, and the spiciness of dried and fresh chillies cut by the sweetness of rock sugar.

I'm beginning to prefer this noodle soup over *pho*. Sweat dripping from my temples, my scalp itchy from the spices, I cool down with a tall glass of iced jasmine tea.

We hop on our bikes and cruise towards the centre of town. The streets of Hue are wide and lined with trees, monuments are covered in green moss, the architecture reminiscent of ancient China — palaces, temples, tombs, tall bamboo and exquisite landscaped gardens, all giving the city an air of serene majesty. If I were a scholar, poet or painter, I would come here for inspiration.

> **❝ IT IS BELIEVED IF YOU HAVE THE SURNAME OF NGUYEN, YOU WILL BE A POWERFUL AND PROSPEROUS FAMILY. AND FOR THOSE WHO ARE SAYING TO THEMSELVES, 'HOW ON EARTH DO I PRONOUNCE THAT SURNAME?', TRY SAYING 'NU-WIN' AND YOU'LL BE CLOSE ENOUGH. ❞**

Hue served as Vietnam's capital under the emperors of the Nguyen dynasty from 1802–1945. The city is situated right on the border of North and South Vietnam, leaning more towards the South. During the Vietnam War, Hue fell victim to much damage, and her battle scars can still be seen today.

We ride over the 'old bridge' across the romantically named Perfume River, which winds itself through the city. It feels like it was not long ago that this country was ruled by emperors, for their opulent palaces and tombs are still standing. We pass the Ancient Citadel, which is surrounded by water-filled moats, covered in breathtakingly beautiful purple lotus.

I stop and soak in the history and realise how much I don't know about Vietnam's past. My parents had little free time to educate me about my country of origin and now I'm keen to discover my roots. It was only recently, when I was reading about the history of Hue and its emperors, that I learned why half of Vietnam's population has the surname Nguyen. We are all named after Lord Hoang Nguyen, the ruler of southern Vietnam, who took control of Hue from the Chinese Han Army in 1558, creating the Nguyen Dynasty. It is believed if you have the surname of Nguyen, you will be a powerful and prosperous family. And for those who are saying to themselves, 'How on earth do I pronounce that surname?', try saying 'nu-win' and you'll be close enough.

Like its elegantly designed streets and architecture, most Vietnamese generally regard the food from Hue to be the most refined in all the country. Hue is famous for its flamboyant imperial banquets, designed to please the ruling emperor of the time, who decreed that their banquets be innovative and that their dishes be set apart from the rest of the country. Emperors demanded that they must not eat the same dish in the same year, and that the imperial dining table must be set with more than fifty dishes. Hence royal cooks were forced to be creative and play around with ingredients, offering an assortment of canapé-sized dishes. From this, Hue cuisine was formed.

We continue to ride, through small streets where front paths of shops and houses are covered with incense sticks — green, gold, orange and red — drying

in the sun. I want to see how these sticks are made. We enter a courtyard with a manicured garden, brightly coloured flowers bloom from their hanging pots, and bundles upon bundles of incense sticks are stacked everywhere, tied together with bamboo bark. A Buddhist nun sits rolling the incense by hand, and throws it in a basket as she finishes. She gets up as soon as she sees us, slapping the dust from her grey robe. 'Come in, would you like some tea?'

Another nun appears from the house with a pot and four small teacups and greets us with a slight bow of her head. The nun pours some tea and asks us where we are from.

'Australia? Wow, such a prosperous country; you must both make so much money. This house was left here by the French, fourteen nuns live here now, and we make incense to raise enough money to eat and to keep the temples open. We need to rebuild our home; it's old and falling apart. Can you help us?'

We are quite surprised at her forwardness. She takes my hand and guides us through the house. 'See, look at the ceiling, it's going to collapse soon, the paint on the walls is peeling off and the floor is about to fall through. We need at least (US) $20,000 to rebuild. Can you help?'

I look at her with confusion and tell her that I think the house looks great, that I love the old rustic worn look, which adds character and charm. 'We really don't have $20,000 to spare, but we can buy some incense off you.'

She laughs and hands us a packet of cinnamon-scented incense. She asks for $2.00, then suggests we have lunch at her pagoda, where fellow nuns cook up a vegetarian banquet. She gives us the directions.

Hidden in a green jungle of jackfruit, mango and fig trees we find the pagoda. We enter a square, tiled courtyard surrounded by oversized bonsai trees, where we are greeted by three nuns with friendly, welcoming smiles. Shoes come off and we sit down at a long narrow table. It is hot and sticky — no fans, no air-con — I'm glad I don't have to wear those long robes.

There is no menu, no ordering; the food continuously comes out. Within minutes our table is covered with small dishes, twenty-five to be exact. I find it fascinating that the nuns can create dishes from tofu, vegetables and gluten to look like prawn, fish, crab, beef, chicken, beef and pork. The inner side of a jackfruit shell is shredded and fried to imitate whitebait, silken tofu is fried into cubes to resemble chicken, strips of gluten are coloured and wok-tossed like beef, tofu is flattened and layered to imitate fish cutlets, and corn and tofu are combined for crab soup. When we begin to eat, we can't believe how closely the texture of these mock meats resembles the real thing. I guess they use plenty of MSG in their cooking, but it all tastes so good.

Eating these dishes triggers memories of when I was younger. My mother would come home from the temple with containers of mock meats for us kids to eat for dinner, as we could not eat meat on the first and fifteenth days of the lunar calendar. So, instead of forcing us to eat vegetables, mum would give us these mock meats and we wouldn't even know the difference. I don't know how to make mock meats, but I plan to return to Hue one day and cook with these nuns.

> **66** ... THE RICE PAPER IS TRULY DECADENT; IT FEELS SO GRACEFUL AND DELICATE IN MY HANDS AS I ROLL PORK AND HERBS WITH IT. EACH MOUTHFUL IS TENDER AND SOFT, YET HAS CRUNCH AND ENOUGH 'GIVE' TO MAKE ME SIGH DEEPLY WITH EVERY BITE. **99**

Unlike the city of Hanoi, where street food is found on every corner and local specialities are easy to find, Hue's unique dishes have to be hunted down, and are not condensed in one area but spread throughout the city. We had met a local lady from Hue on one of our long bus trips and she had told us that we had to try a restaurant, a little north from the city, which was well known for its unique rice paper. Rice papers are usually left out in the sun to dry, but these were dried in the cool air of the early morning mist. I had not heard of or seen this technique anywhere else in Vietnam, so I was curious to try it.

The locals tell us the restaurant is quite a way out of town, too far to go by bicycles, so we hire a scooter and set off on our journey.

The ride is longer than we thought, the busy city streets slowly giving way to dusty dirt roads and thick jungle — we hope we are on the right track. Just as we're beginning to think we are lost, I spot a woman wearing an elegant white traditional dress, the *ao dai*, signalling for us to park.

It's the restaurant we are looking for, an imperial-style building made of engraved dark wood, filled with furniture made for a king. We stroll through the area, amazed at its grandeur and tranquillity: open dining rooms are set amongst an acre of manicured gardens, fish ponds are filled with striking purple lotus flowers and colourful lanterns swing from trees.

We sit at our table and gaze over the extensive menu, but I already know what I want — we are here for only one dish. We order, then out comes a platter laden with a variety of fresh herbs, many that I don't recognise. The waiter tells me these herbs are not found anywhere else in Vietnam; they are native to Hue and only people in Hue eat them. There are more than eight varieties, with colours of light to dark green, pale yellow and purple, all with different flavours and textures. This platter is to accompany slow-cooked pork belly, thinly sliced and, of course, the mist-dried rice paper.

The rice paper comes out as a stack; they are dry but remain soft so there is no need to immerse them in water. The emperors of Hue certainly had it good — the rice paper is truly decadent; it feels so graceful and delicate in my hands as I roll pork and herbs with it. Each mouthful is tender and soft, yet has crunch and enough 'give' to make me sigh with every bite.

I stop the scooter in a narrow lane where I notice two ladies, wearing matching pink silk pyjamas, kneading flour in huge aluminium pots. 'We are preparing *bot cho banh bot loc*,' they tell me, which is a batter for special Hue dumplings. They point to the kitchen and tell us to pop our heads in.

Four ladies, cramped in a dark kitchen, sit on tiny stools, crouched over baskets filled with prawns, pork, wood ear mushrooms and banana leaves, each ingredient piled so high, they roll out from the baskets. Their hands work at lightning speed, shaping hundreds of glutinous dumplings and rice cakes, and folding intricate parcels of bamboo leaf and sticky rice. I ask them to slow down so I can learn a trick or two, but they giggle, then fold, tuck, knot and tie even faster, masters of a craft that takes years and years to perfect.

They ask how many serves we want, and with no clue to what we are getting, I ask for only one. Minutes later one of the ladies places a large round metal tray in the middle of the table, and on it, six varieties of many small Hue delights, all in different shapes and sizes, served with two kinds of fish sauce: one sweet, one salty.

I ask what we are eating and she responds with the same speed as her hands. 'Banh beo, banh loc, banh it, banh trang, banh quai vat, banh uot!' Each little parcel is slightly sticky, some are chewy, some soft, some stringy, but all have such great flavours, each with a texture probably foreign to a Western palate, but for Vietnamese it is these elements of texture that we enjoy so much.

Feeling guilty for eating them all so fast, considering just how much work, time and skill went into making each one, I show them my respect by folding my arms, then thank them profusely, acknowledging their master skills. Before leaving I ask them to recommend their favourite eating spot. A scribble on a napkin and we have an address for our next destination. It's an eating house called Banh Khoai, simply translated as, 'Happy Pancake'.

We arrive at an unusually clean-looking place, with a sparkling white tiled floor, polished silver-rimmed chairs and shiny tables — the well-dressed lady who works there wears gloves while she cooks. I feel a little uncomfortable here; it's not dirty enough for me — it's too organised and clean — this isn't the authentic dining experience I'm looking for … but the dish she's making looks fantastic.

She stands alone behind six blackened iron pans, the flame tall. From left to right she generously pours oil into each, followed by ladles of silky turmeric batter. Sounds of sizzle sing out from the pans, quickly muffled by additions of spring onion, prawn, pork and then the clang of the heavy domed lid. After a short while, lids are lifted, one after the other, pancakes folded in half, revealing a crisp browned base. I feel like I am sitting in front of an orchestra, watching a musician skilfully playing her instrument. Moments later, she places half a dozen pancakes, fresh herbs and a thickened sauce in front of us.

The pancake reminds me of a Saigon dish called banh xeo, a larger version and not as crisp and thick-based as this one.

Why is it called Happy Pancake? Is it because it makes you happy watching her prepare the dish, or is it because when you eat it you are instantly happy. Or maybe it's because when the pancake is folded in half it looks like a smile. Whatever the answer, we had just spent the whole day eating, exploring and discovering the local delicacies and beauty of imperial Hue, and I couldn't be happier.

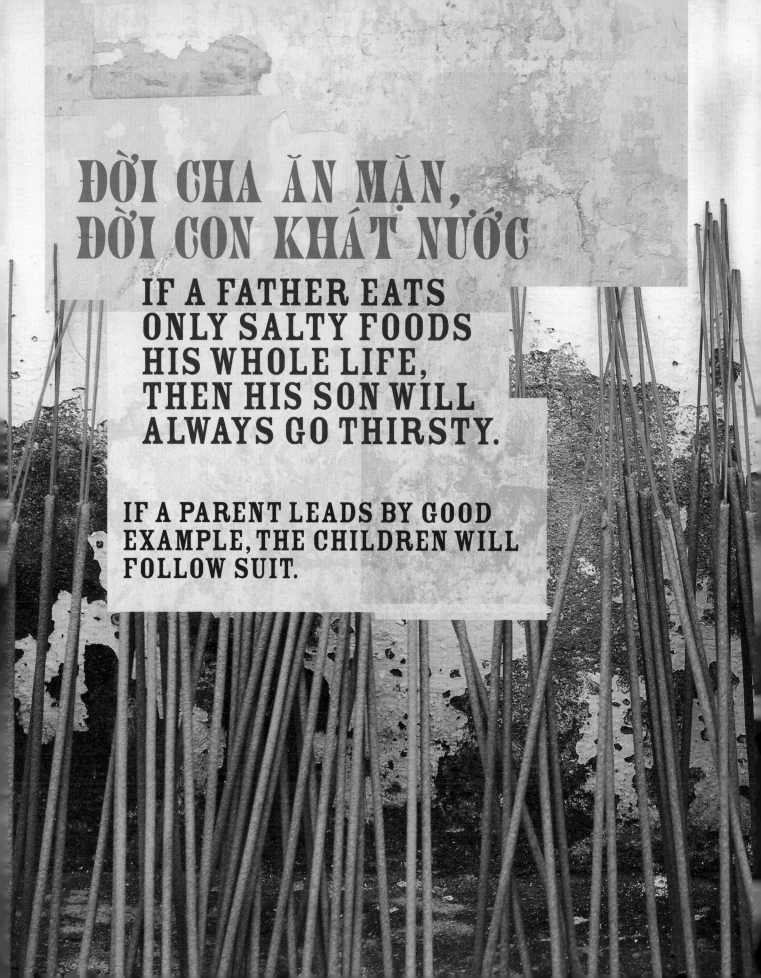

ĐỜI CHA ĂN MẶN,
ĐỜI CON KHÁT NƯỚC

IF A FATHER EATS
ONLY SALTY FOODS
HIS WHOLE LIFE,
THEN HIS SON WILL
ALWAYS GO THIRSTY.

IF A PARENT LEADS BY GOOD
EXAMPLE, THE CHILDREN WILL
FOLLOW SUIT.

HAPPY HUE PANCAKE
BÁNH KHOÁI

BANH KHOAI IN VIETNAMESE MEANS 'HAPPY PANCAKE', SO YOU NEED TO SMILE WHEN YOU PREPARE THIS DISH. THE PANCAKE NEEDS TO BE EXTRA CRISP AND CRUNCHY, SO DON'T TAKE IT OFF THE HEAT UNTIL THIS HAS BEEN ACHIEVED. A HAPPY VEGETARIAN VERSION CAN ALSO BE CREATED BY SUBSTITUTING FRIED TOFU AND AN ASSORTMENT OF ASIAN MUSHROOMS FOR THE PORK AND PRAWNS.

I'VE USED SCHOOL PRAWNS HERE: BECAUSE THEY ARE SMALL THEY ARE VERY TENDER. THE VIETNAMESE ONLY TRIM OFF THE LEGS AND HEADS — THE SHELLS AND TAILS ARE EATEN.

100 g (3½ oz) dried mung beans
vegetable oil, for stir-frying
2 garlic cloves, finely chopped
200 g (7 oz) raw school prawns
    (shrimp), legs and heads
    trimmed, or peel if preferred
200 g (7 oz) boneless pork belly,
    fat trimmed, thinly sliced
1 green oak lettuce or butter lettuce
1 bunch perilla
1 bunch mint
1 bunch Vietnamese mint
1 bunch Vietnamese fish mint
1 Lebanese (short) cucumber,
    thinly sliced (optional)
1 star fruit, thinly sliced (optional)
1 onion, thinly sliced into rings
500 g (1 lb 2 oz) bean sprouts
2 spring onions (scallions), sliced
250 g (9 oz/1 cup) sticky soya
    bean and pork sauce (page 331)

BATTER
125 g (4½ oz/1 cup) cornflour
    (cornstarch)
75 g (2½ oz/½ cup) plain
    (all-purpose) flour
½ teaspoon ground turmeric
½ teaspoon sugar
½ teaspoon bicarbonate of soda
    (baking soda)
100 ml (3½ fl oz) coconut milk

Put the dried mung beans in a bowl, cover with water and set aside to soak for 20 minutes, then drain. Transfer to a steamer over a saucepan of boiling water and steam for 20 minutes.

Place a frying pan over medium heat, add 1 tablespoon of oil, half the chopped garlic and the prawns and stir-fry for 3 minutes. Remove the prawns and set aside. Wipe the pan clean, then repeat this process with the remaining garlic and the pork belly. Set aside.

To make the batter, combine all the ingredients in a large bowl, adding ½ teaspoon salt and 400 ml (14 fl oz) of water. Whisk well and set aside for 10 minutes.

Wash the lettuce leaves and herbs. Pick the leaves off the herbs and arrange the herbs and lettuce on a large platter, along with the cucumber and star fruit, if using.

Place a small heavy-based non-stick frying pan (about 20 cm/8 inches) over medium heat. Add 2 tablespoons of oil to the pan. When the oil is hot, add 2 tablespoons of batter, swirling to coat the base of the pan. Now add a few onion rings, then sprinkle a small handful of the mung beans, followed by some prawns, pork, bean sprouts and spring onions. Fry for 2 minutes, or until the base is crisp and browned, fold the pancake in half to make it 'smile', and remove from the pan. Repeat this process with the remaining batter and filling ingredients.

To serve, wrap up the pancake in a lettuce leaf, adding some herbs, cucumber and star fruit, and spoon on some of the sticky soya bean sauce.

SERVES 4–6 AS PART OF A SHARED MEAL

BEEF AND MUSTARD GREEN SOUP
CANH CẢI CHUA THỊT BÒ

I SAW THIS SOUP SERVED TO AN ELDERLY COUPLE IN A LOCAL HUE RESTAURANT. THEY DIDN'T HAVE IT WITH ANYTHING ELSE — NO RICE OR FISH — JUST BEER. THE SOUP DID HAVE SOME PEANUTS IN IT, SO I GUESS YOU COULD CALL IT A 'DRINKING DISH'.

2 tablespoons vegetable oil

1 garlic clove, crushed

350 g (12 oz) pickled mustard greens (page 335)

2 tomatoes, cut into 3 cm (1¼ inch) cubes

100 g (3½ oz) blanched raw peanuts

2 tablespoons fish sauce

2 slices peeled ginger, bruised

1 teaspoon sugar

350 g (12 oz) beef sirloin, trimmed and thinly sliced

2 tablespoons sliced spring onion (scallion)

1 tablespoon sliced sawtooth herb

1 tablespoon sliced rice paddy herb

1 small handful coriander (cilantro) leaves

1 bird's eye chilli, thinly sliced

fish sauce, for dipping

Place a large saucepan over medium heat, add the oil and fry the garlic until fragrant. Add the mustard greens and stir-fry for 5 minutes, then add the tomatoes and peanuts and stir-fry for a further 5 minutes.

Add 1.5 litres (52 fl oz/6 cups) of water to the pan along with the fish sauce, ginger, sugar, 1 teaspoon salt and ½ teaspoon freshly ground black pepper. Bring to the boil, then reduce the heat and simmer for 10 minutes. Add the beef slices and simmer for a further 5 minutes, skimming any impurities off the surface.

Transfer to large soup bowls. Garnish with spring onion, sawtooth herb, rice paddy herb and coriander. Serve with jasmine rice, and a small bowl of sliced chilli and fish sauce for dipping.

SERVES 4-6 AS PART OF A SHARED MEAL

PORK HOCK BRAISED WITH LOTUS ROOT
MÓNG HEO KHO CỦ SEN

THIS DISH MUST BE EATEN WITH YOUR HANDS, SO DON'T EVEN ATTEMPT TO USE CHOPSTICKS. IF YOU HAVE TROUBLE FINDING DRIED MANDARIN PEEL, MAKE IT YOURSELF BY LEAVING MANDARIN PEEL AT ROOM TEMPERATURE FOR A DAY OR SO UNTIL CRISP. IT WILL NOT ONLY ADD GREAT DEPTH TO THE DISH, BUT IT ALSO RELEASES MANY MEDICINAL ANTIBACTERIAL QUALITIES. THE AROMATIC FRAGRANCE OF THE SPICES REMINDS ME OF HOME-COOKED COMFORT FOOD.

To make the spice pouch, dry-roast the mandarin peel and each spice separately in a small frying pan over medium heat until fragrant. Cool, then coarsely grind using a mortar and pestle or electric spice grinder. Wrap the ground mandarin peel, spices and garlic in a piece of muslin and tie up tightly in a knot. Set aside.

In a bowl, combine the sugar, fish sauce, light and dark soy sauce, garlic, 1/2 teaspoon salt and 1 teaspoon freshly ground black pepper. Stir well, then transfer to a large saucepan. Add the pork hocks, lotus root, muslin spice pouch and 2 litres (70 fl oz/8 cups) of water. Bring to the boil, constantly skimming any impurities off the surface for 5 minutes, then reduce the heat to low and simmer for 1 hour, or until the pork hocks are tender. Transfer to a serving bowl and garnish with star anise and cassia bark, and serve with jasmine rice.

SERVES 4-6 AS PART OF A SHARED MEAL

2 tablespoons sugar
4 tablespoons fish sauce
4 tablespoons light soy sauce
1 tablespoon dark soy sauce
2 garlic cloves, finely chopped
2 fresh pork hocks, cleaned and cut into 4 cm (1½ inch) pieces (ask your butcher to do this for you)
200 g (7 oz) lotus root, peeled and sliced into round pieces, about 5 mm (¼ inch) thick
1 star anise, to garnish
piece of cassia bark, to garnish

SPICE POUCH
4 cm (1½ inch) piece of dried mandarin peel
5 cm (2 inch) piece of cassia bark or cinnamon
2 star anise
½ teaspoon sichuan peppercorns
½ teaspoon coriander seeds
½ teaspoon cumin seeds
½ teaspoon fennel seeds
6 garlic cloves, bashed

HUE PRAWN AND PORK STICKY DUMPLINGS
BÁNH ÍT TRẦN TÔM THỊT

WHEN BUYING GLUTINOUS RICE FLOUR, MAKE SURE IT IS LABELLED AS GLUTINOUS, AS REGULAR RICE FLOUR CANNOT BE USED FOR THIS RECIPE. GLUTINOUS RICE FLOUR IS SWEETER AND IS MADE FROM GLUTINOUS SHORT-GRAIN RICE; THE FLOUR TURNS FIRM AND STICKY WHEN COOKED. YOU MAY FIND THE TEXTURE TO BE AN ACQUIRED ONE, AS THESE DUMPLINGS ARE THE CHEWY AND STICKY KIND.

2 tablespoons vegetable oil
1 garlic clove, finely chopped
1 onion, finely chopped
150 g (5½ oz) raw prawns (shrimp), peeled and deveined, chopped
150 g (5½ oz) minced pork
½ teaspoon fish sauce
½ teaspoon sugar
100 g (3½ oz) drained, tinned water chestnuts, finely chopped
350 g (12 oz) glutinous rice flour
300 ml (10½ fl oz) boiling water
2 tablespoons spring onion oil (page 329)
2 tablespoons fried red Asian shallots (page 329)
125 ml (4 fl oz/½ cup) dipping fish sauce (page 331)

Heat a frying pan over medium heat, add the oil, garlic and onion and fry until fragrant. Add the prawns and pork and season with the fish sauce, sugar and ½ teaspoon each of salt and freshly ground black pepper. Stir-fry for 3 minutes, then add the water chestnuts and fry for a further 2 minutes. Remove from the heat and set aside.

Put 300 g (10½ oz) of the glutinous rice flour in a bowl. Slowly add the boiled water in small amounts, mixing until the dough is smooth. Dust the work surface with the remaining rice flour, then turn the dough out and flatten it using a rolling pin, rolling it out to a 3 mm (1/8 inch) thickness. Using a 9 cm (3½ inch) round pastry cutter or a small Chinese teacup, cut out rounds from the dough, rerolling the scraps to make more rounds.

Place a tablespoon of the prawn and pork mixture in the centre of each round, then bring the edges of the dough up and around the mixture to meet in the middle and form a ball. Press the edges together to seal.

Bring a large saucepan of water to the boil, then reduce the heat to a simmer. Add the dumplings in two batches and cook for 10 minutes. Remove each batch using a slotted spoon, drain, then plunge briefly into cold water, then drain well.

Serve the dumplings immediately as a starter or snack, garnish with spring onion oil and fried shallots and spoon over some dipping fish sauce.

MAKES ABOUT 20

IMPERIAL PRAWN AND PORK CLEAR DUMPLINGS
BÁNH QUAI VẠT

THIS IS NOT THE KIND OF DUMPLING THAT YOU MAY BE USED TO. THESE ARE AUTHENTIC HUE STYLE — TRANSLUCENT AND STICKY. IT TAKES MANY PRACTICE RUNS TO PERFECT THEM, SO KEEP TRYING; IT'S ALL ABOUT GETTING TO UNDERSTAND YOUR TAPIOCA FLOUR.

Put the dried shrimp in a bowl, cover with water and soak for 20 minutes, then drain.

Heat a large frying pan over medium heat, add 1 tablespoon of the oil, then stir-fry the garlic and shallots until fragrant. Add the prawns and pork and season with the fish sauce, sugar and a pinch of salt and freshly ground black pepper. Stir-fry for 2 minutes, then remove and set aside.

Pound the shrimp using a mortar and pestle or in a food processor. Heat a small frying pan over medium heat, add the shrimp and dry-roast for 5 minutes. Remove from the pan and set aside.

Put 125 ml (4 fl oz/^{1}/$_2$ cup) of water into a saucepan with the remaining 1 tablespoon of oil and bring to the boil. Sift the tapioca flour into a bowl, then gradually pour the boiled water into the bowl, mixing with a fork until a smooth dough forms. This should take no more than 3 minutes. Now rest the dough, covered with a tea towel, for 15 minutes. Once rested, oil your hands and knead the dough for 2 minutes, or until smooth. Divide the dough into two parts, covering one half with a damp tea towel.

Dust the work surface with tapioca flour. If your dough is still sticky, knead it again for a few minutes, but otherwise roll the dough into a log, 2 cm (^{3}/$_4$ inch) wide and 16 cm (6^1/$_4$ inches) long. Now slice the log into 16 equal parts. Using a small rolling pin, gently roll out each piece to make a flat, round disc, about 6 cm (2^1/$_2$ inches) in diameter. Top each round with ^{1}/$_2$ teaspoon of the prawn and pork mixture, fold the rounds in half and seal the edges by pressing down with a fork. Transfer the dumplings to an oiled tray, cover with a damp tea towel, and repeat this process with the remaining dough. You should end up with 32 dumplings.

Bring 2 litres (70 fl oz/8 cups) of water to the boil in a large saucepan, then reduce the heat to a simmer. Working in two batches, carefully drop the dumplings into the simmering water and cook for 2 minutes. Remove each batch using a slotted spoon, drain, then plunge briefly into cold water, then drain well again. Transfer to a large platter. Dress the dumplings with hot spring onion oil and dipping fish sauce. Garnish with the fried shallots and shrimp. Serve as a snack or starter.

MAKES 32

50 g (1^3/$_4$ oz/^{1}/$_2$ cup) dried shrimp
2 tablespoons vegetable oil
1 garlic clove, finely chopped
2 red Asian shallots, finely chopped
100 g (3^1/$_2$ oz) raw prawns (shrimp), peeled and deveined, chopped
100 g (3^1/$_2$ oz) minced pork
1 tablespoon fish sauce
2 teaspoons sugar
125 g (4^1/$_2$ oz/1 cup) tapioca flour, plus extra for dusting
2 tablespoons spring onion oil (page 329), heated
125 ml (4 fl oz/^{1}/$_2$ cup) dipping fish sauce (page 331)
2 tablespoons fried red Asian shallots (page 329)

PORK SPARERIBS BRAISED IN COCONUT
SƯỜN RAM MẶN

YOUNG COCONUT WATER, OR COCONUT JUICE, IS THE LIQUID FOUND IN YOUNG GREEN COCONUTS, PLUCKED FROM THE TREE BEFORE THEY MATURE. BRAISING THE PORK IN COCONUT WATER ALLOWS THE MEAT TO ABSORB ALL ITS SWEETNESS, GIVING A UNIQUE CHARACTER TO THE DISH. IF YOU BUY A WHOLE YOUNG COCONUT, USE A HEAVY CLEAVER TO MAKE FOUR INCISIONS IN THE TOP OF THE COCONUT, POUR THE JUICE OUT AND SCRAPE OUT ITS TENDER FLESH WITH A SPOON AND NIBBLE ON IT WHILE YOU COOK. MANY VIETNAMESE RECIPES USE COCONUT WATER INSTEAD OF STOCK.

In a bowl, combine 1 tablespoon of the garlic, the shallot, fish sauce, oyster sauce, sugar, 1/2 teaspoon salt and 1 teaspoon freshly ground black pepper. Mix well, then add the pork ribs and stir to coat well. Cover and place in the fridge to marinate for 20 minutes.

Pour the oil into a wok and heat to 180°C (350°F), or until a cube of bread dropped into the oil browns in 15 seconds. Add the undrained pork in batches and deep-fry over medium heat for 3 minutes, or until brown. Remove the pork and drain on paper towel.

Put the coconut water in a saucepan and bring to the boil. Add the pork ribs, reduce the heat and simmer for 5 minutes, then increase the heat and cook for a further 3 minutes, or until the coconut water has reduced to a quarter of its original amount.

Add the remaining garlic, the onion, chilli sauce and a pinch of freshly ground black pepper. Stir constantly for 5 minutes, then turn off the heat. Transfer the ribs to a serving bowl and garnish with the coriander sprigs. Serve with jasmine rice.

SERVES 4-6 AS PART OF A SHARED MEAL

2 tablespoons finely chopped garlic
1 red Asian shallot, chopped
2 tablespoons fish sauce
1 teaspoon oyster sauce
2 tablespoons sugar
500 g (1 lb 2 oz) pork spareribs, cut into 2 x 3 cm (3/4 x 1 1/4 inch) pieces
vegetable oil, for deep-frying
300 ml (10 1/2 fl oz) young coconut water
1 onion, sliced into thin wedges
2 teaspoons chilli sauce
2 coriander (cilantro) sprigs

CHARGRILLED CHICKEN SKEWERS IN PRESERVED WHITE BEAN PASTE
GÀ NƯỚNG CHAO

I WANTED TO TRY THIS DISH WHEN I WAS IN HUE BUT I COULDN'T FIND IT, SO I DECIDED TO MAKE IT MYSELF. I WENT TO THE MARKETS AND BOUGHT SOME CHICKEN, BEAN PASTE, GARLIC AND LEMONGRASS. ONE THING I COULDN'T FIND WAS BAMBOO SKEWERS, SO I ASKED A FEW LADIES AND THEY LAUGHED: 'YOU WANT TO BUY BAMBOO SKEWERS? HAH! JUST GO OUTSIDE TO THE BAMBOO TREE AND SNAP IT OFF FRESH.' IT FELT SO GOOD THREADING THE MEAT ONTO FRESH BAMBOO, A LUXURY YOU CAN ONLY HAVE IN ASIA.

50 g (1¾ oz) preserved white bean curd
2 teaspoons lemon juice
2 teaspoons sugar
½ teaspoon finely chopped garlic
½ teaspoon finely chopped lemongrass, white part only
2 teaspoons thinly sliced spring onion (scallion), green part only
1 teaspoon thinly sliced coriander (cilantro)
450 g (1 lb) boneless, skinless chicken thighs, cut into 3 x 5 cm (1¼ x 2 inch) pieces
2 teaspoons vegetable oil
salt, pepper and lemon sauce (page 332), for dipping

Soak 12 bamboo skewers in cold water for 30 minutes to prevent them from burning.

In a large bowl, mash the bean curd with a fork, then add the lemon juice, sugar, garlic, lemongrass, spring onion and coriander. Mix well, then add the chicken, stirring to coat it in the marinade. Stir in the oil, then cover the bowl and place in the fridge to marinate for 2 hours, or overnight for a better flavour.

Thread the chicken onto the skewers evenly. Heat a barbecue grill or chargrill pan to medium–high and cook the skewers for 4 minutes on each side, or until cooked through. Serve with jasmine rice, and a small bowl of salt, pepper and lemon sauce for dipping.

MAKES 12 SKEWERS

CHARGRILLED TENDER BEEF SKEWERS
BÒ LỤI

THIS IS A TRADITIONAL DISH I FOUND IN MANY RESTAURANTS IN HUE. IF YOU FEEL THAT USING PORK FAT IS A BIT NAUGHTY, DON'T OMIT IT; JUST USE LESS. THE PORK FAT ROLLED WITH THE BEEF WILL GIVE ADDED TENDERNESS TO THE MEAT AND RELEASES SO MUCH EXTRA FLAVOUR.

THIS IS THE TYPE OF DISH THAT VIETNAMESE LIKE TO ASSEMBLE AT THE TABLE. PUT THE PLATTERS OF MEAT, FRESH HERBS AND VEGETABLES ON THE TABLE, AND MAKE EACH ROLL, ONE AT A TIME, AS YOU EAT IT.

Soak 12 bamboo skewers in cold water for 30 minutes to prevent them from burning.

In a bowl, combine the coconut milk, oyster sauce, fish sauce, honey, garlic, lemongrass, paprika and oil. Add the beef, stir to coat well, then cover and place in the fridge to marinate for 1 hour.

Bring a saucepan of water to the boil, add the pork fat and cook for 3 minutes. Drain and cool. Drain the beef, then roll each piece around a piece of pork fat, and then thread a piece of beef onto a skewer, followed by a wedge of onion. Repeat the process so each skewer has 2 pieces of meat and 2 pieces of onion.

Heat a barbecue grill or chargrill pan to medium and cook the skewers for 4 minutes on each side, or until cooked through. Remove to a serving plate and garnish with peanuts. Place the beef skewers on the table along with the rice papers, cucumber, lettuce, herbs and star fruit.

To assemble the rolls, use kitchen scissors to cut 6 rounds of rice paper in half. Fill a large bowl with warm water and dip one whole sheet of rice paper in the water until just softened, then lay it flat on a plate. Dip a half sheet of rice paper in the water and lay it vertically in the middle of the round sheet. This will strengthen the roll, preventing the filling from breaking through. In the middle of the rice paper, place 2 pieces of beef and 2 pieces of onion (remove them from the skewer) in a horizontal line about 4 cm (1½ inches) from the top. Below this, add some cucumber, lettuce, herbs and star fruit. To form the roll, first fold the sides into the centre over the filling, then fold the bottom of the rice paper up and over. Roll from bottom to top to form a tight roll, and serve with the dipping fish sauce.

MAKES 12 SKEWERS

125 ml (4 fl oz/½ cup) coconut milk
½ teaspoon oyster sauce
2 teaspoons fish sauce
1 teaspoon honey
2 garlic cloves, finely chopped
1 lemongrass stem, white part only, finely chopped
1 teaspoon hot paprika
2 teaspoons vegetable oil
350 g (10½ oz) beef sirloin, trimmed and sliced into 24 thin 3 x 5 cm (1¼ x 2 inch) pieces
100 g (3½ oz) pork back fat, sliced into 1 x 2 cm (½ x ¾ inch) pieces
2 onions, each cut into 12 wedges
40 g (1½ oz/¼ cup) roasted peanuts, crushed (page 328)
18 dried round rice paper wrappers (22 cm/8½ inch diameter)
1 Lebanese (short) cucumber, sliced into batons
1 green oak lettuce or butter lettuce, leaves separated
1 bunch perilla, leaves picked
1 bunch mint, leaves picked
1 bunch Vietnamese mint, leaves picked
2 star fruit, halved lengthways, then thinly sliced
250 ml (9 fl oz/1 cup) dipping fish sauce (page 331)

FLOURLESS CASSAVA CAKE
BÁNH KHOAI MÌ

SUZE AND I PUT OUR DIRTY CLOTHES IN FOR A WASH AT A SMALL SHOP THAT SOLD EVERYTHING: BEER, CIGARETTES, HATS, MODEL BOATS AND CAKES. WE CAME BACK A FEW HOURS LATER TO PICK THEM UP BUT ENDED UP IN THE WRONG SHOP. ALL THE SHOPS LOOKED THE SAME AND THEY ALL SOLD THE SAME GOODS, THIS CASSAVA CAKE INCLUDED. IT WAS WORTH BEING LOST JUST SO I COULD HAVE ANOTHER SLICE.

500 g (1 lb 2 oz) cassava, thawed if using frozen
3 eggs
120 g (4¼ oz) palm sugar (jaggery), crushed or grated
40 g (1½ oz) butter, melted and cooled
½ vanilla bean, halved lengthways and seeds scraped
2 tablespoons sweetened condensed milk
125 ml (4 fl oz/½ cup) coconut milk
250 ml (9 fl oz/1 cup) sweet coconut milk (page 337)

Preheat the oven to 190°C (375°F/Gas 5). Grease a 22 cm (8½ inch) round cake tin with butter.

If using fresh cassava, remove the thick skin, then finely grate the flesh. If using frozen cassava the skin has already been removed, so finely grate it into a bowl. Squeeze the cassava with your hands to extract the juice, and discard the juice.

Beat the eggs in a bowl with the sugar, then add the butter, vanilla seeds, condensed milk and coconut milk. Mix well, then add the grated cassava and mix again. Pour the batter in the greased tin and bake for 40 minutes, or until the cake is firm and golden and a skewer inserted into the centre of the cake comes out clean. Cool, then cut into slices or squares and top with sweet coconut milk.

SERVES 6-8

CHARMING
HOI AN

4

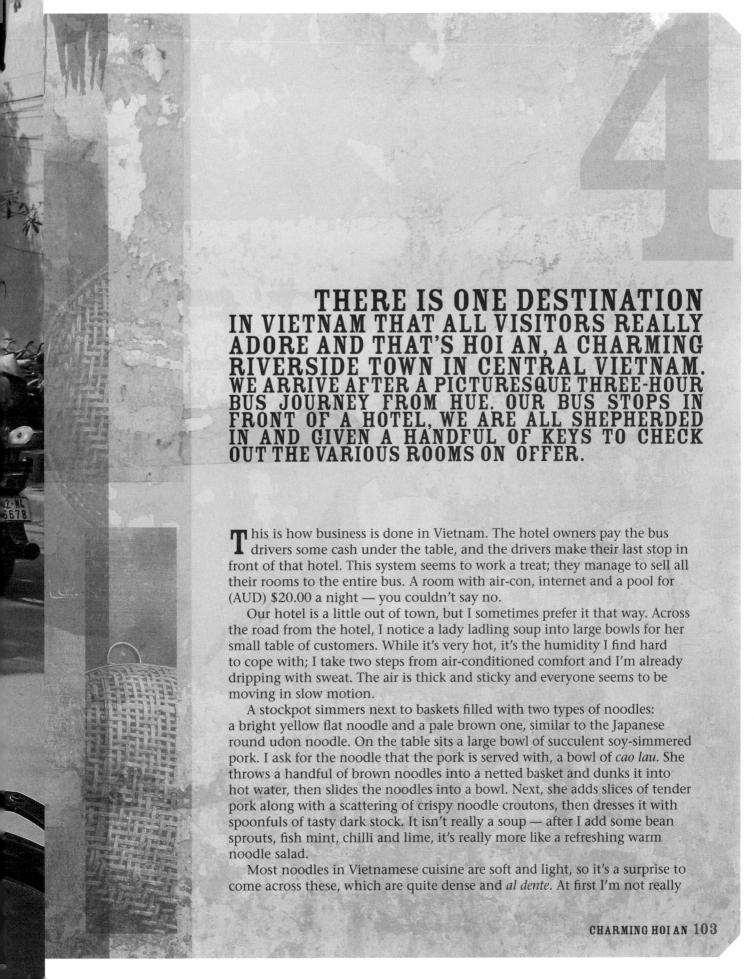

THERE IS ONE DESTINATION IN VIETNAM THAT ALL VISITORS REALLY ADORE AND THAT'S HOI AN, A CHARMING RIVERSIDE TOWN IN CENTRAL VIETNAM. WE ARRIVE AFTER A PICTURESQUE THREE-HOUR BUS JOURNEY FROM HUE. OUR BUS STOPS IN FRONT OF A HOTEL, WE ARE ALL SHEPHERDED IN AND GIVEN A HANDFUL OF KEYS TO CHECK OUT THE VARIOUS ROOMS ON OFFER.

This is how business is done in Vietnam. The hotel owners pay the bus drivers some cash under the table, and the drivers make their last stop in front of that hotel. This system seems to work a treat; they manage to sell all their rooms to the entire bus. A room with air-con, internet and a pool for (AUD) $20.00 a night — you couldn't say no.

Our hotel is a little out of town, but I sometimes prefer it that way. Across the road from the hotel, I notice a lady ladling soup into large bowls for her small table of customers. While it's very hot, it's the humidity I find hard to cope with; I take two steps from air-conditioned comfort and I'm already dripping with sweat. The air is thick and sticky and everyone seems to be moving in slow motion.

A stockpot simmers next to baskets filled with two types of noodles: a bright yellow flat noodle and a pale brown one, similar to the Japanese round udon noodle. On the table sits a large bowl of succulent soy-simmered pork. I ask for the noodle that the pork is served with, a bowl of *cao lau*. She throws a handful of brown noodles into a netted basket and dunks it into hot water, then slides the noodles into a bowl. Next, she adds slices of tender pork along with a scattering of crispy noodle croutons, then dresses it with spoonfuls of tasty dark stock. It isn't really a soup — after I add some bean sprouts, fish mint, chilli and lime, it's really more like a refreshing warm noodle salad.

Most noodles in Vietnamese cuisine are soft and light, so it's a surprise to come across these, which are quite dense and *al dente*. At first I'm not really sure if I like them, but by the third and fourth mouthful I'm really beginning to enjoy the chewiness and springiness of the noodle, and the dish as a whole is full of intense flavour and texture.

The *cao lau* lady senses my curiosity. 'It is Hoi An's special noodle,' she says. 'You can only find it in our town. People from all over Vietnam travel to Hoi An to eat this dish. It is made from rice that has been infused with ash, then made with water from the Ba Le well; it's this unique water that gives the noodle its unusual texture.'

She tells me that there is only one family that makes this noodle — for the whole town, for the restaurants, cafés and markets. The family that created the noodle have kept the recipe secret for generations; many have attempted to make the noodle but all have failed. So what started as a small family of noodle makers, has now grown to become a whole village of noodle makers, with hundreds of uncles, aunties, cousins, nephews and nieces working together, all vowed to secrecy.

I love this tradition of protecting old recipes — it makes the experience of eating that dish much more special. We pay about (AUD) 75 cents for the noodles, then are swarmed by other street vendors, who had been sitting patiently next to their fridges on wheels, waiting until we had finished eating.

Six ladies, all lined up next to each other, selling the same goods, all chirp in unison, 'Want to hire bicycle, want water, mars bar, want beer, want chips?' I wonder why they don't all come to an agreement and each offer something different. To make things fair, I hire my bicycle from one lady, Suze's bicycle from the second lady, water from another and nick knacks from the others. They all seem to like that idea.

We ride into town, passing shop after shop, all selling clothes or shoes, most with signs out front saying, 'Recommended by *Lonely Planet*' — surely they weren't all recommended. 'Come buy from me sir, madame!' Shop after shop after shop ...

I had been thinking of getting a suit made here, but I feel too overwhelmed, so we keep riding until we reach the central markets of Hoi An, where goods from the stalls overflow onto the streets. We get off our bikes and manoeuvre our way through the bustling market, find a bicycle parking station, grab a number, pay our 2 cents and leave our bikes there to be looked after.

It is impossible to simply take a pleasant stroll through this market — people are on the move, buying, haggling, doing business — you get pushed out of the way or nudged by a motorbike if you don't walk fast enough, their horns honking in all directions. Stallholders grab your arm, forcing you to look at their goods for sale — chopsticks, cinnamon toothpicks, incense holders and tourist junk. Herb and vegetable sellers display their produce on any floor space available; this would have to be the most cramped and energetic market I have seen in Vietnam.

We make our way to the river's edge, to the seafood corner. I fold up the bottom of my pants and walk through pools of water, littered with fish guts and scales. Ladies sit on tall stools, with huge sacks of multi-coloured snails the size of rice grains, picking the flesh out with a safety pin. I'm glad I don't have that job.

The seafood market is run by women only. The men return from fishing at 4.30 a.m. and drop off their catch to the women waiting at the dock. The women then sling 50 kilograms of mackerel over their backs and head back to their stalls.

> **"'ARE YOU MARRIED?' SHE ASKS. I SHAKE MY HEAD. 'WELL, MARRY ONE OF THE DAUGHTERS, THEN MAYBE THEY'LL TEACH YOU THEIR SECRET FAMILY RECIPE. THEN COME BACK HERE AND TELL ME THE RECIPE. THEN WE CAN BOTH BE RICH!' ALL THE NOODLE SELLERS BREAK OUT IN LAUGHTER, SENDING ME WALKING AWAY IN EMBARRASSMENT. "**

These old women are tough and extremely aggressive, their dark skins wrinkled like leather, their rotting teeth ruby red from chewing beetle nut. A lady shouts at me, a burning cigarette hanging from her mouth, 'Don't just bloody look at the seafood, buy something! And if you're going to take a photo, it's going to cost you a dollar!'

I move on to the food section, where vendors squat on long wide wooden benchtops, selling noodles. The noodles are stacked as round sheets on bamboo trays and sliced fresh. A woman turns the wheel, feeding the noodle sheet through the slicing machine, then her phone rings. 'How many kilos? Twenty? What restaurant? O.K., I'll be five minutes.' She hangs up, feeds the sliced noodle into a bag and onto the scales, then another call — an order for three types of noodles: soft white rice noodles, a vibrant yellow rice noodle and the chewy *cao lau* noodle. As I approach, her phone rings again. 'Hah? I'm too busy, come get it yourself, I'm not going to deliver for only 5 kilograms!' She slams the phone down and politely asks me what she can do for me.

'I want to find out where they make this *cao lau* noodle and if I'm able to visit the village?'

'Are you married?' she asks. I shake my head. 'Well, marry one of the daughters, then maybe they'll teach you their secret family recipe. Then come back here and tell me the recipe. Then we can both be rich!' All the noodle sellers break out in laughter, sending me walking away in embarrassment.

I take refuge at a juice stand, heaving under mounds of mangoes, sour sop, passionfruit, avocados, bananas, jackfruit and mangosteens. A small girl appears from behind the counter and asks me what I would like. I take a seat and order a mango smoothie. She peels the mango with a sharp knife, with such grace and skill; it is like watching my experienced mother do it. Perfect slices of mango into the blender, three spoons of condensed milk, shaved ice, and whizz. She pours the smoothie into my glass — it fills the glass exactly to the top. She sits down next to me and we begin to chat.

Her name is Que, which means cinnamon in Vietnamese. She is twelve years old and her family is from a small village two hours from Hoi An. I'm surprised, as I thought her mother was the stall owner.

The owner appears. 'No, she's not my daughter; she works for me. Que came walking through the market looking lost and hungry. Her family can't afford to raise her, so she had no choice but to leave home, travelled to Hoi An on her own and came asking for work in the markets. There's no work here, no one can afford to pay her a wage, but when I saw her cute face, I had to help.'

> ## 66 I THINK HOW I COULD SO EASILY GIVE HER ENOUGH MONEY TO PAY FOR HER WHOLE SECONDARY SCHOOLING — I SOMETIMES SPEND 150 BUCKS JUST ON A MEAL OR A PAIR OF JEANS — BUT I WANT TO DO MORE. 99

Que is such a happy girl. She tells me that her boss feeds her and lets her sleep in her home. In return, she works at the juice stand; she doesn't get paid but she is looked after well. I ask if she ever went to school.

'Yes, but I had to finish in primary school, because once you reach secondary level, school gets really expensive. So I had to leave and find a job.'

'So do you plan to find a job where you can earn some money?'

'Well, that's what I wanted to do, but there's not much work around here. School costs about 2 million dong (about (AUD) $150.00) per year, and I don't know how I can ever save that kind of money!'

My mind begins to race as I start to think of all the things I could do to help her. I think how I could so easily give her enough money to pay for her whole secondary schooling — I sometimes spend 150 bucks just on a meal or a pair of jeans — but I want to do more. Que is not the only child in need of an education; there are millions of children in Vietnam in the same situation. I have ideas of opening a hospitality training school in Hoi An, perhaps building a guesthouse with a restaurant and bar. We could train young adults in hotel operations, cookery, front of house and also teach English, in the hope that these students can build enough skills to get them jobs in hotels and restaurants. The revenue raised from the guesthouse and restaurant would then fund kids in need of schooling.

I quietly give Que all the money I have in my pockets and promise her we will come back to see her again.

❧ ❧ ❧

Suze and I walk to the Old Quarter of Hoi An, along the river lined with ancient wooden houses that are now home to cafés, restaurants and shops. The architecture is a blend of cultures and influences: between the fifteenth and nineteenth centuries Hoi An was home to an international trading port. The aged buildings reflect Hoi An's diversity — colonial, Chinese and Japanese — and the streets are lined with textured walls of gold, blue, green and red.

I think back to the secret *cao lau* noodle, which I'm sure was influenced by the Japanese udon noodle. I start thinking how Vietnamese food has been influenced by so many of the best countries in the culinary arts, making it the most delicate and refined cuisine in all of southeast Asia.

Down a narrow lane we see metal coffee filters on display; we head towards the shop. Folk music plays from speakers dotted about, the locals are relaxed, laid back and happy — there's a swing to our step as we stroll down the lane.

We order a coffee and sit next to a table of men playing cards for money. It seems like a serious game, the men slamming the cards down one after the other. They ask if I want to join them but I dare not. One of the men, slimly built with silver hair, wearing a shirt two sizes too big asks where we are from.

When we tell him, he moves to our table, excited to hear about Australia. He tells us that he comes from a family of shoemakers and his favourite customers are from Australia, as 'Aussies are easy going and friendly, just like the people of Hoi An'. He is Lam, and after I tell him I have a Vietnamese restaurant in Sydney, he jumps out of his chair and rushes to phone his wife.

'My wife is an amazing cook. She would be honoured to have you over for dinner tonight. She works as a chef at Hoi An's most expensive hotel. Where are you staying? I'll pick you up at 8 p.m!'

Night begins to fall as we wander back to our hotel. Hoi An starts to come alive: night vendors set up their carts, thousands of coloured lanterns become luminous throughout the town, giving it an old world charm. Tourists venture out of their air-con rooms to drink freshly brewed beer for (AUD) 50 cents a glass. I'm tempted to do the same, but we have dinner plans.

Lam picks us up on his motorbike. He sits up front, Suze in the middle, and I sit at the back, the bags of beer that we've bought delicately balanced on the handlebars. We cross the bridge and head out of town, into remote darkness. In any other situation, in any other country, I would be more cautious, maybe even a little scared, but in Vietnam, meeting people, making new friends and getting invited to strangers' homes for dinner is, for me, a regular occurrence. It is these experiences that I look forward to most.

Their house is painted blue with yellow wooden window panels. His whole family come out to greet us: his wife, son, father and mother. I catch a scent in the night air — fragrant wafts of tamarind, prawns and ash are coming from a room beside the house. My nose leads me to the most impressive kitchen; it's primitive but 'real Vietnam'. The dimly lit room is warm and homely, wood is stacked high against the wall, there is no clutter and only a few pots and pans. A blackened pot is burning over a wood fire, and inside the pot a tamarind broth bubbles away. Beside it a pan of school prawns sizzle in oil; Lam's wife controls the heat by waving a handmade paper fan over the coals.

I offer to help but Lam tells me to leave the cooking to the women. I explain to him that in my family the men do most of the cooking, and that I'm delighted to help his wife. We add sliced beef and water spinach to the sweet and sour tamarind broth. We stir-fry some prawns and pork belly with fish sauce, while Lam fetches some pumpkin flowers from his father's vegetable garden to make a light salad. This is my first experience tasting pumpkin flowers, which we simply blanch then toss in the salad.

While we are cooking, Lam comes back with some paper and a pencil. He asks me to take my shoes off and to place each foot on a sheet of paper. He draws an outline of my feet and then leads me to his workshop. Inside, the walls are lined with shelves holding hundreds of different sized shoe lasts; the floor is covered in a rainbow of leather scraps. He asks me to choose my favourite colours and he'll make me a pair of boots. 'They'll be ready by tomorrow morning,' he says.

I return to the kitchen to help serve the dinner. We take the plates out to the table in the backyard, beside the vegetable garden. From there we can see the moonlit river as we eat this wonderful, authentic Hoi An family dinner with newly made friends. This is the beginning of my love affair with Hoi An.

TAMARIND BROTH WITH BEEF AND WATER SPINACH
CANH CHUA RAU MUỐNG THỊT BÒ

THIS TAMARIND BROTH IS ONE OF MY ALL TIME FAVOURITE VIETNAMESE DISHES; IT REALLY DEFINES WHAT VIETNAMESE CUISINE IS ALL ABOUT — SWEET, SOUR, SALTY, SPICY, LIGHT AND VERY WELL BALANCED. TRADITIONALLY, SOUTHERNERS SERVE THIS DISH WITH FISH OR PRAWNS, AND IN CENTRAL VIETNAM I FOUND LOCALS USING BEEF AND WATER SPINACH. YOU CAN USE WHATEVER YOU PREFER — TRY CALAMARI, MUSSELS, SCALLOPS OR CHICKEN.

WHEN SHOPPING FOR THE HERBS FOR THIS DISH, YOU'LL NEED TO GO TO A GOOD ASIAN MARKET TO FIND THEM. WRITE DOWN THEIR VIETNAMESE NAMES — RICE PADDY HERB (*NGO OM*) AND SAWTOOTH HERB (*NGO GAI*) — AND SHOW THE SHOP ATTENDANT, AS THEY MAY NOT BE FAMILIAR WITH THE ENGLISH.

2 tablespoons vegetable oil
2 garlic cloves, finely chopped
1 lemongrass stem, bruised and cut into 5 cm (2 inch) pieces
350 g (12 oz) beef sirloin, trimmed and thinly sliced
2 tablespoons fish sauce
2 tablespoons sugar
4 tablespoons tamarind water (page 332)
1 bunch water spinach, washed and drained, torn into 4 cm (1½ inch) pieces
1 bunch rice paddy herb, leaves chopped
1 bunch sawtooth herb, leaves chopped
1 teaspoon fried garlic (page 329)
2 bird's eye chillies, sliced
fish sauce, for dipping

Heat a large saucepan over medium heat, add the oil and fry the garlic and lemongrass until fragrant. Add the beef and cook, stirring, for 2 minutes. Add 1.5 litres (52 fl oz/6 cups) of water, the fish sauce, sugar and 1 teaspoon salt, and bring to the boil. Reduce the heat and simmer for 2 minutes, constantly skimming any impurities off the surface. Add the tamarind water and water spinach, bring back to the boil, then turn off the heat.

Transfer the soup to large serving bowls. Garnish with rice paddy herb, sawtooth herb, fried garlic and half the chilli. Serve with jasmine rice, and a small bowl of the remaining sliced chilli and fish sauce for dipping.

SERVES 4–6 AS PART OF A SHARED MEAL

BITTER MELON AND FISH BALL SOUP

CANH KHỔ QUA CHẢ CÁ

BITTER MELON LOOKS LIKE A PALE GREEN CUCUMBER BUT IT HAS A BUMPY EXTERIOR, SIMILAR TO A KAFFIR LIME. ITS FLESH IS CRUNCHY AND WATERY IN TEXTURE WITH A BITTER TASTE, AS THE NAME WILL TELL YOU. THE VEGETABLE SHOULD BE EATEN GREEN AS IT GETS SWEETER AS IT RIPENS.

IN VIETNAM, SOUPS SUCH AS THESE LIGHT BROTHS ARE USUALLY SERVED TO COMPLEMENT THE OTHER DISHES THAT MAKE UP THE MEAL. THEY HELP BALANCE OUT THE SALTIER FLAVOURS OF OTHER FOODS AND ALSO CLEANSE THE PALATE.

Put a large saucepan over medium heat and add 1.5 litres (52 fl oz/6 cups) of water, the fish sauce, sugar and 1 teaspoon each of salt and freshly ground black pepper. Bring to the boil.

Using a teaspoon, shape small balls of fish paste, then slide them into the boiling water, dipping the teaspoon into the water each time to prevent the paste sticking to the spoon. Repeat this process until all the paste is transferred into the soup.

Bring the soup to a simmer and cook for 5 minutes, skimming any impurities off the surface, until all the fish balls float to the top. Now add the bitter melon to the pan, bring the water back to the boil and then turn off the heat.

Transfer the soup and fish balls to large soup bowls and garnish with the spring onion and coriander sprigs. Serve with jasmine rice.

SERVES 4-6 AS PART OF A SHARED MEAL

1 tablespoon fish sauce
1 teaspoon sugar
300 g (10½ oz) fish paste
   (page 334)
500 g (1 lb 2 oz) bitter melon,
   halved, seeded and thinly sliced
2 tablespoons sliced spring onion
   (scallion), green part only
coriander (cilantro) sprigs,
   to garnish

TAMARIND BEEF AND CUCUMBER SALAD
BÒ THẤU MẸ DƯA LEO

MY FRIEND VY, FROM MORNING GLORY RESTAURANT IN HOI AN, ASKED ME TO MAKE A FRESH VIETNAMESE SALAD THAT SHE HAD NEVER TRIED BEFORE. I WAS A LITTLE NERVOUS, AS SHE IS A GURU OF VIETNAMESE CUISINE. I STEPPED INSIDE HER SMALL KITCHEN AND NOTICED ONE OF HER COOKS SQUEEZING TAMARIND PULP, WHICH GAVE ME THE INSPIRATION. WITHIN MINUTES I HAD COMPLETED HER SALAD AND, TO MY RELIEF, VY REALLY ENJOYED IT. IF YOU STORE SOME TAMARIND WATER IN YOUR FRIDGE, YOU CAN WHIP UP THIS SALAD IN NO TIME.

300 g (10½ oz) telegraph (long) cucumber, finely shaved with a vegetable peeler

1 carrot, peeled and finely shaved with a vegetable peeler

2 tablespoons caster (superfine) sugar

2 tablespoons vegetable oil

2 garlic cloves, finely chopped

350 g (10½ oz) beef eye fillet, trimmed and sliced into thin strips

2 tablespoons tamarind water (page 332)

1 handful sawtooth herb, leaves sliced

1 handful Vietnamese mint leaves

2 tablespoons fried garlic (page 329)

2 tablespoons Aunty Nine's salad dressing (page 330)

50 g (1¾ oz/⅓ cup) roasted peanuts, chopped (page 328)

2 bird's eye chillies, finely chopped

In a bowl, combine the cucumber, carrot and sugar. Mix well and set aside for 10 minutes, then drain.

Place a frying pan over high heat, add the oil and fry the garlic until fragrant. Add the beef, season with ½ teaspoon freshly ground black pepper, then stir-fry the beef for no more than 3 minutes. Remove the beef to a bowl, add 1 tablespoon of the tamarind water and toss to combine.

In another bowl, combine the cucumber and carrot, sawtooth herb, Vietnamese mint, fried garlic and tamarind beef. Add the remaining tablespoon of tamarind water and Aunty Nine's salad dressing, then toss the salad to combine all the ingredients. Pile the salad onto a serving platter and garnish with the peanuts and chilli.

SERVES 4–6 AS PART OF A SHARED MEAL

PUMPKIN FLOWER SALAD WITH PRAWN AND PORK
GỎI BÔNG BÍ

PUMPKIN FLOWERS ARE FOUND AND GROWN EVERYWHERE IN HOI AN, AND THIS IS WHERE I HAD MY FIRST PUMPKIN FLOWER EXPERIENCE — IT WAS THE HIGHLIGHT OF THE MEAL. IF YOU CAN'T GET YOUR HANDS ON SOME PUMPKIN FLOWERS, USE ZUCCHINI FLOWERS INSTEAD. PUMPKIN FLOWERS CAN ALSO BE STUFFED AS YOU WOULD A ZUCCHINI FLOWER, AND ARE DELICIOUS WHEN SIMPLY WOK-TOSSED IN GARLIC.

Pour 1 litre (35 fl oz/4 cups) of water into a small saucepan, add the pork neck and bring to the boil. Skim any impurities off the surface, then reduce the heat to a low simmer, add a pinch of salt and freshly ground black pepper, then cover the pan and cook for 20 minutes. Drain the pork and allow to cool, then thinly slice.

Bring a saucepan of water to the boil. Blanch the pumpkin flowers for 30 seconds and refresh in iced water, then drain.

In a bowl, combine the pork, prawns, pickled vegetables, fried garlic and pumpkin flowers. Pour over Aunty Nine's salad dressing and toss well to combine. Transfer to a serving plate, garnish with coriander sprigs and serve with a small bowl of dipping fish sauce.

SERVES 4-6 AS PART OF A SHARED MEAL

200 g (7 oz) pork neck

500 g (1 lb 2 oz) pumpkin or zucchini (courgette) flowers, washed

200 g (7 oz) cooked tiger prawns (shrimp), peeled and deveined, halved lengthways

250 g (9 oz/1 cup) pickled vegetables (page 335)

1 tablespoon fried garlic (page 329)

4 tablespoons Aunty Nine's salad dressing (page 330)

coriander (cilantro) sprigs, to garnish

4 tablespoons dipping fish sauce (page 331)

GREEN MANGO SALAD WITH PRAWN AND DRIED WHITEBAIT
GỎI XOÀI SỐNG

WE DECIDED TO EAT DINNER ONE EVENING IN A RESTAURANT BY THE RIVER IN HOI AN. WE ORDERED A FEW DISHES AND THIS GREEN MANGO SALAD WAS ONE OF THEM. THE CHEF CAME OUT WITH A LONG BAMBOO POLE AND PLUCKED SOME GREEN MANGOES FROM THE TREE BESIDE US.

GREEN MANGOES ARE UNRIPENED MANGOES, THEY ARE OFTEN EATEN DIPPED IN SALT AND CHILLI, AND ARE ENJOYED FOR THEIR CRUNCHY TEXTURE AND SOURNESS. WHEN CHOOSING GREEN MANGOES, MAKE SURE THEY ARE NICE AND FIRM. I ALSO USE DRIED WHITEBAIT HERE, WHICH YOU SHOULD BE ABLE TO FIND IN AN ASIAN MARKET; IF NOT, USE DRIED ANCHOVIES INSTEAD, THE SMALLER THE BETTER.

50 g (1¾ oz) dried whitebait or dried anchovies

vegetable oil, for deep-frying

2 green mangoes, peeled and julienned

1 long red chilli, julienned

1 handful Vietnamese mint leaves, torn

1 handful mint leaves, torn

1 handful perilla leaves, torn

1 teaspoon fried garlic (page 329)

2 tablespoons fried red Asian shallots (page 329)

10 cooked tiger prawns (shrimp), peeled and deveined, halved lengthways

4 tablespoons Aunty Nine's salad dressing (page 330)

1 tablespoon roasted peanuts, crushed (page 328)

dipping fish sauce (page 331), to serve

Wash the dried whitebait, drain them and pat dry with paper towel. Pour the oil into a wok or saucepan and heat to 200°C (400°F), or until a cube of bread dropped into the oil browns in 5 seconds. Deep-fry the whitebait for 1 minute until crisp. Remove from the oil using a slotted spoon and drain well on paper towel.

In a bowl, combine the green mango, chilli, Vietnamese mint, mint, perilla, fried garlic, fried shallots, prawns and whitebait. Pour over Aunty Nine's dressing and toss well to combine. Garnish with crushed peanuts and serve with a small bowl of dipping fish sauce.

SERVES 4-6 AS PART OF A SHARED MEAL

WOK-TOSSED BEAN SPROUTS AND GARLIC CHIVES
GIÁ HẸ XÀO

MY BUS WANTS TO LEAVE WITHOUT ME; THE DRIVER REPEATEDLY HONKS THE HORN. IT WILL BE A THREE-HOUR DRIVE WITH NO BREAK; I HADN'T EATEN AND JUST NEEDED SOMETHING QUICKLY. THE STREET FOOD VENDOR FLAMES HIS WOK, ADDS A DASH OF OIL, THROWS IN A HANDFUL OF BEAN SPROUTS AND GARLIC CHIVES. HE TOSSES IT WITH THE MOST DELICATE TOUCH — IT'S SO SIMPLE, SO FAST AND STILL RETAINS ITS CRISP TEXTURE.

Place a wok over high heat, add the vegetable oil, garlic and shallots and stir-fry for 1 minute, or until fragrant. Add the bean sprouts, garlic chives and spring onions and toss for 1 minute. Add the fish sauce, sugar, 1 tablespoon of water and a pinch of salt and freshly ground black pepper. Toss for a further minute, then finish with a drizzle of sesame oil. Serve with jasmine rice.

SERVES 4-6 AS PART OF A SHARED MEAL

2 tablespoons vegetable oil
1 tablespoon finely chopped garlic
2 red Asian shallots, finely chopped
300 g (10½ oz) bean sprouts
50 g (1¾ oz/1 bunch) garlic chives, roots trimmed, cut into 5 cm (2 inch) lengths
2 spring onions (scallions), cut into 5 cm (2 inch) lengths
1 tablespoon fish sauce
1 teaspoon sugar
½ teaspoon sesame oil

STIR-FRIED CALAMARI WITH PINEAPPLE AND VEGETABLES
MỰC XÀO KHÓM

I PREPARED THIS DISH FOR MY PARENTS WHEN I WENT TO VISIT THEM AFTER I GOT BACK TO SYDNEY. MY MOTHER CALLED ME AT ONE O'CLOCK IN THE MORNING TO TELL ME THAT SHE COULDN'T SLEEP BECAUSE THEY WEREN'T ENTIRELY HAPPY WITH THE DISH AND THOUGHT I SHOULD CHANGE THE RECIPE. 'IT NEEDS MORE SOUR, MORE SPICY,' SHE SAID. OF COURSE I TOLD THEM THAT THEY WERE RIGHT AND THAT I WOULD CHANGE THE RECIPE — BUT I DIDN'T.

300 g (10½ oz) calamari tubes, cleaned
2 tablespoons vegetable oil
2 red Asian shallots, finely chopped
3 garlic cloves, finely chopped
½ green capsicum (pepper), seeded and cut into 2 cm (¾ inch) cubes
1 Lebanese (short) cucumber, halved, seeded and cut into bite-sized pieces
100 g (3½ oz) sweet pineapple, cut into bite-sized pieces
2 tablespoons fish sauce
1 tablespoon sugar
1 onion, cut into thin wedges
4 spring onions (scallions), cut into 4 cm (1½ inch) lengths
½ bunch Asian celery, cut into 4 cm (1½ inch) pieces
1 small handful coriander (cilantro) leaves
1 bird's eye chilli, thinly sliced
light soy sauce, for dipping

SWEET AND SOUR SAUCE
1 teaspoon cornflour (cornstarch)
5 teaspoons sugar
5 teaspoons white vinegar
2 teaspoons tomato sauce (ketchup)
2 teaspoons lemon juice or pineapple juice

To make the sweet and sour sauce, combine the cornflour with 2 teaspoons of water in a bowl until smooth. Add the remaining sauce ingredients, mix well and set aside.

Score the calamari tubes on the inside, then cut into bite-sized pieces, about 3 x 5 cm (1¼ x 2 inches).

Place a wok over high heat. When the wok is hot, add 1 tablespoon of the oil followed by the shallots, half the garlic and all the calamari. Stir-fry for 3 minutes, then remove from the wok and set aside. In the same hot wok, add the remaining oil, the capsicum, cucumber and pineapple. Stir to combine, then add the fish sauce, sugar and 1 teaspoon freshly ground black pepper, and stir-fry for a further 3 minutes.

Now add the prepared sweet and sour sauce and stir until the sauce thickens slightly. Return the calamari to the wok and add the remaining garlic, the onion, spring onions and Asian celery. Combine well, then transfer to a serving bowl and garnish with coriander. Serve with jasmine rice, and a small bowl of sliced chilli and soy sauce for dipping.

SERVES 4-6 AS PART OF A SHARED MEAL

SCHOOL PRAWNS WOK-TOSSED WITH PORK BELLY
TÉP RANG BA RỌI

IT'S 5.30 A.M. AND BOATS WITH FISH, SQUID AND PRAWNS HAVE JUST ARRIVED. THE PRAWNS ARE ALMOST JUMPING OUT OF THEIR BASKETS, THEIR FRESHNESS IRRESISTIBLE. I BOUGHT A FEW HUNDRED GRAMS AND TOOK IT TO THE MARKETS AND ASKED ONE OF THE COOKS IF SHE COULD MAKE SOMETHING FOR SUZE AND ME. SOME PORK, SHALLOTS AND FISH SAUCE LATER, SHE HAD MADE US A SIMPLE, FLAVOURSOME DISH THAT REMINDED ME OF MUM'S HOME COOKING ... COMFORT FOOD.

SCHOOL PRAWNS ARE VERY SMALL AND ARE BEST EATEN WITH THEIR SHELLS STILL INTACT; THEIR SHELLS ARE NOT AT ALL TOUGH, AND THEY ADD CRUNCH TO THE DISH.

2 tablespoons finely chopped garlic
2 tablespoons fish sauce
1 tablespoon finely chopped lemongrass, white part only
1 tablespoon sugar
200 g (7 oz) lean, boneless pork belly, skin on, thinly sliced
1 teaspoon shaoxing rice wine
200 g (7 oz) raw small school prawns (shrimp), legs and heads trimmed, or peel if preferred
2 tablespoons vegetable oil
2 red Asian shallots, finely chopped
2 tablespoons sliced spring onion (scallion)
1 bird's eye chilli, thinly sliced
fish sauce, for dipping

In a bowl, combine 2 teaspoons of the garlic, 1 tablespoon of the fish sauce, 2 teaspoons of the lemongrass, 2 teaspoons of the sugar and a pinch of salt and freshly ground black pepper. Mix well, then add the pork belly, stir to coat in the marinade, then set aside to marinate for 15 minutes.

In a large bowl, combine 1 teaspoon salt, the rice wine and 250 ml (9 fl oz/1 cup) of cold water. Add the prawns and wash thoroughly in the liquid. Strain the prawns and discard the washing liquid.

In another bowl, combine 2 teaspoons of the garlic, the remaining fish sauce, lemongrass and sugar and a pinch of salt and pepper. Mix well, then add the prawns and marinate for 15 minutes.

Heat a wok until very hot, then add the oil, shallots and pork. Stir-fry until the pork is browned, then add the prawns and continue to stir-fry until the prawns change colour. Add the remaining garlic and the spring onion and stir-fry for a further minute, then transfer to a serving plate. Serve with jasmine rice, and a small bowl of sliced chilli and fish sauce for dipping.

SERVES 4–6 AS PART OF A SHARED MEAL

BEEF WOK-TOSSED WITH BETEL LEAVES
BÒ XÀO LÁ LỐT

BETEL LEAVES ARE NATIVE TO MALAYSIA AND ARE NOW USED THROUGHOUT SOUTHEAST ASIA. THEY ARE HEART-SHAPED, DARK GREEN IN COLOUR, AND ONE SIDE IS GLOSSY. YOU HAVE MOST LIKELY SEEN THEM IN MODERN THAI RESTAURANTS, SERVED RAW WITH MIXED TOPPINGS ON THEM. IN VIETNAM WE LIKE THE LEAVES WOK-TOSSED OR GRILLED, AS THEY RELEASE A FRAGRANCE LIKE NOTHING ELSE. WRITE DOWN ITS VIETNAMESE NAME WHEN YOU GO TO THE ASIAN MARKET, AND ASK FOR *LA LOT*.

Heat the oil in a wok and swirl to coat the wok with oil. Add the lemongrass, garlic and chilli and cook, stirring, for 2 minutes over medium–high heat until fragrant. Add the beef and toss for 2 minutes. Now add the fish sauce, soy sauce, sugar, a pinch of salt, onion and betel leaves. Toss the ingredients for another 2 minutes, then transfer to serving bowls and garnish with the peanuts. Serve with jasmine rice.

SERVES 4–6 AS PART OF A SHARED MEAL

2 tablespoons vegetable oil

1 lemongrass stem, white part only, finely chopped

2 garlic cloves, finely chopped

2 bird's eye chillies, finely chopped

350 g (12 oz) beef sirloin, trimmed and thinly sliced

1 tablespoon fish sauce

2 teaspoons light soy sauce

2 teaspoons sugar

1 onion, thinly sliced

300 g (10½ oz/2 bunches) betel leaves, roughly chopped

2 tablespoons roasted peanuts, crushed (page 328)

HOI AN WHITE CHICKEN RICE
CƠM GÀ HỘI AN

I AM WAITING WITH A SMALL GROUP OF LOCALS FOR THIS ROADSIDE CHICKEN STALL TO OPEN. IT IS 4.59 P.M., AND THE RICE IS STEAMING, FRAGRANT WITH JASMINE AND GINGER. WE SIT AND WAIT PATIENTLY, SALIVATING AS WE WATCH THE CLEAVER CHOP THROUGH SKIN AND BONES. THIS DELICIOUS DISH WAS INTRODUCED TO HOI AN BY THE CHINESE, AND IS SIMILAR TO THE CHINESE DISH CALLED HAINAN CHICKEN. IF YOU HAVE ANY EXTRA GINGER, FINELY JULIENNE IT AND ADD IT TO YOUR DIPPING SAUCE.

To cook the chicken and make the stock, stuff the chicken with the onions, spring onions and ginger. Place the chicken in a stockpot with 5 litres (175 fl oz/20 cups) of cold water and bring to the boil for 15 minutes, constantly skimming any impurities off the surface. Now add the fish sauce, sugar, 1 teaspoon salt and 2 teaspoons freshly ground black pepper. Cover the pan and simmer for 20 minutes, then turn off the heat and set aside for 45 minutes. Remove the chicken and cool. Strain the stock through a piece of muslin — you will need 750 ml (26 fl oz/3 cups) of stock. Set the stock aside. With a cleaver, chop the chicken in half, then chop each half into 8 pieces. Set the chicken aside.

To make the ginger rice, place a heavy-based saucepan over medium heat. Add the oil, garlic and ginger and fry for 2 minutes, or until light brown, then add the rice and stir-fry for 5 minutes. Add the chicken stock and bring to the boil, then reduce the heat to low, cover the pan and cook for 20 minutes. Turn off the heat and allow the rice to stand for 10 minutes still covered.

Garnish the chicken with coriander sprigs and serve warm or at room temperature with the ginger rice. Serve with a bowl of dipping fish sauce.

SERVES 4-6 AS PART OF A SHARED MEAL

1 whole chicken (1.5 kg/3 lb 5 oz), cleaned
2 onions, peeled and cut into quarters
4 spring onions (scallions), knotted
100 g (3½ oz) ginger, peeled and sliced
3 tablespoons fish sauce
2 teaspoons sugar
coriander (cilantro) sprigs, to garnish
dipping fish sauce (page 331), to serve

GINGER RICE
2 tablespoons vegetable oil
3 garlic cloves, crushed
15 g (½ oz) ginger, peeled and julienned
400 g (14 oz/2 cups) jasmine rice, washed twice and drained

SAUTEED JUMBO PRAWNS
TÔM KHO TÀU

WITH JUMBO PRAWNS COMES PRAWN 'BUTTER', ALSO KNOWN AS TOMALLEY. PRAWN BUTTER IS A DELICACY IN VIETNAM AND IS FOUND IN THE PRAWN'S HEAD. I USE PRAWN BUTTER IN THIS RECIPE; WHEN COOKED IT HAS A POWERFUL CONCENTRATED PRAWN FLAVOUR. TO OBTAIN THE PRAWN BUTTER, SQUEEZE THE PRAWN HEAD UNTIL ALL THE INNARDS HAVE BEEN EXCRETED, THEN SCOOP OUT THE ORANGE-COLOURED BUTTER.

IT IS COMMON TO FIND PRAWNS COOKED AND SERVED IN VIETNAM WITH THE HEADS STILL INTACT — SUCK OUT THE JUICE IN THE PRAWN'S HEAD BEFORE MAKING YOUR WAY TO ITS BODY. IN THIS RECIPE, YOU'LL NEED TO PEEL THE PRAWNS TO REMOVE THE PRAWN BUTTER FROM THE HEADS, BUT TRY LEAVING A FEW PRAWNS WITH THEIR HEADS ON, AND EAT THEM THE VIETNAMESE WAY.

8 raw jumbo prawns (shrimp)
    or scampi
2 tablespoons fish sauce
1 tablespoon sugar
3 tablespoons finely chopped red
    Asian shallots
3 tablespoons finely chopped garlic
1 tablespoon lemon juice
3 tablespoons vegetable oil
1 long red chilli, julienned
8 spring onions (scallions),
    white part only, cut into 5 cm
    (2 inch) lengths

Peel and devein the prawns, leaving the tails intact. Scoop out the prawn butter from the prawn heads, and reserve the butter. If desired, leave a few of the prawns with their heads and tails intact, and peel only their bodies.

In a bowl, combine the fish sauce, sugar, a pinch of salt, 1 teaspoon freshly ground black pepper, 1 tablespoon of the shallots and 1 tablespoon of the garlic. Add the prawns, toss to coat in the marinade, then cover and place in the fridge to marinate for 20 minutes. Drain, reserving the marinade.

To make the sauce, mix the prawn butter with the lemon juice and 1 tablespoon of the oil. Set aside.

Place a large frying pan over medium–high heat, add the remaining oil, then sauté the prawns for 1 minute on each side to seal. Remove the prawns and set aside.

Wipe the pan clean and turn the heat to low, then add the sauce along with the reserved marinade from the prawns, and simmer for 2 minutes. Now add the prawns, the remaining shallots and garlic, the chilli and spring onions, and stir-fry for 2 minutes. Serve with jasmine rice.

SERVES 4–6 AS PART OF A SHARED MEAL

5

QUIET
QUY
NHON

WE BOTH STAND AT THE BUS STATION — I'M WAITING FOR A BUS TO QUY NHON AND SUZE IS WAITING FOR A BUS TO TAKE HER TO THE AIRPORT — THIS IS OUR FAREWELL. SUZE HAS TO RETURN TO SYDNEY TO START HER NEW JOB. WE'VE HAD SUCH A FANTASTIC TIME TRAVELLING THE FIRST HALF OF VIETNAM TOGETHER, BUT THE NEXT HALF I WILL BE DOING SOLO.

I know very little about Quy Nhon, and when I ask the locals in Hoi An about this small seaside town, I find that they don't know much about it either. It sounds like just the place I am looking for — a relaxing break from the more travelled path.

I am never bored in this wonderfully diverse country. Visiting a new town or city in Vietnam is like visiting a different country each time, offering different landscapes, different fauna and stirring different emotions.

I catch a rickety mini bus with locals and tourists. A few hours into the trip we start to descend a winding, steep mountain; we turn a sharp corner and as we come out of the bend, a breathtakingly peaceful scene slowly appears before me — a calm, clear turquoise sea dotted with brightly coloured fishing boats, their large nets suspended above the water, the crystal-clear ocean fringed by stretches of soft powdered sand. Everything is still, there's hardly a soul in sight — it's as if someone has pressed the pause button. I am in coastal bliss.

At the bus station I brace myself for the onslaught of badgering motorbike taxis and touts, but there is none. I have arrived to an untouched Vietnam.

I wake up two Westerners, who are still asleep in the back of the bus. They get off the bus, dazed and confused, telling me that they had to pop sleeping pills to knock themselves out because they were in too much pain and discomfort in the back seat.

The couple, Dan and Timea, are from California. They are both in the hospitality industry and are big 'foodies', so it is refreshing to meet fellow travellers who are as passionate about food as I am. We share a taxi and find a small family-run guesthouse a few blocks from the beach. We talk about Vietnamese cuisine, and I tell them about all the delicious food I've been eating. With growing appetites, we quickly freshen up and head out, eager to experience the food of Quy Nhon.

Not far from the guesthouse, we come across a small group of people crouched over a low table, eating. The table is covered with baskets of duck eggs, the floor beneath littered with broken egg shells.

'Oh yes,' I think to myself. 'The first test for the adventurous foodies: Vietnam's famous duck embryo.'

I describe for them in fine detail what the eggs actually are. They both look horrified but are keen to give them a try. We take a seat, our feet crunching over the egg shells. The egg lady along with her six customers eye us curiously as if to say, 'Are you sure you want to eat this? Do you know what it is?'

> **66 I COUNT TO THREE AND WE ALL PUT THE DUCK EMBRYO INTO OUR MOUTHS AND START TO CHEW, ALL EYES UPON US, ESPECIALLY THE TWO AMERICANS. THEY BOTH FINISH THE EGG, THEN TURN TO THE REST OF THE TABLE, WITH TWO THUMBS UP, 'NHON — DELICIOUS!' EVERYONE CHEERS AND CLAPS, TAPPING THEM BOTH ON THEIR BACKS. 99**

Everyone looks in our direction, eagerly anticipating our reactions. The egg lady asks me if I want her to take the embryo out for the Americans and put it on a plate. 'No, let them go through the whole ritual,' I say.

As I peel my egg, Timea and Dan follow cautiously, watching every move I make. Then, when the duck reveals itself, Timea swiftly turns her head away, shutting her eyes. The whole table burst into hysterical laughter, slapping their hands on their thighs. Timea turns back to the egg, scoops the duck onto her little spoon and has a long look at it. 'Eeww, it's got hair on it!'

I count to three and we all put the duck embryo into our mouths and start to chew, all eyes upon us, especially the two Americans. They both finish the egg, then turn to the rest of the table, with two thumbs up, 'Nhon — delicious!' Everyone cheers and claps, tapping them both on their backs.

We move from food stall to food stall; they are keen to discover more, and I am more than happy to be the host for the evening. I suggest dishes that I think will be unusual to their palates: bitter melon salads, luffah squash soup, dried bassa fish and pork hock cooked with Quy Nhon seaweed.

As I watch Dan and Timea's reaction after each mouthful, I feel very proud of my heritage and fortunate to have such a strong understanding of Vietnam's regional dishes and delicacies. Every day I am surrounded by the most delectable food, and to be able to introduce others to the food of my country and see how much they enjoy and appreciate it, gives me a real sense of satisfaction and joy.

I ask them what seafood they had eaten in Nha Trang. They had tried very little, and explained that it was very hard for non-Vietnamese speaking foreigners to find traditional dishes or even know about local specialities or where to go. I couldn't believe what I was hearing — all that fantastic seafood they had missed out on! I couldn't let them leave Vietnam's coastal region without a colourful culinary memory.

I ask five different food vendors where the best seafood restaurant is and they all point in the same direction. This restaurant is one of a few favoured by the locals; it doesn't have a name, everyone just knows where it is. After getting a little lost we arrive at four restaurants, side by side, all serving live seafood, a thick smoky aroma coming from the barbecues out the front. We hesitate to choose one; they all look good. I point towards the restaurant with the most women in it — all Vietnamese women are taught at a young age about the importance of fresh produce, so I follow their lead.

We sit down at one of the tables. I go into the kitchen and pick out a dozen live scallops, three live lobsters and a catfish. The waiters take our seafood to the cooks and they prepare the scallops and lobsters, chargrilled in their shells, dressed with spring onion oil and fish sauce; the catfish is steamed at the table with glass noodles, mushrooms and Asian celery.

I'm happy to say that this was the best meal that my new friends had experienced in Vietnam. They were impressed by the flavour, fragrance and balance of Vietnamese food, and were very disappointed that they hadn't discovered the beauty of Vietnamese cuisine earlier.

66 ... I REALLY FEEL LIKE A FOREIGNER HERE. IN THE BIG CITIES I CAN USUALLY BLEND IN WITH THE LOCALS ... 99

The next morning I head out on my own to have breakfast at the markets. Easy enough to find: second left, then third right. I take the second left and already I'm lost. The whole street is buzzing — street vendors take up all of the footpaths and most of the road, barely leaving room for even a motorbike to pass. For two whole blocks, three long streets are pumping with activity.

There are carts selling brightly coloured flowers, and vendors on the road sell baskets of rambutans, lychees and rose apples. An elderly lady peels jackfruit, a large spiky tropical fruit, and places the flesh into small containers. I buy one for (AUD) 40 cents and ask her if she can direct me to the markets.

She smirks and tells me that I'm already there. 'A few years ago there was a fire and the whole market building burnt down. The government didn't relocate us anywhere else, so we all sprawled out onto the street. What you see on the street here is the local market.'

The street markets give this town such energy; I hope they are able to continue to sell their goods like this for many more years to come.

Against a long wall, six ladies have set up their noodle stalls, all offering different varieties of noodle soups for breakfast, their stockpots busy with bubbles. I go over to check it out but can't decide what I want. There are no available tables so I wait for the first free stool, then sit down without ordering and just eat what I'm given: a spicy vermicelli noodle soup with fish cakes. As I eat my noodles I look around — I really feel like a foreigner here. In the big cities I can usually blend in with the locals as many dress like me and wear similar shoes, but in this small coastal town, not yet exposed to modernisation, I look very different; I am a tourist again.

I watch a vegetable wholesaler at work across the road. She has an old, dark, wooden shop front, over two levels with no doors, the whole building seemingly on the verge of collapse. There is one lady on the top level and another lady on the bottom. A motorbike pulls up and the driver places his order. The lady at the bottom screams out the order to the lady above, who grabs a rusty hook and attaches it to a heavy brown basket filled with potatoes. She slowly lowers the basket down by the rope, directly onto the bike. The buyer signs off in an accounts book and rides off. It all flows like clockwork; they make hard work look easy. Watching them reminds me of my Aunty Nine and her fruit business in Saigon. I can't wait to see her again.

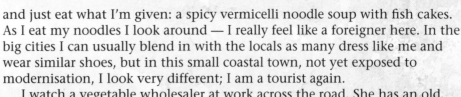

A man with no teeth and no sandals, his pants rolled up to his knees, is selling coconuts. He chooses one from the mound, chops it in perfect halves, then presses the flesh against a motorised rotating grinder, which removes the flesh from its hard shell. It is then sold, to be squeezed into coconut milk.

I ask if I can have a go. It can't be that hard — cut the coconut in half, rotate with pressure and out comes the grated flesh. Chopping the coconut in half with a long machete is the hardest part; there is definitely a technique involved, one that I obviously don't have. After my third go, I'm successful — perfect halves! I press the coconut against the machine but the electricity suddenly cuts out. At first I think I've broken his machine.

The man sits down and shakes his head. 'Not again! How can I earn a living if the electricity cuts out all the time? No electricity means no grinding machine, no shredded coconut, no customers, no money.'

I ask him why this happens so regularly. He explains that the government shuts off electricity in certain areas on certain days due to lack of power supply in the area. It's just something we all have to live with. He takes a puff of his cigarette. 'Oh well, it will come back on tomorrow.'

I am riding my bicycle around one afternoon when I pass a building with a sign: 'Don't feel sorry for us and our disabilities, just give us encouragement'. I lean my bicycle against the wall, grab my bag out of the pink plastic basket on the front, and go to check it out.

The centre is called 'NNC (Nguyen Nga Centre)'. I'm greeted by a young girl who points me upstairs. On the first level, I catch the attention of five students and their teacher, communicating in sign language and learning embroidery. Their teacher stops the class and introduces herself as Miss Nga, apologising for still having her pyjamas on. I tell her not to worry as I'm quite used to it — many Vietnamese women wear their pyjamas all day. She laughs, then directs a young deaf boy to show me around while she goes to get changed.

The boy takes my hand and leads the way. I ask him what his name is, then immediately feel silly for forgetting that he can't hear me. On the first floor, children are sewing bags using old sewing machines; colourful rolls of material are piled up to the ceiling, scattered remnants on the floor. There's a small area allocated for musical instruments, and a sunroom off to one side is filled with artists' easels and beautiful paintings by the students.

We make our way up to the second floor, where students are hammering away, carving precious stones into sculptures of Buddha and dragons; others are making rings, bracelets and necklaces out of silver and special gems. On the top floor, he shows me the kitchen and the students' living quarters.

Miss Nga meets us back downstairs. She has shiny long black hair, a sincere smile and such a gentle manner and energy that you feel instantly drawn to her. I'm curious to know more about the centre, so I ask her how it all began. Nga fetches two stools and asks me to sit down; I figure it's going to be a long story …

MISS NGA'S STORY

'I was born in a small country town called Dap Da, about 30 kilometres from Quy Nhon. Both my parents were farmers and worked very hard to put their two daughters through good schooling. I graduated from high school in 1990, the same year my sister was involved in a motorbike accident, which caused permanent damage to her legs.

'During the time I cared for my sister, I was surrounded by people with disabilities: some were disabled from exploded mines or traffic accidents, and others were children affected by dioxin poisoning.

'Their misfortune made it clear to me that these children would suffer even more losses in their lives in the future. These young people share the same desire of rising in life as us, they want to work and live on their own, and not be a burden to their families and the community. They want to live usefully. I was determined to do something about it. I wanted to create a centre that would contribute to the improvement of life for people with disabilities.

'I told my mother about my plans but she disapproved. She wanted me to go to university, get a good job and have a bright future. I tried to convince her. I told her how lucky I was to have both my arms and legs, my sight and hearing; I told her I could do anything, that I could help these children, but she wouldn't agree to it.

'One day I came up with an idea. I went to visit the monk at our local temple. This monk had the gift of telling the future, and my mother would visit him often. I told the monk of my goals and the situation with my mother. He listened, nodded his head and told me that my spiritual guides would help me.

'The next week my mother left for the temple. A few hours later she came rushing home and called out to me, telling me I had all of her blessings if I still wanted to go ahead with my plans for the centre.

'In June 1993, I started knitting and embroidery classes for ten children with disabilities. Now, thirteen years later, the Nguyen Nga Centre schools 250 children with impaired sight, impaired hearing and physical and intellectual disabilities, and offers programmes in literacy, braille, sign language, computer skills, music, art, knitting, embroidery and dress making.'

I am in awe of this lady. She has such strength and determination, and love and dedication to these children.

'I'm so proud of my kids,' she tells me. 'In the last fifteen years, sixteen of my students have made it to university and have found great jobs in Saigon. My visually impaired students are hired to play and sing at weddings and functions, and twelve of my students are now married.'

I want to do more for these young adults, but I have no musical talent, I can't draw or paint and I definitely can't sew or create a sculpture of any kind, but I can cook, so I ask Nga if I can prepare dinner for the students. Nga looks very surprised that a Vietnamese male has offered to cook dinner; she welcomes the idea and calls her daughter, Kim Anh, and asks her to take me to the markets to buy the ingredients.

After a quick phone call to Dan and Timea to invite them to join us for dinner, I hop on the back of Kim Anh's scooter and we rush to the local markets, just as most of the stalls are closing. I have fifteen mouths to feed, with very little produce available. We buy some fresh mint, green papaya, Asian eggplant, water spinach, tomatoes, preserved bean curd, chilli, live prawns, a whole mackerel and some pork.

Back at the centre, we begin preparations in the small kitchen and dining room area, which doubles as the bedroom at night. With only a few pots and pans the going is a bit slow, but the students are all so keen and willing to learn. Through hand movements and facial expressions we find we can communicate with each other quite well. I ask the blind students to pluck all the mint leaves off the stems, and shell the prawns. I teach them how to shave a green papaya and let them finish it, which they do with ease. I show the deaf students different meat marinades and how to make sauces and dressings, and demonstrate very basic knife skills. We each have our assigned jobs and tasks; we sit together, busily chopping, plucking and marinating, enjoying every quiet moment of it.

Dan and Timea turn up and join in with the preparations. A few students cook a prawn and vegetable stir-fry, we all prepare charred Asian eggplant topped with fish sauce and spring onion oil, and then we stuff some tomatoes. We take turns stir-frying the beef with wing beans, we pan-fry mackerel fillets with green papaya, and then prepare tiger prawns with water spinach, wok-tossed with preserved bean curd.

I elect the blind students as the tasting panel. I ask them before plating each dish: 'More fish sauce? Enough chilli? Too sour? Is it balanced?'

With dinner ready, we all huddle around a small square table. Nobody begins to eat until Miss Nga takes her first mouthful, such is the respect they have for her.

That evening there was a sense of magic. We ate with people who could not hear, could not see, could not walk, could not speak English, and could not speak Vietnamese. But somehow we could all understand each other well, and Dan and Timea were finally able to understand and communicate with the locals without having to speak or understand the Vietnamese language —

a stroke to the side of the right cheek (the food is beautiful);

a rub of the belly in a circular motion (we are full);

a roll of the fist under the chin, then opening the palm (thank you).

I wanted the evening to never end, but it was getting late and the three of us had an early trip the next morning.

ĂN KỸ NO LÂU, CÀY SÂU TỐT LÚA

IF YOU EAT SLOWLY, IT'S GOOD FOR YOUR STOMACH; PLOUGHING DEEPLY IS GOOD FOR THE RICE FIELDS.

DO EVERYTHING WITH CARE AND PATIENCE, AND THINGS WILL TURN OUT WELL.

DIN DAENG FISH CAKES
CHẢ CÁ DIN DAENG

I BOUGHT SOME FISH CAKES FROM A STALL IN THE OPEN MARKETS ON THE STREETS OF QUY NHON. I ASKED THE LADY WHO OWNED THE STALL WHERE SHE GOT HER RECIPE FROM. 'FROM MY BIRTH PLACE, DIN DAENG IN THAILAND,' SHE SAID. I WAS EXCITED AS I WAS ALSO BORN IN DIN DAENG, AND SHE WAS THE ONLY PERSON THAT I'VE EVER MET FROM THERE. WE HAD SIMILAR STORIES: BOTH OUR FAMILIES ESCAPED VIETNAM IN 1977 AND WE WERE BOTH BORN IN THE SAME YEAR, IN THE SAME PROVINCE. SHE DIDN'T HESITATE TO SHARE HER RECIPE WITH ME.

IF YOU DON'T FEEL LIKE WRAPPING THE FISH CAKES IN LETTUCE LEAVES AND MINT, TOSSING THEM THROUGH A SALAD WORKS REALLY WELL TOO.

FISH CAKES

500 g (1 lb 2 oz) boneless, skinless red fish fillets (or any firm white fish fillets), thinly sliced
1 tablespoon Thai red curry paste
1 egg, lightly beaten
1 garlic clove, crushed
2 spring onions (scallions), white part only, thinly sliced
1 tablespoon fish sauce
50 g (1¾ oz) snake (yard-long) beans, thinly sliced
5 kaffir lime leaves, thinly sliced
vegetable oil, for shallow-frying

50 g (1¾ oz) dried rice vermicelli noodles
1 green oak lettuce or butter lettuce, leaves separated
1 bunch perilla, leaves picked
1 bunch mint, leaves picked
1 bunch Vietnamese mint, leaves picked
dipping fish sauce (page 331), to serve

Put the rice vermicelli in a saucepan of boiling water and bring back to the boil. Cook for 5 minutes, then turn off the heat and leave in the water for 5 minutes. Drain the noodles, rinse under cold water, and set aside.

To make the fish cakes, put the fish, curry paste, egg, garlic, spring onions, fish sauce and ½ teaspoon freshly ground black pepper in a food processor and process to form a paste. Transfer the fish paste to a bowl and add the snake beans and lime leaves. Using wet hands, knead together well. Form the fish paste into 5 cm (2 inch) patties, about 2 cm (¾ inch) thick.

Heat the oil in a large non-stick frying pan over medium heat. Add the fish cakes in batches and fry for 4 minutes on each side until golden. Remove and drain on paper towel.

Put the fish cakes on one platter, the vermicelli on another, and the lettuce leaves and herbs on a third platter. Wrap the fish cakes in lettuce leaves, adding some vermicelli and herbs to the parcel. Serve with the dipping fish sauce.

MAKES 12

CHICKEN AND LUFFAH SQUASH SOUP
CANH MƯỚP NẤU GÀ

LUFFAH SQUASH IS ALSO KNOWN AS RIDGED GOURD, AND IS DISTINGUISHED BY TEN RIDGES THAT RUN FROM TOP TO BOTTOM — IF THE RIDGES LOOK WILTED, IT IS NOT FRESH. WHEN COOKED, THE SQUASH ACTS AS A SPONGE AND ABSORBS ALL THE FLAVOURS AND JUICES IT IS COOKED IN.

In a bowl, combine the fish sauce and 1 teaspoon each of salt and freshly ground black pepper, and mix well. Add the chicken pieces, stir to coat in the marinade, then set aside to marinate for 15 minutes. Drain well.

Heat a large saucepan over medium heat, add the oil and lightly brown the garlic. Add the chicken and cook, stirring, for 3–4 minutes, or until the chicken is well sealed on all sides. Add 1.5 litres (52 fl oz/6 cups) of water to the pan and bring to the boil, then increase the heat to high and cook for 15 minutes, constantly skimming any impurities off the surface. Now add the luffah squash and mushrooms and cook for a further 5 minutes.

Turn off the heat and transfer the soup to large serving bowls. Garnish with the spring onions and coriander. Serve with jasmine rice.

SERVES 4-6 AS PART OF A SHARED MEAL

2 tablespoons fish sauce
300 g (10½ oz) boneless, skinless chicken thighs, sliced into 2 x 4 cm (¾ x 1½ inch) pieces
2 tablespoons vegetable oil
2 garlic cloves, finely chopped
500 g (1 lb 2 oz) luffah squash (ridged gourd), peeled, halved and sliced into 2 x 4 cm (¾ x 1½ inch) pieces
100 g (3½ oz) button mushrooms, halved
2 spring onions (scallions), thinly sliced
1 small handful coriander (cilantro) leaves

BITTER MELON SALAD WITH DRIED SHRIMP
GỎI KHỔ QUA TÔM KHÔ

BITTER MELON IS THE VEGETABLE THAT MOST VIETNAMESE KIDS DESPISE EATING — ITS SKIN IS ALL WRINKLY AND IT HAS A BITTER AFTERTASTE, HENCE ITS NAME. WHEN WE WERE KIDS, WE WERE FORCED TO EAT IT, FOR IT WAS 'COOLING' FOR THE BODY. IT WAS THE YIN THAT BALANCED OUT THE YANG. YIN FOODS COOL THE BODY, REDUCE TENSION, LOOSEN THE MUSCLES AND SLOW THE BODY DOWN, AND YANG FOODS DO THE COMPLETE OPPOSITE. I HAVE GROWN TO LOVE BITTER MELON, AND IF YOU HAVEN'T TRIED IT BEFORE, THIS SALAD IS A GREAT INTRODUCTION. THE BITTERNESS IS BALANCED BY THE SALTY DRIED SHRIMP AND TART PICKLED VEGETABLES.

50 g (1¾ oz/½ cup) dried shrimp
1 green bitter melon (350 g/ 12 oz), washed, seeded and thinly sliced
¼ teaspoon caster (superfine) sugar
3 tablespoons Aunty Nine's salad dressing (page 330)
2 tablespoons vegetable oil
2 garlic cloves, crushed
250 g (9 oz/1 cup) pickled vegetables (page 335)
1 handful Vietnamese mint leaves, roughly sliced
1 handful mint leaves, roughly sliced
2 tablespoons roasted peanuts, crushed (page 328)
dipping fish sauce (page 331), to serve

Put the dried shrimp in a bowl, cover with water and soak for 20 minutes, then drain.

In a bowl, combine the bitter melon, sugar, Aunty Nine's salad dressing and ¼ teaspoon each of salt and freshly ground black pepper. Toss well and set aside.

Heat a small frying pan over medium heat and add the oil. When the oil is hot, fry the shrimp for 5 minutes until crisp. Add the garlic and cook for 2 minutes. Turn off the heat, remove the shrimp and garlic and set aside.

In a bowl, combine the bitter melon, pickled vegetables, mint leaves and the shrimp mixture. Toss well, then transfer to a serving bowl. Garnish with crushed peanuts and serve with dipping fish sauce.

SERVES 4–6 AS PART OF A SHARED MEAL

CHARGRILLED EGGPLANT WITH PRAWNS
CÀ TÍM NƯỚNG

I PREPARED THIS DISH FOR FELLOW TRAVELLERS I MET IN QUY NHON, ONE OF THEM A 'VEGEQUARIAN'. I WENT SHOPPING FOR INGREDIENTS AT THE MARKETS AND FOUND A LADY SELLING READY-CHARRED EGGPLANT, AND A LADY NEXT TO HER SELLING READY-DICED ASIAN SHALLOTS AND CRUSHED ROASTED PEANUTS — HALF THE PREP WAS DONE! JAPANESE EGGPLANTS ARE LONG AND SLENDER, PALE PURPLE IN COLOUR AND ARE SWEETER THAN THE LARGER ROUND VARIETY.

Poke some holes evenly in the eggplants with a toothpick to ensure the eggplants don't explode when they are cooked.

Brush the skins of the eggplants with vegetable oil and place them on a barbecue grill or in a chargrill pan heated to high. Char the eggplants, turning them occasionally, until the skin becomes blackened and cracks, and the flesh is tender. This should take about 10 minutes in total. Allow to cool, then remove the charred skin and discard it.

Place the eggplants on a serving plate. Using a knife, slice out a shallow pocket along the middle of each eggplant, reserving the flesh. Roughly chop the reserved flesh and stuff it in the pockets, then place the prawns on top of the soft eggplant. Dress with dipping fish sauce and spring onion oil and garnish with the shallots and peanuts. Serve with jasmine rice.

SERVES 4-6 AS PART OF A SHARED MEAL

4 long purple Japanese eggplants (aubergines)

2 tablespoons vegetable oil

150 g (5½ oz) cooked small tiger prawns (shrimp), peeled and deveined, roughly chopped

3 tablespoons dipping fish sauce (page 331)

1 tablespoon spring onion oil (page 329)

1 tablespoon fried red Asian shallots (page 329)

1 tablespoon chopped roasted peanuts (page 328)

PAN-FRIED SPANISH MACKEREL WITH SPICY TOMATO SAUCE
CÁ THU SỐT CÀ

YOU WILL FIND SPANISH MACKEREL IN MANY VIETNAMESE RECIPES. THEY ARE ENJOYED FOR THEIR FIRM FLESH AND THEIR DEEP SAVOURY FLAVOUR. THEY ARE A CLOSE RELATIVE TO THE TUNA, SO TUNA CUTLETS WOULD BE A GOOD SUBSTITUTE IF MACKEREL IS UNAVAILABLE.

3 mackerel cutlets (600 g/
    1 lb 5 oz)
200 g (7 oz) tomatoes
125 ml (4 fl oz/½ cup) vegetable oil
2 garlic cloves, finely chopped
1 onion, cut in half (then ½ finely
    chopped, ½ diced)
2 red Asian shallots, finely chopped
2 spring onions (scallions), sliced
2 teaspoons fish sauce
1 teaspoon sugar
2 bird's eye chillies, sliced
2 tablespoons Mum's vinaigrette
    dressing (page 330)
1 teaspoon cornflour (cornstarch)
1 small handful coriander (cilantro)
    leaves

Season the cutlets with ½ teaspoon each of salt and freshly ground black pepper. To seed the tomatoes, cut them in half horizontally, then squeeze out the seeds or use a teaspoon to scoop them out. Finely chop the tomato flesh and set aside.

Heat the oil in a frying pan over medium heat. Add the fish cutlets and fry for 3 minutes on each side until browned. Remove from the pan and drain on paper towel.

Transfer 2 tablespoons of the hot oil to a clean, hot frying pan. Add the garlic, finely chopped onion and shallots and fry until fragrant. Add the tomatoes, diced onion, spring onions, fish sauce, sugar, chilli, Mum's vinaigrette and ½ teaspoon salt to the pan, and simmer for 3 minutes. Combine the cornflour with 1 teaspoon of water to make a paste, then add to the pan and stir for 30 seconds, or until the sauce thickens.

Place the cutlets on a serving platter, pour over the tomato sauce and garnish with coriander. Serve with jasmine rice.

SERVES 4-6 AS PART OF A SHARED MEAL

PORK NECK COOKED IN LEMONGRASS AND CHILLI
THỊT HEO XÀO XẢ ỚT

I HAD ONLY EVER COOKED CHICKEN WITH LEMONGRASS AND CHILLI BEFORE I TRIED IT IN QUY NHON MADE WITH PORK NECK. IT WAS JUST AS SUCCULENT AS THE CHICKEN VERSION, AND THE PORK SOAKED UP THE DELICIOUS SAUCE BEAUTIFULLY.

In a bowl, combine the sugar and fish sauce, stirring to dissolve the sugar. Once the sugar has dissolved, add 1 tablespoon of the oil, 1 tablespoon of the lemongrass, 2 teaspoons of the garlic and 2 teaspoons of the chilli. Mix well, then add the pork neck and toss to coat in the marinade. Cover and place in the fridge to marinate for 20 minutes.

Heat the remaining 2 tablespoons of oil in a large saucepan over medium heat. Add the remaining lemongrass, garlic and chilli and stir-fry until fragrant, then add the pork and stir-fry for 3 minutes. Add 150 ml (5 fl oz) of water, then cook over low heat for a further 10 minutes. Transfer to a serving bowl and garnish with the coriander sprigs. Serve with jasmine rice and a side bowl of cucumber.

SERVES 4-6 AS PART OF A SHARED MEAL

2 tablespoons caster (superfine) sugar
3 tablespoons fish sauce
3 tablespoons vegetable oil
2 lemongrass stems, white part only, finely chopped
3 garlic cloves, crushed
4 bird's eye chillies, finely chopped
300 g (10½ oz) skinless pork neck, cut into 2 cm (¾ inch) cubes
2 coriander (cilantro) sprigs
1 Lebanese (short) cucumber, sliced

TOMATO STUFFED WITH PORK AND WOOD EAR MUSHROOMS
CÀ CHUA NHỒI THỊT

I COOKED THIS DISH WITH THE HELP OF SOME AMAZING YOUNG PEOPLE I MET AT THE NGUYEN NGA CENTRE. TWELVE KIDS, ALL OF WHOM WERE HEARING OR VISUALLY IMPAIRED, WERE THE FASTEST LEARNERS I HAVE MET IN A KITCHEN.

WHEN BUYING INGREDIENTS FOR THIS RECIPE, CHOOSE TOMATOES THAT ARE SLIGHTLY UNDERRIPE, AS THEY TEND TO WORK BEST HERE, AND ASK YOUR BUTCHER TO GRIND THE REGULAR PORK MINCE MORE FINELY FOR YOU.

4 dried wood ear mushrooms
6 tomatoes, slightly underripe
250 g (9 oz) finely minced pork
3 garlic cloves, finely chopped
3 red Asian shallots, finely chopped
2 tablespoons fish sauce
2 tablespoons sliced spring onion (scallion)
125 ml (4 fl oz/½ cup) vegetable oil
1 teaspoon tomato paste (concentrated purée)
2 teaspoons sugar
1 small handful coriander (cilantro) leaves

Put the mushrooms in a bowl, cover with water and soak for 20 minutes, then drain and thinly slice. Cut the tomatoes in half horizontally, then scoop out the flesh with a teaspoon. Reserve the flesh and set the tomato shells aside.

In a bowl, combine the mushrooms, pork, half of the garlic, half of the shallots, 1 tablespoon of the fish sauce, 1 tablespoon of the spring onion, ½ teaspoon salt and 1 teaspoon freshly ground black pepper. Knead all the ingredients together, then mould the mixture into 12 individual even portions. Tightly stuff each of the tomato shells with a portion of the mushroom and pork mixture, and then set aside on a tray.

To make the tomato sauce, heat 2 tablespoons of the oil in a small saucepan over medium–high heat. Add the remaining garlic and shallots and fry until fragrant, then add the reserved tomato flesh along with 4 tablespoons of water, the remaining 1 tablespoon of fish sauce, the tomato paste and sugar. Stir for 5 minutes, then turn off the heat and set aside.

Heat 2 tablespoons of the oil in a large frying pan over medium heat. Add 6 tomatoes to the pan, stuffing side down, and fry for 5 minutes, or until brown. Turn the tomatoes over, increase the heat to high and fry for a further 3 minutes. Remove the tomatoes from the pan and place on a serving plate. Repeat with the remaining oil and tomatoes. Add the tomato sauce to the pan and cook for 3 minutes.

Drizzle the tomato sauce over the tomatoes and garnish with the remaining spring onion and the coriander.

SERVES 6 AS PART OF A SHARED MEAL

KOHLRABI AND SCHOOL PRAWN STIR-FRY
SU HÀO XÀO TÉP

I WAS INTRODUCED TO KOHLRABI WHILE IN SAPA AND SINCE THEN I HAVE KEPT MY EYE OUT FOR ANY RECIPES THAT USE THIS UNIQUE VEGETABLE. THE TEXTURE OF BOTH KOHLRABI AND SCHOOL PRAWNS COMPLEMENT EACH OTHER WELL. BUT THAT'S ONLY IF YOU STICK TO THE RULES AND EAT THE PRAWN SHELLS!

Pour 1 litre (35 fl oz/4 cups) of water into a saucepan and bring to the boil. Add the kohlrabi and boil for 2 minutes. Drain well, then plunge into iced water, drain and set aside.

Place a frying pan over medium heat, add 1 tablespoon of the oil and stir-fry the garlic until fragrant. Increase the heat, then add the prawns and stir-fry for 3 minutes. Remove the prawns from the pan and set aside.

In the same pan, heat the remaining oil and stir-fry the kohlrabi for 3 minutes, then add the fish sauce, sugar, spring onions, ½ teaspoon salt and 1 teaspoon freshly ground black pepper, and stir-fry for 5 minutes. Return the prawns to the pan and toss for a further minute to heat through.

Transfer to a serving bowl and garnish with coriander sprigs. Serve with jasmine rice.

SERVES 4-6 AS PART OF A SHARED MEAL

500 g (1 lb 2 oz) kohlrabi, peeled and sliced into 1 x 4 cm (½ x 1½ inch) pieces
2 tablespoons vegetable oil
2 garlic cloves, finely chopped
200 g (7 oz) raw small school prawns (shrimp), legs and heads trimmed, or peel if preferred
2 teaspoons fish sauce
1 teaspoon sugar
2 spring onions (scallions), sliced into 4 cm (1½ inch) pieces
coriander (cilantro) sprigs, to garnish

香油　合樂助　越幣　壹拾萬元正

香油　合樂助　越幣　壹拾萬元正

香油　合樂助　越幣　壹拾萬元正

香油　合樂助　越幣　伍萬元正

香油　合樂助　越幣　貳拾萬元正

香油　合樂助　越幣　壹拾萬元正

香油　越幣　伍萬元正

胡廣昌　家　合樂助　香油　越幣　壹拾...

美國　蘇紅燕　家　合樂助　香油　越幣　貳萬...

蘇偉世　家　合樂助　香油　越幣　伍萬...

合眾　香油　合樂助　越幣　貳萬...

中國　王艷　家　香油　合樂助　越幣　肆萬...

蘇克民　家　合樂助　香油　越幣　壹拾萬...

何扼偉　家　香油　合樂助　越幣　壹...

6

MISS NHA TRANG

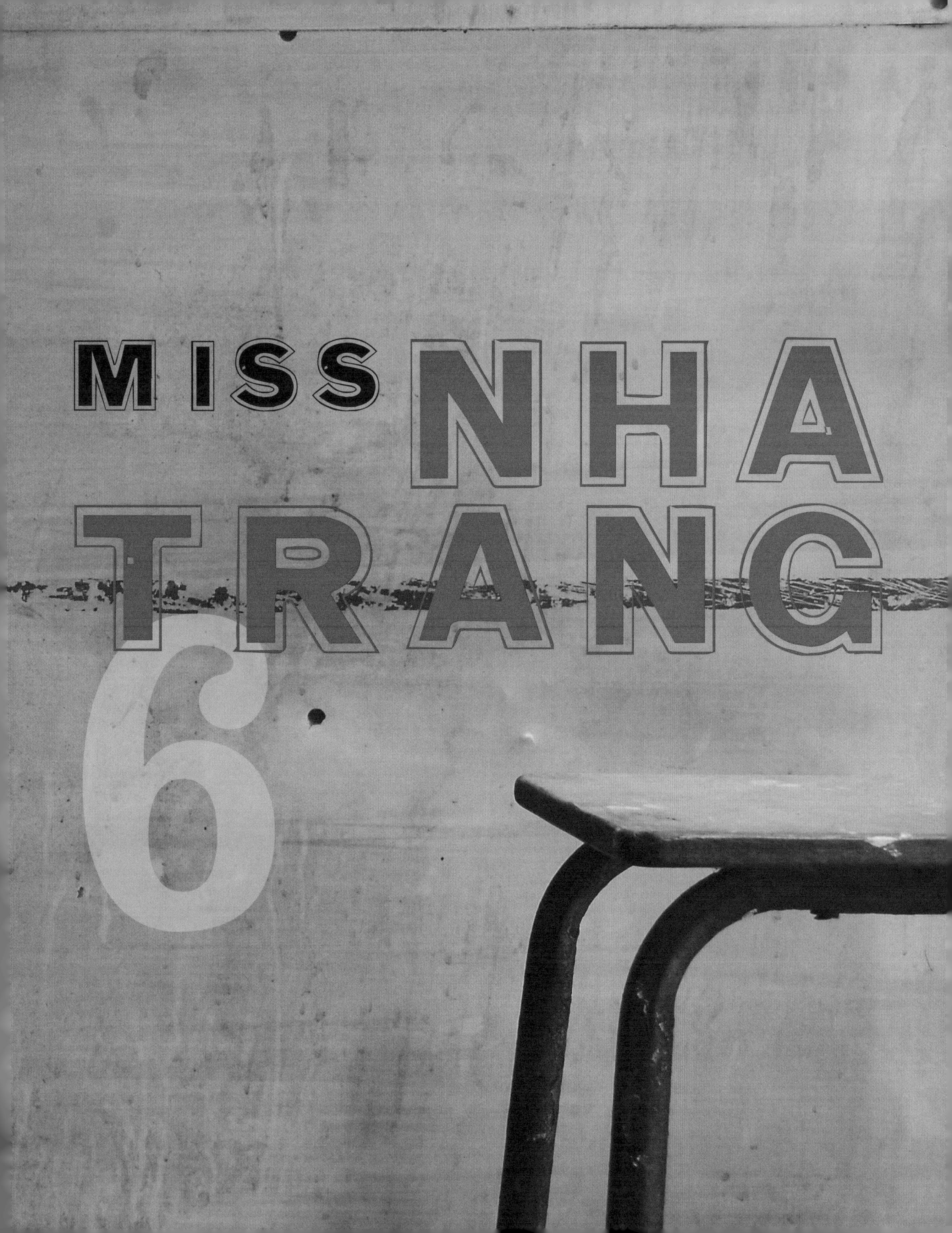

A FEMALE VOICE CALLS OUT IN A HIGH, DRAWN-OUT TONE, 'XOI GA DAY! XOI GA DAY! I WAKE UP AND LOOK THROUGH THE DUSTY BLINDS. IT'S DARK, WITH ONLY A HINT OF LIGHT, BUT I CAN MAKE OUT AN ELDERLY WOMAN WALKING DOWN THE STREET, BALANCING A BAMBOO POLE ACROSS HER SHOULDERS, HER BASKETS FILLED WITH STICKY RICE, CHICKEN AND BANANA LEAF. EARLY RISERS ON THEIR WAY TO WORK STOP HER FOR BREAKFAST, THEY EAT SQUATTING AROUND HER BASKETS, THEN THEIR DAY BEGINS.

A car arrives at 7 a.m. to transfer me to the bus station. There are already six people packed in the car: two on top of each other in the front passenger's seat and four in the back, with their backpacks on their laps. I'm somehow shoved in; I can barely breathe and hope we don't have far to go. Thankfully, it's only fifteen minutes before we stop and are briskly transferred to a larger bus, ready for our 200 kilometre, five-hour journey to Nha Trang.

Our bus driver is dressed like a soldier; he has a thin moustache, wears a green military cap and an army jacket studded with red stars, his matching cammo pants tucked into his shiny black boots.

Ready for battle, he firmly orders his young assistant to count heads. The boy does so as he hands each person a wet towel, a bottle of water and two small plastic bags. This was to be the start to the longest and most frightening bus trip I have ever had.

With his boot pressed heavily on the pedal and his hand firmly on the horn, we're off. At break neck speed he manoeuvres the bus down snake-like roads, overtaking slower cars and trucks directly into oncoming traffic, swerving back onto the right side of the road only at the last minute. We all breathe a sigh of relief as he narrowly misses a motorbike, only millimetres away from clipping his back wheel. We continue on like this for almost an hour, when the lady behind me begins to vomit. This starts a dreadful domino effect. Directly opposite me a man rubs the back of his partner as she leans forward, groaning; halfway down the back another person is following suit, and then another.

'Make sure you use the plastic bags,' the driver screams over his shoulder.

At this point I too feel a little queasy. An English couple stumble to the front of the bus and plead with him to slow down. He shakes his head wildly and points at his watch; he has a deadline to meet! Distraught, they walk back to their seats. There is nothing any of us can do; we just have to sit, white-knuckled, through this nightmare and wait for it to be over.

Two hours later we make it to a flat stretch of highway where, thankfully, the going is a little better. We stop at a roadside restaurant, pulling up next to half a dozen buses. We are given 30 minutes to get some lunch and use the toilet. The restaurant is filled with small tables, each seating six. There's no menu; diners all share a soup, greens, fish, meat and rice.

Unable to stomach anything, I decide to check out the kitchen instead, curious to learn how they manage to feed groups of hundreds of people, all within a 30-minute time frame. I watch as waiters zip back and forth carrying huge trays with platters of various dishes. No one has time to stop, so I enter the kitchen and park my back against a wall, out of harm's way.

66 DISHES ARE READY IN UNISON AND SKILFULLY TRANSFERRED TO HUNDREDS OF PLATTERS, THEN BRISKLY TAKEN OUT TO HUNGRY DINERS. THE FIRST SEATING IS OVER AND THE MOUNTAIN OF WASHING UP BEGINS ... 99

The kitchen is staffed with women, wearing silky patterned pyjamas and green rubber boots; I count thirty cooks in total. The ladies begin their theatrical show.

Eight very large rice cookers whistle with steam, gas burners roar under half a dozen hot woks, which clank, bang and char; the air is filled with smoking chilli, which brings water to my eyes. A blue tiled work bench is covered in a rainbow of colanders filled with an array of vibrant green herbs. Clear broths bubble in large stockpots, heavy cleavers chop through catfish, which are then thrown into piping hot oil, while lemongrass-coated beef is chargrilled under tall orange flames. Dishes are ready in unison and skilfully transferred to hundreds of platters, then briskly taken out to hungry diners.

The first seating is over and the mountain of washing up begins, ready for the next round. Blackened pots and pans are slid over the wet concrete floor to be washed. There's no sink; five women fill red plastic tubs with water and detergent and frantically scrub everything by hand. Out the back, clean bowls, spoons and chopsticks are spread out on bamboo mats to dry in the sun.

The cooks take a break and wait for the next bus to arrive. One of the cooks notices me and asks me what I want to eat. Keen to be part of the action, and

with my stomach feeling more settled, I ask if I could befriend her mighty wok and prepare my own dish. They all laugh with raised eyebrows as she playfully hands me her wok.

Excited to grip a wok again, I use the ingredients before me and prepare a simple dish of wok-tossed beef, chilli, water spinach, oyster sauce and basil. I finish within minutes; she samples my dish and gives me a nod of approval, puts her arms around my shoulders, smiles and asks me if I'm married. I retreat to a table and quickly eat my lunch — my 30 minutes is up.

I move to the back of the bus, pop in my earphones and turn the music up. We drive past lush rice fields, all in different shades of bright green; underfed buffaloes cross the road to the fields, ready to begin ploughing; and orange corn, drying in the sun, carpets the fronts of house after house. The landscape is breathtakingly diverse. We travel past rural rice fields, then climb slowly up into the mountains and drive through areas of thick jungle then, finally, we reach the blue coastal waters of the South China Sea.

We have been on the road for four long hours and, thanks to some perilous driving, we've arrived in Nha Trang an hour early. I hurry off the bus and am instantly hit by a thick wall of heat. I check my map; luckily my intended mini hotel is not far from the bus station.

After I've checked in, I take a walk down Tran Phu Boulevard, a pleasant waterfront promenade dotted with tall palm trees, which sway beside a beautiful white sandy beach — a picture-postcard paradise but for the big blocks of ugly resort-style hotels, tourist shops and noisy Western-style bars that line the street behind me.

Back in the early 1900s, when the French colonised Vietnam, they recognised that the beauty of this tranquil bay, its pristine waters and surrounding islands, made it a perfect getaway spot. Slowly they began to transform Nha Trang into a resort town, and it later became very popular with American soldiers during the Vietnam War. Today Nha Trang has a reputation for being a bit of a party town.

I lay out my towel on the hot sand, strip down to my swimmers and dive into the ocean, dodging the plastic bags floating beside me; the water is an unrefreshing 30 degrees Celsius. I find a little spot on the beach and sit down and have a bit of a whinge to myself; it hasn't been a great day.

I'm snapped out of my mood by a lady balancing a long bamboo yoke across her shoulders, carrying a hot heavy pot and a basket filled with live crabs called *ghe*, a crab similar to our blue swimmer. She plunks it down next to me and asks me if I want to eat. Things are suddenly looking a lot brighter.

She is covered from top to toe: on her head she wears a conical hat and a silk scarf is pulled across her face, she wears elbow-length gloves, sandals with socks, two layers of shirts, long pants and a loose jacket. I can't help but ask if she's hot and why she wears so many clothes.

'In Vietnam, women of darker skin are seen as being less feminine, poor and hard working, so our skin must stay white and pure; it's a sign of beauty.'

I look along the beach and see pale-skinned tourists wearing next to nothing, embracing the sun's rays, desperate to get a tan. What different worlds we live in, how differently we all think.

'And of course I'm hot,' she continues. 'I spend all day under the sun, lugging burning coal under a boiling pot of water. This makes me perspire a lot, but if I only wear one shirt then the wind will get to my chest, I'll catch a cold and I won't be able to work. So I wear lots of layers to break the wind.'

She hands me two crabs on a round platter — one steamed, one grilled — and a dipping sauce of salt, pepper and lime, half a bunch of Vietnamese mint and a cold beer. After sucking all the delicious meat out of the crabs and chewing on its charred crispy legs, a young boy walks past. On his head he is balancing a tray, stacked with little sugar-coated buns filled with sesame and mung beans — things really couldn't get much better than this.

☜ ☜ ☜

'Would you like to see the nicer parts of Nha Trang?'

I look round to see who has spoken to me and see an elderly man sitting on concrete steps near my hotel.

Impressed by his excellent English and his ability to read my mind, I sit down to have a chat. His name is Thanh and he is an easy rider, a person who takes tourists on guided motorbike tours. We end up talking for some time, then, keen to hear more of his story, I hop on the back of his motorbike and he takes me on a half-day trip around the outskirts of Nha Trang. We visit secluded beaches, galleries and mud baths. We stop at Po Nagar Cham Towers, where I learn about the Cham Kingdom, their architecture, spiritual life, traditions and religion. The four towers were built between the seventh and twelfth centuries by the Chams, and were used (and still are) for worship and offerings. I walk up the steep steps of the 28-metre-high northern tower to enjoy the amazing view. It is here that Thanh tells me about his life during the Vietnam War.

THANH'S STORY

'My family moved to Nha Trang in 1955. My father set up a successful business here, which allowed me to study in Saigon, graduating at the English Language University.

'In 1964, when the United States bombed North Vietnam for the first time, I was only nineteen. Because I could speak English well, I was assigned to be an interpreter for the US troops. I spent a year at the US base in Danang, and helped to plan strategic moves and attacks, and became as much an advisor as an interpreter. I had to accompany the US troops wherever they went and during all battles. I remember the attack in Cam Ranh Bay.

'We were in a M48A3 battle tank; I was petrified, I had no prior combat training at all — I was just an interpreter — but I was the soldiers only means of communication with the locals. It was dark with very little space in the tank, and I was trembling with fear. I knew we were in enemy grounds and feared the worst. As we rolled through, bullets began to rain down on us — continuous shots from several DKZ-75 machine guns — and the tank was soon engulfed in flames. I froze; I thought I was already dead because I couldn't move, then I realised that half my body was alight. One of the troops dragged me out and took me to safety. I lost all my hair and eyebrows, my burns were severe, and I don't even remember how I broke my leg. But I'm very lucky to be alive and the scars on my face remind me every day of that horrific time.

'On the 30th of April 1975, Saigon fell to the North Vietnamese. Shortly after that I was captured and sent to a 're-education camp', where I spent many years learning strict communist policy. It was tough: we were beaten and we were worked hard, day and night, spending endless hours in rice fields

and fetching firewood in the jungle. Many of my friends didn't make it. There wasn't enough food; we were all very weak. When I was released, I had no home and many of my family members were dead. I was moved to a new economic zone, and this was where I met my wife. We were struggling farmers but we managed to raise six lovely children, who are all now in their twenties. I tried to flee Vietnam with my family five times; I failed every time. Somehow, someone always knew about our plans and informed the authorities, and each time we were caught meant six months for me in jail, so I gave up in the end.'

I take a long, deep breath. Thanh's story makes me realise how fortunate my family and I were to have made it out of Vietnam and into Thailand as boat people, on our first attempt. Yes, we had nothing when we arrived there and nothing for many years, but at least we made it out.

I thank Thanh for sharing his story with me, as I know how hard it must have been to talk about. My own father never talked about his time in the war. It was an extremely sensitive topic and something he would rather block out of his mind completely. The one time I did ask him about it was when I was fourteen or so. He glared at me with a stare that could send even a grown man running with fear, and sternly said, 'You cannot begin to imagine how many men I have killed.'

As a young boy, I dared not push the boundaries too far. But now, after hearing Thanh's story, I make a promise to myself that I will try again to talk to my father about his time and experiences during the war.

We leave Cham Towers in silence and ride south across dusty gravel roads to visit the salt fields of Nha Trang. The fields resemble a serene frozen lake, the salt white as snow, reflecting the blue sky and white clouds above. Ten barefoot workers, dressed in black with conical hats, collect the salt into their baskets. I watch in awe while they work under the scorching sun.

Salt production is one of the area's main sources of income, along with tourism and the fishing industry. When seawater enters the fields at high tide, the thick mud dykes surrounding the fields capture and retain the water once the tide goes down. The seawater evaporates after many hot days, leaving only the dry white salt powder, ready to be shovelled and collected for sale. Thanh tells me that he knows many farming families who have switched to producing salt, as the price of salt in Vietnam has soared four to five times the price of the previous year.

All this talk of salt starts me thinking about flavour, which then starts me thinking about food. I ask Thanh to recommend a place for me to try Nha Trang's freshest seafood.

'My house! My wife is a good cook,' he replies.

We ride to the seafood markets. I am a little concerned about arriving late, worried that the seafood may not be as fresh as early in the morning, but it doesn't matter, everything is alive and kicking — fish, eels, squid, lobsters, prawns, snails, mussels, clams, crabs and many other unfamiliar species of the South China Sea. I buy three whole lobsters, 2 kilograms each of calamari and large tiger prawns, rice paper and beer, all for (AUD) $28.00.

Thanh's house is about twenty minutes from town, in the slum area of Nha Trang. As we carefully ride through the dirty narrow lanes, neighbours peek out of their houses, surprised to see a foreigner. I duck under a line of drying clothes across their front door as Thanh's wife frantically runs out, apologising, pushing them to one side. Thanh, his wife, Vang, and her mother live in this tiny weathered shack, its rusted tin roof scattered with patches of dried mud to fill up holes. Inside, there's a mat on the ground for sleeping, a dusty fan, a foam esky, a rice cooker, a mortar and pestle, a guitar, and an open squat toilet in the corner. I cannot hide my feelings of shock and sadness.

'We live a very poor but simple life,' Thanh says. 'We can barely get by with my wage, and there are times when we don't have enough money for dinner. But there are many people who are a lot worse off than us,' he says, lowering his voice. 'My next door neighbours, for instance. Their kids, who are eight and nine years old, sell lottery tickets on the streets all day long, while the parents rummage through rubbish, collecting plastic bottles and aluminium cans to sell for recycling. They earn less than a dollar a day.' I begin to feel extremely guilty for spending so much on a seafood dinner.

Thanh takes out a blue guitar pick from his wallet and starts to sing and play John Lennon's 'Imagine' with his guitar, while Vang and I prepare dinner.

We heat some oil in a saucepan and add spring onions, salt and fish sauce, which we use to baste the lobsters and calamari while they are grilling. Vang makes a delicious dipping sauce with fish sauce, vinegar, garlic, sugar and pounded ginger, and her mother squeezes some juicy limes into a mix of sea salt, freshly ground black pepper and chopped green chilli. I am in charge of the grilling; all is done within twenty minutes. Vang brings out some mint and other herbs from her esky, which we wrap up with the prawns in rice paper.

An hour into dinner and the electricity cuts out, leaving us with no light or fan, but it doesn't bother us. We have great food, cold beer, live music and interesting discussions about day-to-day life in Vietnam. We continue to eat, drink, sing and laugh well into the evening.

A sign on the lobby's notice board reads, 'Volunteer English Teachers Needed!' I write down the address and make my way to the school, which is run by a lady named Kimmy Le, proud owner of the 'Crazy Kim' bar. For many years she has been running her 'Hands off the Kids' campaign, which aims to prevent paedophilia in Vietnam, and she has recently set up classes to teach English to street kids. There is a full-time teacher employed at the school, and sometimes they need the help of volunteers during group English discussions.

I walk through the bar to an outdoor area where the classrooms are located. I'm surprised to see so many students of all ages, between five and twenty years old, all split into three separate classes. Not sure as to where I should go, I peek into them all, then choose one and nervously enter to meet the teacher, only to find that there isn't one; the teacher hadn't turned up that morning.

'Good morning teacher,' the children say when they see me, rising from their seats. Evidently, I am their man!

I stand there, stunned, unsure of what to do; I'm just a volunteer, not a qualified English teacher. But it seems that I have no choice.

'Take out your text books, please,' I say, resisting all thoughts of running away. 'Continue where you left off yesterday.'

They do so happily and the lesson begins. 'Teacher, teacher, is this the correct pronoun to use in this sentence? Teacher, teacher, is this the right consonant?' They fire questions at me from all directions: nouns, pronouns, verbs, adjectives, adverbs and consonants — it's been so bloody long! I struggle to explain it to them in simple form.

The hours go by slowly, it is exhausting work then, finally, the bell — class dismissed!

I follow the students into the bar area, where we all sit down and share a big lunch. I am so amazed and proud of these kids for wanting to learn; they are so motivated and determined to improve their English so they can have better job opportunities and eventually afford a place to live.

I promise to come back every morning for the rest of the week. They are all very excited and promise me in return to work hard and complete an exercise every class. But, if they do, I have to buy them each an ice cream. I think all volunteers get roped into this deal.

The week quickly goes by, the kids become my new family in Nha Trang, each taking turns after class to introduce me to the different dishes of their region. On the last day of class the older students take me on a street food crawl. Our dinner starts at 5.30 p.m., and we move from street vendor to street vendor, sampling each speciality. We eat at eight different stalls — an eight-course degustation dinner, hawker style. This was the menu.

STALL 1: NEM NUONG Nha Trang barbecued pork sausages, wrapped in rice paper and fresh herbs — (AUD) $2.00.

STALL 2: MUC NUONG DAU HAO Chargrilled cuttlefish marinated in oyster sauce — (AUD) $4.00.

STALL 3: CA TRUNG CHIEN Little crispy fried fish filled with roe — (AUD) $2.50.

STALL 4: GOI XOAI CA COM KHO Green mango salad with dried anchovies — (AUD) $1.20.

STALL 5: GOI SUA Salad of raw jellyfish, banana blossom, green banana and mint — (AUD) $1.80.

STALL 6: BUN CA Vermicelli and fish served in a light fish broth — (AUD) 35 cents.

STALL 7: CA CHUNG TUONG Steamed cod in soya beans — (AUD) $4.50.

STALL 8: THE HIGHLIGHT Kerbside, across the road from the main beach. This last street stall was a metal cart on wheels, filled with live seafood, and with a rusty green scale and a tiny coal grill. I weighed up some white-shelled snails, black mussels, scallops and lobsters. The mussels were dressed with spring onion oil, the scallops and lobsters were topped with a saté sauce and the snails were dipped into a sweet fish sauce. The most expensive — (AUD) $12.80.

That evening I absorbed all that Nha Trang had to offer: its stories, people, culture, food and way of life. The amazing night ended with a very teary farewell to my young family.

SILKEN TOFU AND PORK SOUP
CANH ĐẬU HŨ HẸ HEO XAY

TOFU IS A DIETARY STAPLE THROUGHOUT VIETNAM. IT ACTS AS A SPONGE AND CARRIES THE FLAVOURS IT IS COOKED WITH. I USE MAINLY SILKEN TOFU IN MY COOKING AS I ENJOY ITS SOFT CREAMY TEXTURE. I COOK THIS RECIPE WHEN I'M FEELING UNWELL — IT'S COMFORT FOOD — EVEN PREPARING IT MAKES ME FEEL BETTER. LEFTOVER TOFU SHOULD BE KEPT IN COLD WATER AND REFRIGERATED. CHANGE THE WATER DAILY AND USE IT WITHIN THREE DAYS.

200 g (7 oz) minced pork
1 teaspoon sugar
1 tablespoon fish sauce
250 g (9 oz) silken tofu, cut into
    bite-sized pieces
1 tablespoon preserved cabbage
1 bunch garlic chives, cut into
    4 cm (1½ inch) pieces
4 spring onions (scallions),
    green part only, thinly sliced
    lengthways
1 handful coriander (cilantro)
    leaves, roughly chopped
1 bird's eye chilli, thinly sliced
fish sauce, for dipping

Pour 1.5 litres (52 fl oz/6 cups) of water into a saucepan and bring to the boil. Add the pork and stir for 3 minutes to break up the mince, skimming any impurities off the surface. Now add 2 teaspoons salt, the sugar, fish sauce and tofu. When the tofu rises to the surface, add the preserved cabbage and garlic chives. Remove the saucepan from the heat.

Transfer the soup to large serving bowls and garnish each bowl of soup with some spring onions, coriander and a pinch of freshly ground black pepper. Serve with jasmine rice, and a small bowl of sliced chilli and fish sauce for dipping.

SERVES 4-6 AS PART OF A SHARED MEAL

STEAMED MURRAY COD WITH SOYA BEANS
CÁ CHƯNG TƯƠNG

WHEN I SERVE WHOLE FISH AT RED LANTERN, THERE ARE TIMES WHEN GUESTS ASK ME TO FILLET THE FISH AND REMOVE ITS HEAD. BEFORE SAYING NO, I EXPLAIN THAT FISH SHOULD ALWAYS BE COOKED AND EATEN WITH SKIN, AND ITS HEAD SHOULD DEFINITELY NOT BE WASTED — CHEEKS AND EYES ARE THE BEST PARTS AND SHOULD BE DEVOURED. EATING WHOLE FISH IS LIKE EATING CRAB IN ITS SHELL — YOU NEED TO USE YOUR FINGERS TO PICK OFF THE FLESH FROM THE BODY AND BETWEEN THE BONES. IF YOU GET A BONE STUCK IN YOUR THROAT, DON'T PANIC, JUST SWALLOW A SPOONFUL OF RICE.

FERMENTED SOYA BEANS CAN BE FOUND AT YOUR LOCAL ASIAN MARKET IN JARS; LOOK FOR THE BLACK VARIETY. THEY ARE QUITE SALTY, SO I USE LESS FISH SAUCE HERE THAN IN OTHER RECIPES.

Put the mushrooms in a bowl, cover with water and soak for 20 minutes, then drain and thinly slice. Put the bean thread vermicelli in a bowl, cover with water and soak for 20 minutes, then drain and use kitchen scissors to cut into 4 cm (1½ inch) lengths.

In a small bowl, combine the sugar, fish sauce and 1 teaspoon each of salt and freshly ground black pepper, and mix well. Add the fermented soya beans and stir through. Coat the whole fish with this mixture, then place the fish on a heatproof plate that will fit into your steamer.

Place water in a large saucepan and bring to the boil. Set the steamer over the boiling water and put the fish on the plate in the steamer. Top the fish with the vermicelli, mushrooms, onion, tomatoes, chilli, ginger and garlic oil. Steam, covered, over high heat for 15 minutes, then add the spring onions and celery and steam for a further 5 minutes.

Carefully remove the plate from the steamer. Serve the fish with jasmine rice, and a small bowl of sliced chilli and soy sauce for dipping.

SERVES 4-6 AS PART OF A SHARED MEAL

5 dried wood ear mushrooms
20 g (¾ oz) dried bean thread (glass) vermicelli noodles
1 tablespoon sugar
2 teaspoons fish sauce
2 tablespoons fermented soya beans
1 whole Murray cod (600 g/1 lb 5 oz), cleaned (or use silver perch or barramundi)
1 onion, cut into wedges
2 tomatoes, cut into wedges
1 long red chilli, julienned
1 cm (½ inch) piece of ginger, peeled and julienned
1 tablespoon garlic oil (page 329)
2 tablespoons sliced spring onion (scallion)
½ bunch Asian celery, sliced into 4 cm (1½ inch) pieces
sliced chilli, extra
light soy sauce, for dipping

NHA TRANG PORK SAUSAGE
NEM NƯỚNG NHA TRANG

LOCALS IN NHA TRANG ARE VERY PROUD OF THEIR SPECIALITY. I WAS HAVING MY EARLY MORNING COFFEE WHEN I NOTICED A *NEM NUONG* RESTAURANT ACROSS THE ROAD; I SAT AND WATCHED SIX WOMEN PREPARE 50 KILOGRAMS OF PORK SKEWERS, AND THIS WAS ONLY FOR THE LUNCH SERVICE. I RETURNED HOURS LATER TO A FULL, BUSY RESTAURANT, THE BARBECUE LINED WITH CHARRING PORK SKEWERS. THROUGH THE THICK SMOKE I COULD SEE THE WOMEN STILL PREPARING THE PORK SAUSAGES — THEY HADN'T MOVED FROM THEIR SEATS AND WERE PREPARING ANOTHER 50 KILOGRAMS FOR DINNER.

NEM NUONG IS ALSO FOUND IN SAIGON AND DALAT, PREPARED WITH ONLY PORK MEAT. NHA TRANG, BEING A COASTAL TOWN, ADDS PRAWN AND FISH TO THE RECIPE.

100 g (3½ oz) dried rice vermicelli noodles

150 g (5½ oz) raw tiger prawns (shrimp), peeled and deveined, chopped

400 g (14 oz) minced pork

100 g (3½ oz) fish paste (page 334)

2 garlic cloves, finely chopped

2 red Asian shallots, finely chopped

1 teaspoon sugar

23 dried round rice paper wrappers (22 cm/8½ inch diameter)

1 Lebanese (short) cucumber, sliced into batons

1 bunch perilla, leaves picked

1 bunch mint, leaves picked

1 bunch Vietnamese mint, leaves picked

1 green oak lettuce or butter lettuce, leaves separated

90 g (3¼ oz/1 cup) bean sprouts

2 star fruit, halved and thinly sliced

1 bunch garlic chives, cut into 4 cm (1½ inch) lengths

250 ml (9 fl oz/1 cup) hoisin dipping sauce (page 330)

Soak 15 wooden chopsticks in cold water for 30 minutes to prevent them burning. Put the rice vermicelli in a saucepan of boiling water and bring back to the boil. Cook for 5 minutes, then turn off the heat and leave in the water for 5 minutes. Drain the noodles, rinse under cold water, and set aside.

Using a mortar and pestle, pound the prawns to a fine paste, then set aside. Repeat this process with the minced pork. Alternatively, combine the prawns and pork in a food processor and process to form a fine paste.

In a large bowl, combine the prawn paste, pork paste, fish paste, garlic, shallots, sugar and 1 teaspoon each of salt and freshly ground black pepper. Knead well for 10 minutes, or until the mixture is very elastic. Cover and refrigerate for 20 minutes.

Coat the palm of your hand with oil to stop the mixture sticking, then take a small handful of the prawn and pork mixture. Holding the chopstick in your other hand, wrap the mixture around three-quarters of the length of the chopstick, and shape it like a sausage, smoothing it with your hand. Repeat with the rest of the mixture, oiling your hand each time.

Heat a barbecue grill to medium and chargrill the pork sausages for 8 minutes, rotating the chopsticks every 2 minutes.

To assemble the rolls, cut 8 rice paper wrappers in half. Fill a large bowl with warm water and dip one whole sheet of rice paper in the water until just softened, then lay it flat on a plate. Dip a half sheet of rice paper in the water and then lay it vertically in the middle of the round sheet. This will strengthen the roll, preventing the filling breaking through.

In the middle of the rice paper, place a pork sausage, some vermicelli, cucumber, perilla, mint, Vietnamese mint, lettuce, bean sprouts, star fruit and garlic chives. To form the roll, first fold the sides into the centre over the filling, then the bottom of the rice paper up and over, and roll it up to form a tight roll. Serve with the hoisin dipping sauce.

MAKES 15

CHARGRILLED JUMBO PRAWNS IN OYSTER SAUCE
TÔM NƯỚNG DẦU HÀO

IN THIS RECIPE I SUGGEST PEELING THE PRAWNS, BUT IN VIETNAM THE LOCALS WOULD LEAVE THE SHELLS INTACT AND ENJOY THE CRUNCH OF THE CRISPY CHARCOAL SHELLS. IF YOU ARE FEELING ADVENTUROUS, PLEASE DO THE SAME.

In a bowl, combine the ginger, shaoxing wine, shallots, garlic, brown sugar, oyster sauce, fish sauce and sesame oil. Mix well, then add the prawns and toss to coat in the marinade. Cover and place in the fridge to marinate for 30 minutes. Drain well.

Heat a barbecue grill or chargrill pan to medium–high and cook the prawns for 2 minutes on each side. Remove to a serving plate, garnish with the sesame seeds and serve immediately. Serve with jasmine rice, and with chilli sauce for dipping.

SERVES 4-6 AS PART OF A SHARED MEAL

1 tablespoon julienned ginger
2 tablespoons shaoxing rice wine
2 red Asian shallots, finely chopped
2 garlic cloves, finely chopped
1½ tablespoons soft brown sugar
1 tablespoon oyster sauce
1 tablespoon fish sauce
1 teaspoon sesame oil
500 g (1 lb 2 oz) raw jumbo prawns (shrimp), peeled and deveined, tails intact, or left unpeeled if preferred
1 teaspoon toasted sesame seeds
2 tablespoons chilli sauce

CARAMELISED MACKEREL WITH PINEAPPLE
CÁ THU KHO KHÓM

THIS RECIPE IS A MARRIAGE OF MANY DIFFERENT ELEMENTS, BALANCED TOGETHER PERFECTLY. IT IS A LIGHTER VERSION OF THE POPULAR TRADITIONAL DISH OF CARAMELISED FISH, *CA KHO*. I HAVE BALANCED THE SALT WITH THE PINEAPPLE, THE FISH SAUCE WITH SUGAR AND ADDED DARK SOY SAUCE FOR COLOUR. IF YOU DON'T OFTEN USE PINEAPPLE IN COOKING, GIVE THIS A TRY; YOU'LL BE PLEASANTLY SURPRISED.

WHEN USING A CLAY POT FOR THE FIRST TIME, MAKE SURE YOU IMMERSE IT IN COLD WATER FOR A FEW HOURS. THIS WILL ENSURE THAT IT DOES NOT CRACK OVER INTENSE HEAT. CLAY POTS RELEASE EARTHY, SMOKY FLAVOURS INTO YOUR FOOD AND THEY MAINTAIN THEIR HEAT WELL.

2 garlic cloves, finely chopped
4 spring onions (scallions), white part only, bruised
2 tablespoons fish sauce
1/4 teaspoon dark soy sauce
1 teaspoon oyster sauce
2 tablespoons sugar
3 mackerel cutlets (600 g/1 lb 5 oz in total)
2 tablespoons vegetable oil
300 g (10½ oz) pineapple, cut into bite-sized pieces
200 ml (7 fl oz) chicken stock (page 328)
1 tablespoon fried garlic (page 329)
1 tablespoon garlic oil (page 329)
2 spring onions (scallions), green part only, sliced
1 small handful coriander (cilantro) leaves
1 bird's eye chilli, finely chopped
1 Lebanese (short) cucumber, sliced

In a bowl, combine half the garlic, the white spring onion, the fish sauce, dark soy sauce, oyster sauce, sugar and 1/2 teaspoon salt. Coat the fish with the mixture, then cover and place in the fridge to marinate for 15 minutes, reserving any leftover marinade.

Place a frying pan over medium heat with 1 tablespoon of the vegetable oil. Add the pineapple and stir-fry for 1 minute, then remove from the pan and set aside. Add the remaining oil and heat over medium heat, then brown the fish cutlets on both sides.

Remove the pan from the heat and transfer the fish to a chopping board. Chop each fish cutlet into four pieces with a heavy cleaver. Transfer the fish and pineapple to a clay pot and pour in the reserved marinade. Place the clay pot on the stovetop, turn the heat to high and bring to the boil. Add the chicken stock and bring back to the boil, skimming any impurities off the surface. Reduce the heat to low and simmer for 20 minutes, or until the liquid has reduced by half.

Add the remaining chopped garlic to the pot along with the fried garlic, garlic oil and 1/2 teaspoon freshly ground black pepper, and stir to combine. Spoon the sauce over the fish. Remove the clay pot from the heat, garnish with the spring onion, coriander and chilli, and serve with a side bowl of cucumber and jasmine rice.

SERVES 4-6 AS PART OF A SHARED MEAL

CHARGRILLED SQUID IN OYSTER SAUCE
MỰC NƯỚNG DẦU HÀO

I DECIDED TO TAKE A LONG WALK ALONG NHA TRANG BEACH, AWAY FROM THE NOISE AND TOURISTS. TWO KILOMETRES LATER, I SAW SOME LADIES WEARING CONICAL HATS SITTING ON THE WHITE SAND, GRILLING SQUID. I SAT WITH THEM FOR HOURS, EATING DRIED SQUID, SEMI-DRIED SQUID AND SQUID SIMPLY MARINATED IN OYSTER SAUCE.

2 tablespoons shaoxing rice wine
2 red Asian shallots, finely chopped
2 garlic cloves, finely chopped
2 tablespoons oyster sauce
1 tablespoon fish sauce
1 tablespoon soft brown sugar
1 teaspoon sesame oil
500 g (1 lb 2 oz) squid, cleaned,
    tubes butterflied and scored
    on the inside, tentacles reserved
1 teaspoon toasted sesame seeds
2 tablespoons chilli sauce

In a bowl, combine the rice wine, shallots, garlic, oyster sauce, fish sauce, brown sugar and sesame oil. Add the squid body and tentacles and toss to coat well, then cover the bowl and leave the mixture at cool room temperature for 30 minutes.

Heat a barbecue grill or chargrill pan to high. Cook the scored side of the squid first for no longer than 2 minutes, then turn and cook the other side for about 2 minutes, or until golden in colour. Remove from the heat and cut the squid into bite-sized pieces. Transfer to a serving plate and garnish with sesame seeds. Serve with chilli sauce for dipping, and jasmine rice.

SERVES 4-6 AS PART OF A SHARED MEAL

NHA TRANG FISH AND VERMICELLI NOODLE SOUP
BÚN CÁ NHA TRANG

BUN CA IS ONE OF MANY FAMOUS DISHES FROM NHA TRANG. I SPENT A LONG HOUR LOOKING FOR THIS PARTICULAR RESTAURANT THAT SERVED THE BEST *BUN CA* IN TOWN. THE HUMIDITY WAS HIGH AND THE SUN PUNISHING, AND WHEN I GOT THERE I DIDN'T KNOW IF I STILL WANTED A BOWL OF STEAMING HOT SOUP. I SAT AND RESTED AND REFRESHED WITH AN ICED JASMINE TEA. ALONG THE AQUA WALLS WERE FRAMED ARTICLES WRITTEN FROM ALL OVER THE WORLD, ALL TALKING ABOUT THIS HIDDEN GEM FOUND IN THE BACK LANES OF NHA TRANG, SERVING THIS DELECTABLE NOODLE SOUP. I QUICKLY ORDERED ONE.

Season the fish with 1 teaspoon salt, ½ teaspoon freshly ground black pepper and 1 tablespoon of the dill, then set aside for 15 minutes. Season the pork ribs with ¼ teaspoon salt and 1 tablespoon of the fish sauce, then set aside to marinate for 15 minutes.

Bring the chicken stock to the boil in a large saucepan, add 1 teaspoon salt, the sugar and the remaining fish sauce, stir to combine, then add the pork ribs. Bring back to the boil, skimming any impurities off the surface, then reduce the heat and simmer for 15 minutes.

Put the rice vermicelli in a saucepan of boiling water and bring back to the boil. Cook for 5 minutes, then turn off the heat and leave in the water for 5 minutes. Drain the noodles, rinse under cold water, and set aside.

Meanwhile, using oiled hands, mould the fish paste into small balls — you should have about 16–20 fish balls. Add the fish balls to the simmering stock and cook for 3 minutes, or until they rise to the surface.

Heat 2 tablespoons of the oil in a frying pan over medium heat. Add the fish and briefly cook on both sides for 1 minute, to seal. Add the sealed fish to the stock and simmer for 10 minutes. Take the fish, pork ribs and fish balls out of the stock, and place them on separate platters to cool.

Put the remaining 2 tablespoons of oil in a hot saucepan. Add the chopped tomato, chilli flakes and remaining dill, then reduce the heat to low and simmer the sauce for 3 minutes. Now add the sauce to the stock and bring to the boil, adding the tomato wedges, pineapple, star fruit and fried shallots. Turn off the heat.

To serve, divide the vermicelli among large soup bowls. Place a fish cutlet on top of the vermicelli, along with a few fish balls and a few pieces of chopped pork. Ladle over the hot stock to cover the ingredients. Add the mint, spring onions and bean sprouts, and serve with a bowl of sliced chilli and fish sauce for dipping. For more depth of flavour, add about ¼ teaspoon of shrimp paste to each bowl, stirring to dissolve the paste.

SERVES 6

1 whole Spanish mackerel (about 700 g/1 lb 9 oz), gutted, cleaned and chopped into 2 cm (¾ inch) cutlets
2 tablespoons chopped dill
500 g (1 lb 2 oz) pork spareribs
100 ml (3½ fl oz) fish sauce
2.5 litres (87 fl oz/10 cups) chicken stock (page 328)
2 teaspoons sugar
250 g (9 oz) dried rice vermicelli noodles
300 g (10½ oz) fish paste (page 334)
4 tablespoons vegetable oil
3 tomatoes (½ finely chopped, ½ cut into wedges)
½ teaspoon chilli flakes
½ pineapple, peeled, trimmed and cored, cut into bite-sized pieces
2 star fruit, thinly sliced
2 tablespoons fried red Asian shallots (page 329)
1 large handful mint leaves
4 spring onions (scallions), sliced
180 g (6 oz/2 cups) bean sprouts
1 bird's eye chilli, thinly sliced
fish sauce, for dipping
shrimp paste, to taste (optional)

FISH CONGEE
CHÁO CÁ

I GREW UP EATING THIS DISH, EITHER FOR BREAKFAST, SUPPER OR WHEN I WAS UNWELL AND NEEDED SOMETHING EASY TO DIGEST. CONGEE IS ENJOYED IN MANY ASIAN COUNTRIES, AND EACH HAS THEIR OWN WAY OF MAKING AND SERVING IT. IN VIETNAM, *CHAO* (RICE PORRIDGE) CAN BE SERVED WITH CHICKEN, DUCK, PORK, SALTED EGG OR OFFAL.

In a large frying pan, dry-roast the rice over low heat until fragrant but not brown. Transfer to a large saucepan, then pour in the chicken stock and bring to the boil. Add the fish pieces to the pan and cook for 2 minutes, then remove the fish with a slotted spoon and set aside.

Reduce the heat to a simmer and cook the rice, stirring regularly, for 25 minutes, then add the fish sauce and soy sauce.

Transfer the congee to a serving bowl, place the fish on top and garnish with the spring onion and coriander, and sprinkle each serving with a pinch of freshly ground black pepper.

SERVES 4–6 AS PART OF A SHARED MEAL

150 g (5½ oz/¾ cup) long-grain rice
1.5 litres (52 fl oz/6 cups) chicken stock (page 328)
300 g (10½ oz) ling fillets, sliced into bite-sized pieces
1 tablespoon fish sauce
1 tablespoon light soy sauce
1 tablespoon sliced spring onion (scallion)
1 tablespoon sliced coriander (cilantro) leaves

ROASTED PORK SPARERIBS
SƯỜN NON QUAY

OVENS ARE A RARE FIND IN VIETNAM, SO WHENEVER I SEE THIS ROASTED PORK DISH BEING CHOPPED UP, I ALWAYS STOP AND TRY IT. IT'S EXTREMELY SIMPLE TO MAKE THIS DISH YOURSELF, SO DON'T TAKE YOUR OVEN FOR GRANTED — USE IT.

1 tablespoon shaoxing rice wine
2 teaspoons light soy sauce
2 teaspoons fish sauce
1 tablespoon oyster sauce
1 tablespoon honey
½ teaspoon five-spice
3 garlic cloves, smashed
3 garlic cloves, finely chopped
500 g (1 lb 2 oz) lean pork
     spareribs
6 spring onions (scallions), thinly
     sliced lengthways

In a large bowl, combine the rice wine, soy sauce, fish sauce, oyster sauce, honey, five-spice, 1 teaspoon salt and the smashed and chopped garlic. Mix well, then add the pork ribs, tossing to coat them in the marinade. Cover the bowl and place in the fridge to marinate for at least 2 hours.

Preheat the oven to 200°C (400°F/Gas 6). Place the ribs in a baking dish in a single layer, then roast for 30 minutes, basting the pork with the marinade every 5–10 minutes. The ribs should be crisp and golden brown. Remove from the oven and cut the ribs through the bone with a heavy cleaver into 6 x 2 cm (2½ x ¾ inch) pieces and garnish with the spring onions. Serve with jasmine rice.

SERVES 4-6 AS PART OF A SHARED MEAL

CUTTLEFISH POACHED IN A VINEGAR STEAMBOAT
MỰC NHÚNG GIẤM

STEAMBOATS ARE A FUN AND COMMUNAL WAY OF EATING. YOU NEED A PORTABLE GAS STOVE, WHICH WILL SIT IN THE MIDDLE OF THE TABLE. CHOOSE A POT THAT IS SHALLOW ENOUGH FOR YOUR GUESTS TO BE ABLE TO SEE WHAT IS COOKING, SURROUND THE POT WITH PLATTERS OF FRESH HERBS, THE CUTTLEFISH AND DIPPING SAUCE, ALONG WITH A SLOTTED SPOON. ONCE THE BROTH IS SIMMERING, EACH GUEST SHOULD COOK THEIR OWN CUTTLEFISH, THEN ROLL IT UP IN THE WRAPPER WITH THE HERBS. YOU CAN BUY STEAMBOAT HOTPOTS AND GAS STOVES FROM YOUR LOCAL CHINATOWN OR ASIAN MARKET.

To make the vinegar water, combine the vinegar, 750 ml (26 fl oz/3 cups) of water, 2 teaspoons salt and the sugar in a bowl. Mix well and set aside.

Place a frying pan over medium heat. Add the oil and fry the lemongrass, garlic, onion and chilli until brown.

Place a gas stove in the centre of the dinner table, with the hotpot on medium heat. Add the vinegar water and lemongrass mixture to the hotpot. Assemble all the vegetables and herbs on platters and arrange them around the hotpot. Each person should have a side bowl of anchovy and pineapple dipping sauce.

Increase the heat so the vinegar water is simmering. Using chopsticks, each diner poaches a piece of cuttlefish in the simmering water, and then uses it to make the rolls.

To assemble the rolls, fill a large bowl with warm water and dip one sheet of rice paper in the water until just softened, then lay it flat on a plate. In the middle of the rice paper, place a piece of poached cuttlefish in a horizontal line approximately 4 cm (1½ inches) from the top. On top of the cuttlefish, add some perilla, mint, coriander, cucumber and bean sprouts. To form the roll, fold the sides into the centre over the filling, then the bottom of the paper up and over. Roll from bottom to top to form a tight roll. Dip the rolls into the anchovy and pineapple sauce.

SERVES 4-6 AS PART OF A SHARED MEAL

250 ml (9 fl oz/1 cup) white vinegar
110 g (3¾ oz/½ cup) sugar
4 tablespoons vegetable oil
1 lemongrass stem, white part only, finely chopped
4 garlic cloves, finely chopped
1 small red onion, finely chopped
4 long red chillies, finely chopped
1.5 kg (3 lb 5 oz) cuttlefish, cleaned, scored on the inside and sliced into 3 x 6 cm (1¼ x 2½ inch) pieces
20 dried round rice paper wrappers (16 cm/6¼ inch diameter)
1 handful perilla leaves
1 handful mint leaves
1 handful coriander (cilantro) leaves
1 Lebanese (short) cucumber, cut into batons
90 g (3¼ oz/1 cup) bean sprouts
250 ml (9 fl oz/1 cup) anchovy and pineapple sauce (page 333)

PORK BELLY STIR-FRIED WITH BAMBOO SHOOTS
THỊT BA RỌI XÀO MĂNG

IN THE MARKETS OF VIETNAM, BAMBOO SHOOTS ARE SOLD IN MORE THAN TEN DIFFERENT FORMS, SHAPES, CUTS AND SIZES. IF YOUR LOCAL ASIAN MARKET ONLY HAS THE PACKAGED OR TINNED VARIETY, MAKE SURE YOU BLANCH THEM IN BOILING WATER FOR A FEW MINUTES BEFORE USE.

2 tablespoons vegetable oil
2 garlic cloves, finely chopped
200 g (7 oz) boneless pork belly,
  thinly sliced
300 g (10½ oz) cooked fresh or
  packaged bamboo shoots
2 spring onions (scallions), cut into
  4 cm (1½ inch) lengths
2 teaspoons fish sauce
1 teaspoon sugar
1 long red chilli, thinly sliced on
  the diagonal
125 ml (4 fl oz/½ cup) dipping fish
  sauce (page 331)

Heat a frying pan over medium heat, add the oil and fry the garlic until lightly browned. Increase the heat, then add the pork belly and ½ teaspoon each of salt and freshly ground black pepper, and stir-fry for 3 minutes, or until the pork is brown. Add the bamboo shoots, spring onions, fish sauce and sugar and stir-fry for another 3 minutes. Remove the pan from the heat.

Transfer to a serving bowl and garnish with sliced chilli. Serve with jasmine rice and dipping fish sauce.

SERVES 4-6 AS PART OF A SHARED MEAL

DALAT
IN BLOOM

7

I TAKE TWO STEPS OUT OF MY HOTEL CARRYING MY BACKPACK AND I'M ALREADY DRIPPING WITH SWEAT; THE HUMIDITY IS HIGH AND THE SUN STRONG. I WAVE DOWN A GREEN TAXI AND JUMP IN. I'M OFF TO THE AIRPORT TO CATCH A LIGHT PLANE TO DALAT, WHICH LIES IN THE CENTRAL HIGHLANDS OF VIETNAM.

After a rough and bumpy 45-minute flight, I'm happy to get off the plane. I take a deep breath of the cool, fresh air. At the luggage collection area I'm approached by four short plump women, who ask me if I'd like to share a taxi with them. They are all in their seventies, with dark inked eyebrows and carrying fake Gucci bags, travelling from Singapore to visit the beautiful flower gardens of Dalat.

We bundle into the taxi, the ladies singing in loud, happy, croaking voices their Chinese rendition of 'Guantanamera'. I admire their playfulness and do my best to sing along with the chorus when I can. 'Guantanamera, guajira guantanamera, guantanameraaaaa! Guajira guantanamera …' We are like kids in the back of the school bus.

The taxi driver drops us off in town in front of their hotel and I help them take their luggage inside.

'500,000 dong,' demands the driver as I go to pay him. I'm in shock — (AUD) $40.00 for a 20-minute ride! I realise that while we'd been having our sing-along in the back seat, the driver had been pressing a few secret buttons on the meter and had charged us three times the going rate. I offer him 150,000 dong but he refuses it and starts to get aggressive, shouting, screaming, causing a scene and repeatedly pushing me hard in the chest, demanding that I pay what the meter reads.

Within minutes we are surrounded by onlookers, some running from afar, eager to see some free live entertainment, some standing on their motorbikes to get a better look.

The Singapore grandmas come to my rescue, abusing him in a torrent of Cantonese, hitting them with their Guccis, and pushing and shoving him until he is forced against the car bonnet. I put 150,000 dong in his pocket, he accepts defeat and drives away, while we bow and wave to the cheering crowd.

The hotel manager greets us with a warm smile. 'Welcome to Dalat.'

Dalat is known as 'The City of Eternal Spring', it lies 1500 metres above sea level and the temperature stays between 10 and 24 degrees Celsius all year round, making it a popular getaway for Vietnamese escaping the hot weather. For centuries Dalat has been home to many different hill tribe minorities, and in the early 1900s the city was developed by the French as a hill station. They built villas, churches and chateaus, which still remain today, and the area now looks something like a cross between Vietnam and the French Alps.

It's 7 p.m. on a Saturday night and the centre of the city is closed to all vehicles, allowing the night market to sprawl its goods all over town. Forty or so vendors spread their clothes on the ground, and with their high-pitched nasal tones they try to shout louder than the next, offering their wares for sale.

I move through the night noodle stalls looking at what's on offer — dishes from all over Vietnam, such as *pho* from Hanoi, *bun bo Hue* from Hue and *cao lau* from Hoi An — and although it all looks so delicious, I wonder if Dalat has its own regional speciality. I settle on a dish I haven't tried before: *bun mang vit*, a duck and bamboo broth served with vermicelli noodles. The broth is clear and the noodles soft, yellow pieces of bamboo float on the surface and shredded duck is scattered on top. I tear up my herbs, add tiny chillies and devour it in minutes. Still feeling peckish I move on.

I'm indecisive, the choices many: grilled pungent dried squid, crisp sheets of rice paper covered in sesame seeds and spring onion oil, sticky rice with chicken, deep-fried Vietnamese doughnuts, and baguettes filled with egg.

At the bottom of the stairs sits a lady and her steamer; she is serving *vit lon*, boiled duck embryo. I tried this Vietnamese delicacy recently in Quy Nhon, and seeing it again brings back memories of the first time my parents brought it home. I was seven years old and only knew of boiled chicken eggs. My parents' gave me the egg, their eyes fixed on me, eager to catch my reaction. I gave the tip of the delicate shell three light taps, then slowly peeled off some shell to find a thin layer of membrane, and beneath it what looked like a tiny duck, curled up inside and floating in liquid. I jumped back in shock while my parents broke out in laughter — I remember thinking it was an evil baby alien hiding in its cocoon. Mum broke open the membrane and explained that it was a fertilised duck egg; a lot of women eat it after giving birth and men eat it to stay 'strong'. Not sure what to do first, I sipped on the liquid in the shell, which was surprisingly tasty, almost like sipping on duck broth. I then spooned the duck out, and could see its veins, feathers and beak. I remember worrying about its bones and beak getting stuck in my throat, but I ate it regardless, enjoying all the textures, the crunchiness of the beak, the crushing of bones, and the feathers getting caught between my teeth.

I take a seat, keen to try the eggs again, only today I have some Vietnamese mint to spice it up, and a salt, pepper and lime dipping sauce to give the egg some dimension — it is even more delicious this time round.

I'm making an early start this morning, as I want to explore the beautiful highlands by motorbike. For me, this is no mean feat and, with my limited riding experience, navigating the skinny winding roads that loop in and out of the mountains sets my nerves on edge. I don't have a license but the lady who rents me the Honda cruiser tells me if the police stop me I'll be fine if I just speak English, not Vietnamese.

I set out slowly, taking it pretty easy so I can get used to the bike. The traffic isn't anywhere near as hectic as in Hanoi, so I'm feeling quite relaxed. I make it out of town safely and ride deep into the mountains and find myself surrounded by tall pine forests and luscious green fertile landscapes. There is not a soul in sight — I take a deep breath of the crisp air, the cool wind blows against my face, and I relish in my child-like freedom.

I suddenly press hard on the brake as something catches itself under my helmet strap, it is small but there is a sharp sting. It's only a bee but it has managed to dig its stinger deep into my face, just under my cheekbone. I pry the stinger out and flick it away.

I stop outside a local flower garden where a grower squats, snipping the stems of flowers. I ask permission to enter her garden, curious to see what she is growing and amazed by such an array of vivid colours and sweet scents.

Her name is Thang and she tells me that she moved here with her family from the outskirts of Hanoi twenty years ago to grow flowers. As we speak, I can see only her almond eyes — her head is covered with the traditional conical hat, her face hidden by a surgical mask to protect her skin from the sun.

She walks me through her garden, passionately explaining each flower in detail, its origins, its varieties and their English names. It's her peach blossom tree, with its colours of light purple and ruby red, that she's most proud of. She explains that these blossoms reflect the Vietnamese people: the blossoms are slender and delicate but exude solemnity, strength and determination.

Next to Thang's blossom tree are twenty or more rows of orchids. In Vietnam the orchid is known as 'The Queen in the World of Flowers'. There are about 100,000 types of orchids in the world and Vietnam grows 500 of them, many of which are found in Dalat. We move on to an array of coloured roses — red, soft pink, white and bright yellow — then her gladiolus flowers, also known as sword lilies.

'Legend has it,' Thang says, as she settles down to tell me the story, 'that a Roman general captured two enemies and kept them in his house as prisoners. To the general's dismay, his two daughters fell madly in love with the prisoners. Filled with rage, he demanded that the two men go to battle against each other, and using their swords they must fight to the death.

'The prisoners would not fight; they both refused and stabbed their swords into the ground. The general saw this as a great disrespect and immediately had them both beheaded. But when their heads were sliced off and hit the ground, their swords bloomed into two gladioli, resembling the shape of a short sword.'

As she finishes her story I realise she is looking at me quite strangely. She tells me that one side of my face is bigger than the other. In the mirror of my motorbike I can see that the right side of my face is swollen up like a puffer fish. I've obviously had an allergic reaction to the bee sting. There's nothing much I can do now, so I adjust my helmet strap and continue my journey.

" COFFEE PLAYS A BIG PART IN DAY-TO-DAY LIFE IN VIETNAM. YOU CAN FIND A CUP OF COFFEE JUST ABOUT ANYWHERE, EITHER FROM A SMALL COFFEE SHOP OR ONE OF THE MANY STREETSIDE STANDS. "

I ride further and see more gardens filled with wild sunflowers, hydrangeas and fuchsias. Vegetable patches are dotted about, growing daikon, artichoke, pumpkin, cabbage, cauliflower, potatoes, onions and lettuce; strawberries, mulberries and blueberries wait patiently to be picked; and lemons, mangoes and jackfruit hang from trees. I stop my bike on the top of a hill. It's a scene straight out of a fairy tale book; flowers and coffee trees sway with the breeze, and as far as the eye can see, every stretch of land is covered with patches of different shades of lush greenery, abundant with fresh produce.

Dalat has some of the most fertile land in Vietnam, making this area the premier agricultural land in the country. The top restaurants in Vietnam get all their fresh produce from here, in particular, restaurants that offer western cuisine contract farmers here to grow rocket, basil, thyme, rosemary and many other herbs and vegetables traditionally not grown in Vietnam.

The majority of Vietnam's coffee is grown in these central highlands. In recent years Vietnam has shot up through the world's coffee exporting ranks and is now the second largest coffee exporter in the world, trailing closely behind Brazil. It was the French colonists who introduced coffee to the region late in the nineteenth century. Almost all the coffee trees that grow here are the Robusta variety, one of two principal species of coffee grown in the world, the other being Arabica. Robusta is known to be more robust with a higher caffeine content than Arabica, but is said to have an inferior flavour.

One variety that is more superior to them all, however, is known as 'weasel coffee' or *ca phe chon*. The ripe coffee berries are fed to weasels, the weasels excrete the seeds, the excreta is collected, usually by young children, and the seeds are harvested, a process that is thought to enhance the taste of the bean. Coffee connoisseurs swear by it, as do I; it is definitely stronger, smoother and has a headier flavour, but it is much more expensive.

Coffee plays a big part in day-to-day life in Vietnam. You can find a cup of coffee just about anywhere, either from a small coffee shop or one of the many streetside stands. Locals like to gather together, drinking a cup of coffee at any time of day, chatting and making small talk. I usually have two cups a day; it's not just the flavour that I enjoy but also the ritual of drinking it.

I stop into a home where the family grows and roasts their own coffee. The house is surrounded by hundreds of Robusta plants, all varying in size, and the front pavement is carpeted with coffee beans drying in the sun. I ask for a *ca phe sua da*, an iced coffee with sweetened condensed milk.

A young girl brings out a glass, which has a thin layer of condensed milk sitting in the bottom of it, and a small stainless-steel coffee filter that fits perfectly on top. She places it on the table next to a bowl of ice. I sip from a glass of iced tea while I patiently wait for the hot water to slowly seep through the dense compressed ground coffee, filtering individual drops of thick black coffee onto the bed of condensed milk below.

Once all the liquid has dripped into the glass, I tilt the filter a little to make sure not a drop is wasted. I take the lid off, place it on the table, then put the filter on top of the lid. I stir, add chunks of ice, mixing and rotating it around my glass for at least a minute. I sip slowly, enjoying every last drop; it is sweet, thick, strong and very addictive.

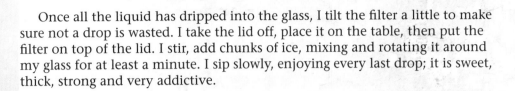

It's lunch time, so I stop at a house that displays a sign that says 'Set lunch'. An elderly man seats me on a creaky wooden balcony overlooking his fruit plantations. He kindly gets me some ice for my swollen face, which has begun to throb, and asks me where I'm from and if I'm married. I tell him I'm not married in the traditional sense but that I am definitely very hungry.

His wife brings out a large metal tray with six different dishes: a whole fried fish, crisp rice paper parcels, rolled egg omelette, grilled pork cutlets, stir-fried water spinach, wok-tossed green beans and some braised chicken. It's far too much food for one, so I ask him to join me.

He sits down and brings out some homemade rice wine and encourages me to down a few shots, then he calls out to his wife to bring the family photo album and proceeds to show me happy family snaps, most of which are shots of his six daughters.

'We have six very beautiful daughters, no boys; our daughters are all single and all very good cooks. Which one do you like, point her out and I'll ask her to come out and meet you.' With a grin, he pours me some more rice wine. I explain to him that just because someone isn't married it does not mean they don't have a partner and are not in a serious long-term relationship.

He can't understand how someone who is in a ten-year relationship cannot be married or have any children. In a stern voice, he explains that in Vietnamese culture you marry young and have as many children as you can, so they can help with the family business and look after you when you grow old and frail. That is their duty.

A young lady comes to clear our dishes and offers us some more rice wine. 'Luke, this is my youngest daughter Huong; she's twenty-three years old. Isn't she pretty?' Huong sits down at the table. She has a fixed fake smile on her face and continuously flutters her eyelids. She tells me I am very handsome and I look like a Hong Kong superstar. I almost choke on my drink in laughter, as I tenderly touch my swollen face. As soon as I take a drink of water, she pours me more, when I have a few spoons of rice, she refills my bowl, then picks up more food with her chopsticks and places it in my bowl.

Huong clears the table and brings out some fat mangoes for dessert. She sits next to me, giggling, feeding me pieces of mango from a fork. I finish the mango and move to the next chair. Undaunted, she takes a cigarette from her father, puts it in my mouth and lights it.

'Wouldn't she make a great little wife, Luke?'

This is a fairly regular occurrence for me and other foreigners in Vietnam, as women (and their fathers) hope to latch onto a 'wealthy' foreigner. I remember many of my father's mates, who were all married men, returning home from a Vietnam trip with new wives by their side. All claimed that it was the work of 'black magic', the spell so strong that all efforts from friends and family could not break it. Their stories were very convincing, back then …

I escape my impending nuptials to a complete stranger and head off again, to the Summer Palace, the home of Bao Dai, the last Emperor of Vietnam. At the entrance, I'm given a pair of military green socks to wear over my shoes to preserve the palace floor. I'm quite impressed by the Art Deco interior in this beautiful villa, built in 1933.

Set in a pine grove, the whole palace, along with its furniture and décor, has been kept in its original state. Dozens of gold-framed portraits of the royal family line the walls. I walk through Bao Dai's office, his living quarters, the meeting room, dining room and his son's room, admiring the ornate design and the tasteful choice in colonial Vietnamese furniture.

I enter Bao Dai's bedroom where a group of young Vietnamese tourists ask me to take their photo. They take their socks off and jump over the ropes onto Bao Dai's bed, and then sit down on it next to the sign, 'Do not touch the bed'. I quickly take the photos just as two armed guards come in, yell at us and kick us out of the house.

As I hop on my motorbike, I see the group approach me. 'No more photos!' I cry. But they have only come to apologise for the trouble they caused me, and invite me to dinner, to eat a speciality of Dalat.

'A speciality of Dalat? I didn't know there was one!' I follow them eagerly back into town.

We arrive at a typical hole-in-the-wall street eatery and sit at low tables. Two ladies are sitting outside, crouched over a burning grill, cooking the only dish they serve here, *nem nuong*, chargrilled pork skewers. The group I'm with are in their late twenties, and have travelled from Saigon for the weekend to celebrate a work colleague's job promotion.

We order six Saigon Red beers and *mot, hai, ba, yo*! (1, 2, 3, cheers!) Out come twelve pork skewers made from minced pork worked into a paste with spring onions, garlic and lemongrass, and a separate platter of fresh lettuce, herbs, green mango, green banana, cucumber and rice paper. We roll all these ingredients together into a chewy textured rice paper roll and dip it into a delicious dipping sauce, which I hadn't had before. The sauce is light orange in colour, quite thick and has a slight prawn flavour. I ask the lady what is in it, and she says those three words that I hear way too often: 'It's a secret.'

The night is long: we eat three lots of skewers and drink plenty of beer, all of us getting more rosy cheeked and louder as the night goes on. I suggest we need a change of scene, so we walk to the famous Xuan Huong Lake, where hundreds of locals sprawl around chatting, cuddling or fishing, many taking a ride around the lake in a pink swan-shaped pedal boat. Next, we make our way through the colourful flower markets and then stagger up to the top of a hill to a large Buddhist temple, where we buy some incense and then make our way inside.

As we light our incense and offer it to the gods, something takes over us; we are suddenly transformed into sensible, sober beings. Four Buddhist monks, dressed in long orange robes, enter and the crowd files in after them, ready for prayer.

The gong rings from behind me, vibrating through my ears. The monks' deep chant calms me; we kneel and begin to follow in prayer. The smoke from the incense fills the room. I feel light and very at peace.

UỐNG NƯỚC NHỚ NGUỒN, ĂN TRÁI NHỚ KẺ TRỒNG CÂY

WHEN DRINKING WATER, REMEMBER WHERE IT FLOWED FROM; WHEN EATING FRUIT, REMEMBER WHO PLANTED THE TREE.

IN LIFE, ALWAYS BE THANKFUL FOR HOW YOU GOT WHERE YOU ARE, AND REMEMBER WHO HELPED YOU GET THERE.

LOTUS STEM AND OYSTER MUSHROOM SALAD
GỎI NGÓ SEN NẤM BÀO NGƯ

I DISCOVERED A PLACE IN DALAT RUN BY BUDDHIST MONKS; THEY SERVED MOCK MEAT DISHES AND A WIDE SELECTION OF FRESH SALADS, USING ONLY LOCALLY GROWN HERBS AND VEGETABLES. ONE OF THE SALADS USED FRESH LOTUS SHOOTS, BUT UNFORTUNATELY IT IS QUITE DIFFICULT TO FIND THESE OUTSIDE OF ASIA, SO I'VE USED PICKLED SHOOTS INSTEAD, WHICH CAN BE FOUND IN JARS AT YOUR ASIAN MARKET.

2 tablespoons caster (superfine) sugar
2 tablespoons soy sauce
1 tablespoon lemon juice
2 teaspoons sesame oil
2 bird's eye chillies, thinly sliced
500 g (1 lb 2 oz) pickled lotus shoots, washed and drained
100 g (3½ oz) pickled vegetables (page 335)
50 g (1¾ oz) oyster mushrooms, halved
1 large handful Vietnamese mint, large leaves torn
1 teaspoon garlic oil (page 329)
2 tablespoons roasted peanuts, chopped (page 328)

To make the salad dressing, combine 1 tablespoon of the sugar, the soy sauce, lemon juice, sesame oil and chilli in a bowl. Stir well to dissolve the sugar, then set aside.

In a large bowl, add the pickled lotus shoots, pickled vegetables, oyster mushrooms, Vietnamese mint, garlic oil, the remaining 1 tablespoon of sugar and 1 teaspoon each of salt and freshly ground black pepper. Pour over the salad dressing and toss well. Garnish the salad with the peanuts.

SERVES 4-6 AS PART OF A SHARED MEAL

VIETNAMESE KIM CHI
KIM CHI

I STOPPED AT A TINY STALL IN THE DALAT MARKETS WITH LARGE PLASTIC TUBS FILLED WITH PICKLED BABY LEEK, PICKLED GARLIC, PICKLED KOHLRABI, PICKLED CHILLI, PICKLED GREEN PAPAYA, PICKLED LEMON, PICKLED WATERMELON SKIN AND *KIM CHI*. SEEING THIS DISH OF PICKLED CABBAGE, REMINDED ME OF MY MUM'S *KIM CHI* RECIPE, WHICH SHE'S BEEN MAKING FOR OVER TWENTY YEARS. I RECENTLY ASKED HER HOW SHE CAME ACROSS THIS RECIPE AND HOW *KIM CHI* ARRIVED IN VIETNAM. 'WHEN THE WAR BROKE OUT, TROOPS FROM ALL PARTS OF THE WORLD WERE IN OUR NEIGHBOURHOOD. I NOTICED A KOREAN SOLDIER EATING A SPICY LOOKING CABBAGE SALAD; I ASKED HIM WHAT IT WAS. HE GAVE ME A SPOONFUL TO TRY; I ENJOYED IT SO MUCH I ASKED HIM FOR THE RECIPE.'

Mix the cabbage well with the salt, and set aside for 1 hour. Rinse the salt out with cold water and drain.

Place the pounded ginger in a piece of muslin. Gather up the cloth to enclose the ginger, then hold it over a bowl and squeeze the ginger firmly to extract the juice — you should have about 3 tablespoons of ginger juice. Discard the ginger solids.

In a large bowl, combine the cabbage, spring onions, garlic, sugar, ground pickled chilli, chilli flakes, paprika, pepper and ginger juice. Toss together well, then transfer the *kim chi* to an airtight container and marinate overnight at room temperature.

Toss the *kim chi* again before transferring to glass jars. Refrigerate for 1 week before eating. Serve as an accompaniment with rice or noodle dishes. *Kim chi* will keep refrigerated for 1 month.

SERVES 6 AS AN ACCOMPANIMENT

1 Chinese cabbage (wong bok), each leaf roughly cut 6 x 10 cm (2½ x 4 inches) in size
250 g (9 oz/1 cup) salt
300 g (10½ oz) ginger, peeled and sliced, then pounded using a mortar and pestle
1 bunch spring onions (scallions), sliced into 4 cm (1½ inch) pieces
10 garlic cloves, peeled and thinly sliced
110 g (3¾ oz/½ cup) sugar
2 tablespoons ground pickled chilli
1 tablespoon chilli flakes
1 tablespoon hot paprika
1 tablespoon freshly ground black pepper

PRAWN AND CORN FRITTERS
BÁNH BẮP CHIÊN TÔM

A YOUNG GIRL FRIES BITE-SIZED FRITTERS IN A SMALL WOK IN FRONT OF HER HOME. SHE TRANSFERS THE FRITTERS TO A SHEET OF NEWSPAPER, GIVES THEM A COOLING BLOW AND GIVES IT TO HER YOUNGER SISTER AS A SNACK. IT TOOK ME BACK TO THE DAYS WHEN MY SIBLINGS AND I WERE YOUNG AND WE HAD TO LOOK AFTER AND FEED ONE ANOTHER WHILE OUR PARENTS WERE OUT WORKING.

100 g (3½ oz/⅔ cup) plain (all-purpose) flour
½ teaspoon paprika
½ teaspoon ground turmeric
200 g (7 oz) raw tiger prawns (shrimp), peeled and deveined, roughly chopped
200 g (7 oz) corn kernels (from 2 corn cobs)
2 spring onions (scallions), sliced
1 garlic clove, finely chopped
2 red Asian shallots, finely chopped
2 eggs, lightly beaten
vegetable oil, for deep-frying
125 ml (4 fl oz/½ cup) dipping fish sauce (page 331)

FOR SERVING (OPTIONAL)
1 green oak lettuce or butter lettuce, leaves separated
1 bunch perilla, leaves picked
1 bunch mint, leaves picked
1 bunch Vietnamese mint, leaves picked

In a bowl, combine the flour, paprika and turmeric and mix well. Put the prawns in another bowl and season with ½ teaspoon each of salt and freshly ground black pepper. Add the corn kernels, spring onions, garlic, shallots and eggs. Mix to coat the prawns, then gradually add the flour mixture, mixing until well combined. The mixture will be very thick.

Pour the oil into a wok and heat to 180°C (350°F), or until a cube of bread dropped into the oil browns in 15 seconds. Shape the batter with wet hands to create small patties. Carefully add to the hot oil and fry for 3–4 minutes, or until crisp and brown. Remove with a slotted spoon and drain on paper towel, then serve immediately.

Eat as a snack, or wrap each fritter in a lettuce leaf, adding perilla, mint and Vietnamese mint leaves. Serve with the dipping fish sauce.

SERVES 4-6 AS A SNACK OR PART OF A SHARED MEAL

HAIRY MELON STUFFED WITH PORK AND BLACK FUNGUS STRIPS
BÍ DỒN THỊT

HAIRY MELON IS IN THE GOURD FAMILY AND IS ALSO KNOWN AS A HAIRY GOURD, FUZZY GOURD OR HAIRY CUCUMBER. IF YOU CAN'T FIND HAIRY MELON IN YOUR ASIAN MARKET, YOU CAN USE BITTER MELON IN THIS RECIPE INSTEAD.

Put the mung beans in a bowl, cover with water and soak for 20 minutes, then drain. Transfer the drained beans to a steamer and place over a saucepan of boiling water, then cover and steam for 20 minutes.

Soak the bean thread vermicelli in water for 20 minutes, then drain and use kitchen scissors to cut into 4 cm (1½ inch) lengths. Put the black fungus strips in a bowl, cover with water and soak for 20 minutes, then drain.

Peel the skins off both hairy melons, cutting the ends off each and reserving the ends to use later. Use a spoon to scoop out the flesh from inside the melons, and discard it.

Combine the mung beans, vermicelli, black fungus, pork, spring onions, fish sauce, sugar, egg white and ½ teaspoon each of salt and freshly ground black pepper. Mix well, then stuff each melon with this mixture. Seal the ends of both melons with the reserved ends and secure with toothpicks.

Place the melons in a large saucepan and cover with 2 litres (70 fl oz/ 8 cups) of water, or as much water as needed so the melons are covered. Bring to the boil, then reduce the heat to a low simmer. Cover and simmer for 1 hour, or until tender.

Remove the toothpicks from the melons and cut into 2 cm (¾ inch) thick slices. Arrange on a long serving platter and garnish with coriander. Serve with jasmine rice, and a small bowl of sliced chilli and fish sauce for dipping.

SERVES 4-6 AS PART OF A SHARED MEAL

1 tablespoon dried mung beans
10 g (¼ oz) dried bean thread (glass) vermicelli noodles
20 g (¾ oz) dried black fungus strips
2 hairy melons, each 20 cm (8 inches) in length
150 g (5½ oz) minced pork
2 spring onions (scallions), white part only, sliced
2 teaspoons fish sauce
½ teaspoon sugar
1 egg white
1 handful coriander (cilantro) leaves
1 bird's eye chilli, thinly sliced
fish sauce, for dipping

WOK-TOSSED BEEF WITH WINGED BEANS
BÒ XÀO ĐẬU RỒNG

THE FIRST TIME I SAW A WINGED BEAN PLANT WAS IN DALAT. THE PLANT HAD BLUE FLOWERS, ITS STEMS CLIMBED HIGH, WHILE THE WINGED BEANS HUNG DOWN, POINTING TO THE SOIL. THEY MUST BE THE PRETTIEST BEAN ON THE MARKET AND THEY ARE DELICIOUS: THINK SNOW PEAS AND ASPARAGUS. WINGED BEANS IN VIETNAMESE ARE CALLED *DAU RONG*, TRANSLATED AS 'DRAGON BEAN'.

250 g (9 oz) beef sirloin, trimmed and thinly sliced
3 tablespoons fish sauce
4 tablespoons vegetable oil
2 garlic cloves, finely chopped
2 red Asian shallots, finely chopped
1 onion, cut into thin wedges
300 g (10½ oz) winged beans, tips and any strings removed, then cut on the diagonal into 1 cm (½ inch) pieces
2 teaspoons sugar
1 small handful coriander (cilantro) leaves, to garnish (optional)

Put the beef in a bowl with 1 tablespoon of the fish sauce, 1 tablespoon of the oil and ½ teaspoon freshly ground black pepper. Stir to coat in the marinade, then cover the bowl and place in the fridge to marinate for 20 minutes.

Heat a wok over medium heat, then add 2 tablespoons oil, half the garlic and half the shallots. Stir-fry until fragrant, then add the beef and stir-fry for 1 minute. Remove and set aside.

In the same wok, heat the remaining 1 tablespoon of oil and fry the remaining garlic and shallots until fragrant. Add the onion, winged beans, remaining fish sauce and sugar. Stir-fry for 1 minute, then return the beef to the wok and toss for a further minute to warm through. Garnish with coriander if desired, and serve with jasmine rice.

SERVES 4-6 AS PART OF A SHARED MEAL

STIR-FRIED BITTER MELON WITH STRAW MUSHROOMS
KHỔ QUA XÀO NẤM RỞM

DALAT IS FULL OF FRESH, VIBRANT AND COLOURFUL PRODUCE. I COULD LIVE ON VEGETABLES AND FRUITS ALONE IF I LIVED THERE. IF YOU ARE VEGETARIAN, OMIT THE OYSTER SAUCE AND ADD ONE TEASPOON OF DARK SOY SAUCE INSTEAD.

Soak the bean thread vermicelli in water for 20 minutes, then drain and cut using kitchen scissors into 10 cm (4 inch) lengths.

Heat a wok over medium heat, then add the oil and garlic and stir-fry for 1 minute, or until fragrant. Add the carrot, bitter melon and mushrooms and stir-fry for 3 minutes. Now add the vermicelli, sugar, soy sauce, oyster sauce and 3 tablespoons of water. Stir-fry for another 2 minutes, then add the sesame oil and a pinch of salt and freshly ground black pepper.

Transfer to a serving bowl and garnish with coriander. Serve with jasmine rice, and a small bowl of sliced chilli and soy sauce for dipping.

SERVES 4-6 AS PART OF A SHARED MEAL

40 g (1½ oz) dried bean thread (glass) vermicelli noodles
2 tablespoons vegetable oil
1 tablespoon finely chopped garlic
1 carrot, peeled and julienned
1 bitter melon (150 g/5½ oz), halved and seeded, then thinly sliced on the diagonal
8 straw mushrooms, halved
1 tablespoon sugar
1 tablespoon light soy sauce
1 tablespoon oyster sauce
½ teaspoon sesame oil
coriander (cilantro) sprigs, to garnish
1 bird's eye chilli, thinly sliced
light soy sauce, for dipping

PORK SPARERIB AND PICKLED MUSTARD GREEN SOUP
CANH SƯỜN DƯA CẢI

VIETNAMESE SOUPS, *CANH*, ARE NOT MEANT TO BE EATEN ALONE — THEY ARE DESIGNED TO COMPLEMENT ALL THE FLAVOURS OF THE OTHER DISHES AND TO HELP WITH DIGESTION. IN THIS SOUP, THE MAIN FOCUS IS THE BROTH, WHICH IS WHY WE COOK THE PORK RIBS FOR LONGER THAN USUAL — TO DRAW OUT ALL THE SWEETNESS FROM THE MEAT AND BONES.

MUSTARD GREENS ARE THE LEAVES OF THE MUSTARD PLANT AND THESE HAVE A STRONG PEPPERY MUSTARD-LIKE CHARACTER. BUY THEM FROM ANY ASIAN MARKET IN THE REFRIGERATION SECTION, SEALED IN ITS PICKLING WATER (RINSE UNDER COLD WATER BEFORE USE), OR TURN TO PAGE 335 FOR THE RECIPE.

350 g (12 oz) pickled mustard greens (page 335)
2 tablespoons fish sauce
1 teaspoon sugar
300 g (10½ oz) pork spareribs, cut into 2 x 4 cm (¾ x 1½ inch) pieces (ask your butcher to do this)
3 tomatoes, cut into wedges
2 spring onions (scallions), thinly sliced
1 small handful coriander (cilantro) leaves

Wash, drain and slice the pickled mustard greens into 5 mm (¼ inch) slices and set aside.

Put 2 litres (70 fl oz/8 cups) of water in a saucepan along with the fish sauce, sugar and 1 teaspoon each of salt and freshly ground black pepper, and bring to the boil. Add the pork ribs and bring to the boil over high heat, skimming any impurities off the surface, then reduce the heat and simmer for a further 10 minutes.

Now add the pickled mustard greens and tomatoes and simmer for another 5 minutes. Transfer to soup bowls and garnish with the spring onions and coriander. Serve with jasmine rice.

SERVES 4–6 AS PART OF A SHARED MEAL

WOK-TOSSED ASPARAGUS IN GARLIC
MĂNG TÂY XÀO TỎI

I WAS SURPRISED TO SEE ASPARAGUS GROWING EVERYWHERE IN DALAT. ASPARAGUS IS BECOMING POPULAR IN VIETNAMESE COOKING, WHICH, I AM TOLD, IS DUE TO ITS APHRODISIAC QUALITIES.

Bring a saucepan or deep frying pan of water to the boil, add the asparagus and blanch for 2 minutes. Drain and refresh in iced water, then drain again and set aside.

Heat a wok over medium heat, then add the oil and stir-fry the garlic and shallots for 1 minute, or until fragrant. Add the asparagus and toss gently for 2 minutes. Add the fish sauce, sugar, 1 tablespoon of water and a pinch of salt and freshly ground black pepper. Toss for a further minute, then transfer to a serving plate and garnish with sliced chilli and toasted sesame seeds. Serve with jasmine rice.

SERVES 4-6 AS PART OF A SHARED MEAL

14 stems asparagus, woody
    ends removed
2 tablespoons vegetable oil
3 garlic cloves, finely sliced
2 red Asian shallots, chopped
1 tablespoon fish sauce
2 teaspoons sugar
1 long red chilli, thinly sliced
    on the diagonal
½ teaspoon toasted sesame seeds

CHOKO STIR-FRIED WITH SCHOOL PRAWNS
TRÁI SU XÀO TÉP

I MET A FELLOW TRAVELLER IN DALAT. HE WAS FROM AUSTRALIA AND HAD HEARD OF MY RESTAURANT, RED LANTERN. HE ASKED ME TO JOIN HIM FOR DINNER, EXCITED THAT I COULD ORDER ALL THE LOCAL DELICACIES FOR HIM TO TRY. WHEN A PLATE OF CHOKO AND PRAWNS ARRIVED, HE COULDN'T HIDE HIS DISAPPOINTMENT. 'IS THAT CHOKO? WHAT'S SO BLOODY SPECIAL ABOUT CHOKO?' I TOLD HIM TO JUST TRY IT (I WAS SURE HE'D ONLY EATEN THEM BOILED). AFTER TASTING THE CHOKOS, WHICH HAD SOAKED UP ALL THE FLAVOURS IN THE STIR-FRY, HE RAISED HIS EYEBROWS IN SURPRISE, 'BLOODY BRILLIANT MATE!'

1 tablespoon caster (superfine) sugar
2 tablespoons fish sauce
150 g (5½ oz) raw small school prawns (shrimp), legs and heads trimmed, or peel if preferred
2 tablespoons vegetable oil
1 tablespoon finely chopped garlic
200 g (7 oz) choko, peeled and cut into batons
2 spring onions (scallions), thinly sliced on the diagonal
coriander (cilantro) sprigs, to garnish
1 bird's eye chilli, thinly sliced
fish sauce, for dipping

In a small bowl, combine the sugar and fish sauce, stirring until the sugar has dissolved. Divide the fish sauce mixture in half, and use one half to marinate the prawns for 10 minutes.

Place a wok over high heat, add 1 tablespoon of the oil and stir-fry the prawns for 1 minute. Remove and set aside.

Wipe the wok clean, add the remaining oil and the garlic and stir-fry for 1 minute, or until fragrant. Add the choko and remaining fish sauce mixture and stir-fry for 2 minutes, then return the prawns to the wok and toss for a further minute.

Transfer to a serving plate and garnish with spring onions, coriander sprigs and ½ teaspoon freshly ground black pepper. Serve with jasmine rice, and a small bowl of sliced chilli and fish sauce for dipping.

SERVES 4–6 AS PART OF A SHARED MEAL

BAKED BANANA CAKE
BÁNH CHUỐI

I HAVE NOT YET MET A VIETNAMESE PERSON WHO HAS NOT SAID THAT THIS CAKE IS THEIR FAVOURITE OR THAT THEIR MOTHER MAKES THE BEST VERSION. BE WARNED, YOU WON'T BE ABLE TO STOP AT ONE PIECE, SO I'VE MADE THIS RECIPE BIG ENOUGH FOR SECONDS ... AND THIRDS.

Slice the bananas thinly on the diagonal and coat with sugar. Cover and set aside at room temperature for 30 minutes.

Preheat the oven to 200°C (400°F/Gas 6). Grease a 24 cm (9½ inch) round baking tin with butter and line the base with baking paper.

Beat the eggs and combine with the condensed milk and melted butter. Now add the flour and mix well, then gently fold the bananas through the batter. Pour the batter into the prepared tin and bake for 1 hour, or until the cake is cooked through and golden brown. Transfer to a wire rack to cool, then cover and refrigerate for 1 hour before serving.

SERVES 12

NOTE For the best flavour, choose bananas that are fairly ripe but not starting to turn black.

12 ripe finger bananas (see note)
60 g (2¼ oz/¼ cup) caster (superfine) sugar
7 eggs
380 g (13½ oz) tin sweetened condensed milk
250 g (9 oz) unsalted butter, melted
200 g (7 oz/1⅓ cups) plain (all-purpose) flour

SWEET POTATO AND CASSAVA PUDDING
CHÈ BÁNH LỌT BÀ BA

A VENDOR SELLING PUDDINGS HAD SET UP HIS CART NEAR THE LAKE, WHERE COUPLES CUDDLE, KISS AND GIGGLE. I WAS MISSING SUZE AND FEELING LONELY — SOMETHING SWEET WOULD MAKE ME FEEL BETTER, SO I ORDERED THIS UNUSUAL SWEET PUDDING WITH VEGETABLES AND NICE TRANSLUCENT CHEWY BITS, TOPPED WITH CREAMY COCONUT. IT WAS STRANGE BUT I REALLY LOVED IT. VIETNAMESE PEOPLE EAT THESE SWEET PUDDINGS AS A SNACK, RATHER THAN AS A DESSERT.

I LIKE TO USE PANDAN LEAVES IN MY DESSERTS AND PUDDINGS AS A VANILLA BEAN SUBSTITUTE; IT HAS A LOVELY FRAGRANCE AND SUBTLE FLAVOUR. USE UP ANY LEFTOVER LEAVES BY ADDING A FEW TO THE POT NEXT TIME YOU COOK RICE.

200 g (7 oz) dried mung beans
300 g (10½ oz) cassava, thawed if using frozen
300 g (10½ oz) orange sweet potato
200 g (7 oz) tapioca flour
125 ml (4 fl oz/½ cup) hot boiled water
500 ml (17 fl oz/2 cups) coconut milk
3 pandan leaves, sliced into 5 cm (2 inch) pieces
250 g (9 oz) sugar
1 tablespoon toasted sesame seeds

Put the mung beans in a bowl, cover with water and set aside to soak for 20 minutes. Transfer the drained beans to a steamer and place over a saucepan of boiling water, then cover and steam for 20 minutes.

If using fresh cassava, first remove the thick skin. If using frozen cassava the skin has already been removed. Cut the cassava into bite-sized pieces, about 1 cm (½ inch) square. Peel the sweet potato and cut it into similar-sized pieces.

Combine the tapioca flour and boiled water in a bowl. Stir to combine, then knead the mixture for about 4 minutes, or until the dough is smooth. Turn out the dough onto a work surface or chopping board and roll it out with a rolling pin to about 5 mm (¼ inch) thick. Now cut the dough into bite-sized pieces, about 2 cm (¾ inch) long and 1 cm (½ inch) wide.

Bring 1 litre (35 fl oz/4 cups) of water to the boil in a saucepan and add pieces of the sliced dough. When they rise to the surface (about 2 minutes), remove with a slotted spoon. Refresh in cold water, then drain well.

In a large saucepan, combine 250 ml (9 fl oz/1 cup) of the coconut milk, 1 litre (35 fl oz/4 cups) of water, ½ teaspoon salt, the pandan leaves and mung beans. Stir, then add the cassava and sweet potato and simmer for 20 minutes, or until the cassava, sweet potato and mung beans are just cooked — they should still be *al dente*. Add the cooked pieces of tapioca dough and bring to the boil. Take out the pandan leaves and discard them, then add the remaining cup of coconut milk and the sugar, stir to combine and bring to the boil. Take off the heat. Serve the pudding warm in small bowls and garnish with toasted sesame seeds.

SERVES 6

STEAMING
SAIGON

8

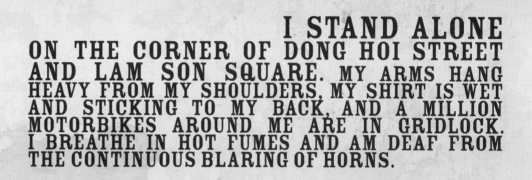

I STAND ALONE ON THE CORNER OF DONG HOI STREET AND LAM SON SQUARE. MY ARMS HANG HEAVY FROM MY SHOULDERS, MY SHIRT IS WET AND STICKING TO MY BACK, AND A MILLION MOTORBIKES AROUND ME ARE IN GRIDLOCK. I BREATHE IN HOT FUMES AND AM DEAF FROM THE CONTINUOUS BLARING OF HORNS.

I do know how to cross a road in Saigon but I'm just not ready. I need to grow accustomed to this chaotic, electric, magnetic and frustrating city. I remember Saigon ten years ago, when the streets moved gracefully with thousands of bicycles, there were kerbside cafés on every corner, and endless streetfood stalls lined the walls.

The Saigon before me is now home to designer brands, five-star hotels, fine dining restaurants, wine bars, night clubs, fast-food chains, constant development and one of the highest real estate prices in the world. Saigon has had a major facelift over the years, and the bicycles and cyclos have been replaced by motorbikes and luxury cars.

I cross the road. I look the drivers directly in the eye and move forward confidently at a constant, even pace, letting the motorbikes swerve around me. If I stop, I'll interrupt the natural flow of things and I may get hit.

I'm on my way to rendezvous with my parents, who have already been in Saigon for a few weeks. I am quite excited to see them, as this will be the first time that we will experience Vietnam together. They are staying with my Aunty Eight, who lives an hour out of town, in an area called Hoc Mon. Mum would kill me if I caught a taxi there, so I'm following her instructions closely: 'Walk to Ben Thanh markets, look for the local green bus going to Cu Chi Tunnels, don't pay more than 2000 dong, and get off at Hoc Mon bus depot.' Fifteen cents and a bus trip later I get off at the Hoc Mon markets.

As I enter these local markets I'm greeted with smiles of interest from stallholders. An area not yet exposed to tourism, being here is like a breath of fresh air, the people friendly and welcoming.

" I ACTUALLY DON'T KNOW THE NAMES OF MY AUNTIES AND UNCLES, I ONLY KNOW THEM BY THEIR NUMBER, OR POSITION, IN THE FAMILY. THE PARENTS ARE ALWAYS NUMBER ONE IN THE FAMILY; THE FIRST CHILD IS ADDRESSED AS NUMBER TWO, THE SECOND AS NUMBER THREE, AND SO ON. "

'Where are you from, do you have family here, are you married, any kids, do you like Vietnam?'

All asking the same questions, curious to know more, and all keen to give me directions to my Aunty Eight's market place.

I actually don't know the names of my aunties and uncles, I only know them by their number, or position, in the family. The parents are always number one in the family; the first child is addressed as number two, the second as number three, and so on. Remembering the numbers is a lot easier than remembering everyone's name, especially when there are ten children in the family. On my mum's side, Aunty Two lives in Paris, Aunty Three and Uncle Four have passed on, Uncle Five lives in Sydney, number six is my mum, Uncle Seven lives in Sydney, Aunty Eight in Hoc Mon, Aunty Nine in Saigon and Aunty Ten lives in Minnesota. I'm not too sure about my dad's siblings. There seems to be much mystery surrounding that side of the family and they are not talked about often.

As I walk down a main road I notice huge trucks ahead, packed with fresh corn, so I know I'm close to Aunty Eight's stall. She buys truck loads of corn from growers in Dalat and then sells corn wholesale to smaller local markets. I follow the trucks down a dirt road and there she is, a short stocky woman, cigarette hanging from her mouth, directing the truck driver as he reverses under her shelter.

She shouts out to her army of workers and six ladies run out with bamboo baskets in hand; they line up facing each other, three on one side and three on the other. She then calls to the driver to tilt the tray, and two men in the tray use their feet to help push the load of corn out onto the concrete floor. The ground is soon carpeted with fresh corn.

The ladies squat on the ground, busily sorting the corn into different sizes and grade levels, throwing the cobs into baskets, which are numbered from one to eight. As the baskets fill, strong shirtless men lift them onto their shoulders and carry them to an area to be packed into hessian bags, which are then tied and weighed, ready to be sold.

The best grade of corn is eaten — grilled, boiled or used in desserts — and the lower grades are sold as pig food. Aunty Eight has been in the wholesale corn business for thirty years now. She lives a very simple, humble life; she likes beer, cigarettes and corn, in that order, and she can definitely drink me under the table.

Aunty Eight greets me with a punch to the arm and asks me if I have eaten. Not that it would matter if I had. She takes a dozen corn from basket number one and orders me to shave the kernels off the cob. Her work place is little more than a corrugated roof supported by rotting wooden frames. Towards the

back is a room with two beds and a small kitchen. Aunty Eight sleeps here with her best friend and business partner, who I also call aunty. An aluminium door opens up to a backyard of water spinach growing in a lake.

A group of young boys tread waist-deep through the lake, spearing small fish. On Aunty Eight's orders they pluck some water spinach out for her. I wash the spinach while she prepares some corn fritters for a quick snack. She then throws more corn into a pot along with freshly pressed coconut milk and sugar, for dessert. My parents did warn me that Aunty Eight would be stuffing my face with corn and water spinach.

We go back out to join the workers; it takes a team of twelve to sort through the corn, and when that truck leaves another quickly takes its place. It takes many hours to complete the work, so I help out where I can. Between us, we manage to go through 2 tonnes of corn, then Aunty needs a break. She sits me down and opens three different kinds of beer for me to try — she forces me to drink them all.

Luckily my parents arrive. 'Luke, we're going into town to meet your cousin Raymond,' they tell me.

'Back to Saigon? Why did you tell me to come all the way out here if we are to go straight back again?' I reply, although I am interested to meet him. Raymond lives in Paris and we haven't met before.

'It's very important to see what your Aunty Eight does and where she lives; she tells all her friends and neighbours about you and your restaurant in Sydney. They all wanted to meet you,' mum replies.

Back in Saigon city, we get off the bus at Ben Thanh markets and my parents begin to give me a guided walking tour of Saigon. I realise how little I know about my parents. When I was growing up all they did was work, work and work, and they never had time to tell me about their life in Vietnam.

'This is where I used to take your mother out on dates,' dad says, pointing to the Majestic Hotel. 'We would have wonderful dinners there, and then continue on to the rooftop bar of the Rex.'

I am shocked. My parents actually went out on dates, and at such swish establishments! I suddenly realise that they'd had a normal life too, before the war broke out.

'Hang on a minute,' I say. 'How could you afford to go out to such expensive places?'

We stop walking, sit down on a bench and mum begins to talk.

'Your grandparents used to own four market stalls, selling wholesale fruit. It was back-breaking work, but they did very well. We made millions and millions of dong a day. Your grandfather bought gold necklaces and bracelets for your aunties and me all the time. Aunty Two was your grandfather's favourite and he spoilt her terribly; she was given money and was allowed to buy anything she wanted. These market stalls were then passed down to your father and me to run, and we continued the success of the business. Your father drove a nice car and we went out to nice restaurants every week.'

I am surprised to hear this, as I have only known us to be poor. We arrived in Australia with nothing, lived in a housing commission home in western Sydney most of our lives, and pretty much struggled until we were old enough to look after ourselves. I had no idea that my parents lived like this in Vietnam; all I knew was that they ran a wholesale fruit business in the markets. I felt happy for them but sad at the same time, for they had given up everything to search for a better life for their children.

> ## 66 IT WAS THE DAY WE WERE TO FLEE VIETNAM. I HAD FINISHED BUILDING OUR ESCAPE BOAT, BUT WE COULD NOT TELL ANYONE, NOT EVEN OUR OWN FAMILY, THAT WE WERE GOING. 99

We walk past my parents' primary school and university, then continue on for a while, when they both stop, their faces sad with pain. After several minutes silence my dad begins to speak.

'It was the day we were to flee Vietnam. I had finished building our escape boat, but we could not tell anyone, not even our own family, that we were going. There were informants everywhere, so I told your mother to take the kids and catch the bus to the docking area at the river. Where we are standing right now is where your mother, sister and brother caught their last bus, which took them to the most heavily guarded area along the river. It was a huge risk, but I thought our best chance of escape was to do so right under the authorities' noses; they would never have imagined that anyone was brave enough to do that. But we did, and we succeeded.'

I want to see the point where they actually set sail along the river, so we walk there and I ask my father to go through the details of that day. I want to have a clear picture in my mind of what they had been through.

It was the first time that my parents spoke freely and comfortably about their ordeal, and I felt it was really important for them to release the emotions and memories that had been hidden away for so many years.

We continue walking to the restaurant where we are to meet our family. My dad used to go to this restaurant when he was a young man. In those days, everyone sat at tables outside, enjoying their meals in the fresh air, but over the years new rules have meant that all the tables had to be moved inside.

'Saigon has changed so much, too many rules and regulations now,' he says.

Inside waits my Aunty Nine and her son, Manh. I haven't seen this aunty for ten years and Manh, whose name means 'strong' has actually grown up to be a strong, healthy boy.

Manh wasn't always called Manh. When he was born, he was named Cuong; he was a very sick baby and was always in and out of hospital, the doctors unable to help him.

Aunty Nine was (and still is) a very superstitious woman and she had heard of a story where a mother 'threw away' her sick son, then took him back under another name, and he was miraculously cured. Hoping for the same result, Aunty Nine wrapped her son up in a blanket, walked into town and dumped him next to the rubbish tip and then went home.

The next morning there was a knock on Aunty Nine's door. A lady stood there, holding a child. 'Miss, I have a child but I can no longer afford to look after him, can you help, can you raise him as your own?'

Aunty Nine accepted the child with open arms and asked what the child's name was.

'His name is Manh,' the lady told her.

I had never believed in these superstitions until I heard of Manh's story. They went through the whole staging process, then gave him a name of strength. But it clearly worked and I'm fascinated every time this story is told.

My cousin Raymond arrives, we all settle down and order a feast. We eat and talk about food and make our way through a case of '333' beer. This is when my father builds enough courage to tell me that he would really like to take me to meet my half siblings in Phan Thiet. I've only recently learned that my father has another family; he had a second wife with whom he had three kids. I've never met them before and I wasn't sure I wanted to, so in typical Nguyen fashion, I ignore the issue, change the subject and keep drinking.

Eating Vietnamese food in a Vietnamese restaurant with my family is always an interesting experience, for they are all foodies and, of course, each can cook 'better' than anyone else. With every mouthful they pick out the faults and tell me how they would do it, how theirs would be so much more flavoursome. This may be true, but it makes it hard to enjoy the meal.

I finish my dinner and make a quick escape to meet my old friend, Bien Nguyen, at his restaurant, XU, in central Saigon. Bien fled Vietnam in 1978 and settled in Perth. He worked in restaurants in Perth and then Sydney, where we met one another, then returned to Vietnam five years ago to set up his own restaurant. I believe this is how Saigon has changed so rapidly. 'Overseas Vietnamese' or *Viet Kieus*, as they are known in Vietnam, are Vietnamese who grow up abroad, learn skills and trades, then return to Vietnam to do business. The government now welcomes *Viet Kieus* coming back to Vietnam to set up a business, so they can build and improve Vietnam's economy and industries.

Bien brought back his experience in fine dining restaurants and his knowledge in international wines, and took a huge gamble by introducing Saigon to contemporary Vietnamese cuisine.

I remember when he first opened the restaurant; it was so quiet that he thought perhaps Vietnamese people were not quite ready for contemporary Vietnamese food. Well, they sure are ready now; the middle class in Vietnam is growing, the majority of Vietnam's population is under thirty years of age and they all want to spend their money and enjoy life.

I arrive at XU to see Bien sitting with a few good friends of mine, actor Dustin Nguyen, and film writer, Vincent Ngo, both from Los Angeles. They too fled Vietnam, lived in Los Angeles for thirty years and are now back, pioneering the film industry in Vietnam.

We move upstairs to the plush cocktail lounge, sip on lychee martinis and mingle with the who's who of Saigon. For a second I don't know where I am — I have definitely experienced the best of both modern and traditional Saigon in one day.

The next morning the car picks me up at my hotel. I had arranged a car and driver to take us all to the Mekong Delta, where we were to meet with my mother's family. My parents and Aunty Eight meet me at the hotel, then we drive to district three to pick up Aunty Nine.

The car stops near her house, then we all get out and walk the rest of the way, through narrow lanes that wind around small homes. Front doors are wide open and families are asleep on the cool tiled floors; others prepare coffee and soup to be sold to neighbouring households. A bicycle, equipped with scales and a basket filled with small fish and calamari, is ready to go; another bike, fitted out with brooms, mops, dusters and cleaning products, is being pushed from door to door. If you were to live here, you wouldn't need to leave your home; everything is at your doorstep or is delivered to you.

Aunty Nine's home is cluttered and cramped. She lives here with Manh. A large shrine dominates the room, with pictures of my uncle, who passed a few years ago, and an offering of plates of mango, with burning incense.

It is extremely humid, an old fan does little to cool the room, and there are no tables or chairs. I thought my aunty was doing OK with the fruit business, which was passed down to her when my parents fled Vietnam, but I dare not ask. We all settle down with a cup of tea, when the power suddenly cuts out. A while later two men in blue uniforms arrive at the front door.

'We've cut your power because you have not paid your last two bills,' they tell us and then walk away, clipboards tucked under their arms.

Aunty Nine breaks down in tears, I think more because my parents were there to see this happen and she felt she had lost face.

'Why didn't you tell me you had financial troubles,' Aunty Eight angrily shouts at Aunty Nine, as she takes money from her shirt pocket and places it in her sister's hands.

I don't know what to do. Why was Aunty Eight giving her money and not mum, dad or me?

'Take back your money,' says my mother to Aunty Eight. 'I would like to pay the money for her outstanding bills.'

This only makes Aunty Eight all the more furious. 'I don't need your money. We have lived and struggled in Vietnam all these years while you and your brothers live in luxury in Australia. Don't come back here now wanting to help us!'

Aunty Eight storms off, Aunty Nine is still in tears, and now so is mum.

'When Tuyen died, I was left to run the business alone,' says Aunty Nine to mum. 'My role in the business was to deal with the sellers and buyers, his job was to look after the books and collect debts. I didn't know who owed us money and who would and wouldn't pay. I ended up trusting too many people and lost too much money and couldn't pay the suppliers. They won't give me fruit on credit, I have to pay cash on delivery. I'm too deep in debt, so I have no fruit to sell and no money to pay the bills. I really don't know how I'm going to put Manh through school.'

Was it my responsibility to help? Or should I leave it to my aunties and uncles? I want to do something but I decide to stay out of it and let my parents sort it out; if they need my help they will ask.

We talk for a while, mum and dad trying to come up with different options. They reassure Aunty Nine that everything will be fine and that they are there to help her.

We pack some cold drinks and baguettes and the five of us walk back to the car. We begin our four-hour drive to the Mekong Delta.

BEEF AND JICAMA NOODLE BOWL
BÚN BÌ BÒ

I ARRIVE AT AUNTY NINE'S HOME IN DISTRICT THREE. 'WHAT SPECIALITY DO YOU FEEL LIKE EATING TODAY LUKE?' SHE ASKS. 'BUN BI BO,' I REPLY. 'THAT'S NOT A SPECIALITY,' SHE SAYS, 'THAT'S STREET FOOD — TOO SIMPLE, WHAT ELSE?' BUT FOR ME, IT'S THE SIMPLE DISHES THAT I CRAVE THE MOST.

THIS RECIPE USES JICAMA, PRONOUNCED HEE-KAM-MAH, WHICH IS A ROOT VEGETABLE, QUITE STRANGE LOOKING, WITH CRISP WHITE FLESH AND A DUSTY BROWN SKIN. UNLIKE ITS RELATIVE THE POTATO, IT CAN BE EATEN RAW. JICAMA IS GREAT NOT ONLY IN SALADS BUT ALSO IN STIR-FRIES AND EVEN AS CHIPS.

2 tablespoons fish sauce

1 tablespoon sugar

500 g (1 lb 2 oz) lean minced beef

3 tablespoons vegetable oil

2 garlic cloves, finely chopped

1 lemongrass stem, white part only, finely chopped

1 onion, finely chopped

500 g (1 lb 2 oz) jicama, peeled and cut into 5 mm (¼ inch) dice

VERMICELLI SALAD

250 g (9 oz) dried rice vermicelli noodles

90 g (3¼ oz/1 cup) bean sprouts

1 Lebanese (short) cucumber, sliced into matchsticks

1 handful perilla, leaves torn

1 handful mint, leaves torn

80 g (2¾ oz/1 cup firmly packed) sliced iceberg lettuce

TO SERVE

250 ml (9 fl oz/1 cup) dipping fish sauce (page 331)

4 tablespoons spring onion oil (page 329)

4 tablespoons fried red Asian shallots (page 329)

4 tablespoons chopped roasted peanuts (page 328)

In a bowl, combine the fish sauce, sugar, a pinch of salt and 1 teaspoon freshly ground black pepper. Mix well, then add the beef and stir to combine. Cover and place in the fridge to marinate for 15 minutes.

Meanwhile, to make the vermicelli salad, cook the vermicelli in a large saucepan of boiling water for 5 minutes. Turn off the heat and leave the noodles in the water for another 5 minutes. Drain into a colander and rinse under cold water. Drain well, then set aside to dry at room temperature, covered with a damp tea towel.

To assemble the salad, divide the bean sprouts evenly among five or six bowls, then top with the vermicelli. Put the cucumber in a bowl with the perilla, mint and lettuce and stir to combine. Divide the herb and lettuce mixture among the bowls, and place on top of the vermicelli. Set aside.

Heat 2 tablespoons of the oil in a wok, then add the garlic, lemongrass and onion. Cook, stirring, over medium–high heat for 1 minute, or until lightly browned. Add the beef and stir-fry over high heat for 3 minutes. Remove the beef and transfer to a strainer. Leave to drain for 5 minutes.

Wipe the wok clean, then add the remaining oil and stir-fry the jicama with a pinch of salt and freshly ground black pepper over medium heat for 5 minutes. Remove from the heat, then transfer the jicama to another strainer. Leave to drain for 5 minutes. Put the warm beef and jicama in a bowl and toss to combine.

To serve, place a cupful of the beef and jicama mixture on top of each vermicelli salad and dress with 2 tablespoons of dipping fish sauce for each serve. Garnish with spring onion oil, fried shallots and peanuts.

SERVES 5-6 AS PART OF A SHARED MEAL

PURPLE YAM AND PRAWN SOUP
CANH KHOAI MÕ TÉP

YAMS ARE OFTEN MISTAKEN FOR SWEET POTATOES, BUT THEY ARE NOT RELATED. YAMS CAN BE FOUND AT YOUR LOCAL ASIAN MARKET, THEY HAVE A BROWN OUTER SKIN AND STRIKING PURPLE FLESH. THIS DISH IS TEXTURALLY AND VISUALLY STUNNING.

First peel the yam, then, holding the yam upright and resting on a chopping board, use a spoon to scrape off the yam flesh from top to bottom, working around the whole yam until it has all been scraped (this is a traditional technique that gives the chunky texture needed for the dish; alternatively coarsely grate the yam).

Put 1.5 litres (52 fl oz/6 cups) of water in a large saucepan and add the reserved prawn shells. Bring to the boil for 10 minutes, then strain the stock, discarding the prawn shells. Bring the stock back to the boil in the same pan and add the yam and fish sauce, then simmer for 10 minutes.

Using a mortar and pestle or a small food processor, pound or process the prawns with the sliced white part of the spring onion until a paste forms. Add ½ teaspoon freshly ground black pepper and mix well into the paste.

Heat a frying pan over medium heat, then add the oil and fry the garlic until brown. Add the prawn paste and stir-fry for 2 minutes until fragrant. Season with ½ teaspoon salt.

Transfer the prawn paste into the saucepan with the simmering stock and yam, and stir for 3 minutes. Add ½ teaspoon freshly ground black pepper, then turn off the heat. Serve the soup in large bowls and garnish with the spring onion, sawtooth herb and rice paddy herb. Serve with jasmine rice.

SERVES 4-6 AS PART OF A SHARED MEAL

500 g (1 lb 2 oz) purple yam
500 g (1 lb 2 oz) raw school prawns (shrimp), peeled, reserving the heads and shells
2 tablespoons fish sauce
1 tablespoon sliced spring onion (scallion), white part only
2 tablespoons vegetable oil
4 garlic cloves, finely chopped
1 tablespoon sliced spring onion (scallion), green part only
½ bunch sawtooth herb, leaves sliced
½ bunch rice paddy herb, leaves sliced

LOTUS STEM SALAD WITH PRAWN AND PORK
GỎI NGÓ SEN

MY AUNTY NINE IS THE QUEEN OF VIETNAMESE SALADS AND DRESSINGS. I HAVE EATEN MANY LOTUS STEM SALADS IN VIETNAM, BUT IT IS HER VERY WELL-BALANCED DRESSINGS AND SAUCES THAT DISTINGUISHES HERS FROM THE REST. YOU CAN BUY THE PICKLED LOTUS STEMS AND CARROTS IN JARS FROM YOUR ASIAN MARKET.

300 g (10½ oz) pork neck
300 g (10½ oz) cooked prawns (shrimp), peeled and deveined, then halved lengthways
300 g (10½ oz) pickled lotus stems, washed and drained
100 g (3½ oz) pickled carrots, washed and drained
100 g (3½ oz) daikon, peeled and thinly sliced
2 Chinese celery stems, sliced into 5 cm (2 inch) pieces
1 large handful Vietnamese mint leaves
2 tablespoons roasted peanuts, crushed (page 328)
2 tablespoons fried red Asian shallots (page 329)
2 bird's eye chillies, sliced
coriander (cilantro) sprigs, to garnish
dipping fish sauce (page 331), to serve
1 plate cooked prawn crackers

DRESSING
125 ml (4 fl oz/½ cup) lemon juice
2 tablespoons caster (superfine) sugar
1 tablespoon fish sauce

To cook the pork neck, pour 1 litre (35 fl oz/4 cups) of water into a small saucepan, add the pork and bring to the boil. Skim any impurities off the surface, then reduce the heat to a low simmer. Add a pinch of salt and freshly ground black pepper, then cover the pan and cook for 20 minutes. Drain the pork and allow to cool, then thinly slice.

Meanwhile, make the dressing by combining all the ingredients in a bowl. Season with 1 teaspoon freshly ground black pepper, then stir well to dissolve the sugar. Set aside.

In a large bowl, combine the pork, prawns (reserving a few prawns for garnishing), pickled lotus stems, pickled carrots, daikon, Chinese celery and Vietnamese mint. Pour over the dressing and toss to combine.

Transfer to a salad platter and garnish with the reserved prawns, peanuts, fried shallots, sliced chilli and coriander sprigs. Serve with dipping fish sauce and prawn crackers.

SERVES 4–6 AS PART OF A SHARED MEAL

GREEN PAPAYA SALAD WITH DRIED BEEF LIVER
GỎI ĐU ĐỦ GAN BÒ KHÔ

GOOD FRIENDS JEAN AND BI TOOK ME TO THEIR FAVOURITE STREET STALL. IT IS ON HAI BA TRUNG, ONE OF SAIGON'S LONGEST AND BUSIEST STREETS. WE APPROACH A LADY WHO GIVES US A PLASTIC TILE EACH, TO SIT ON UNDER A TREE. SHE ASKS HOW MANY GREEN PAPAYA SALADS WE WANT, THEN SCREAMS FROM THE TOP OF HER LUNGS ACROSS THE ROAD, THROUGH THE NOISE OF HUNDREDS OF MOTORBIKES, INTO THE EARS OF A LADY WITH A CART PARKED ON THE ROAD OPPOSITE — 'THREE SERVES!!' MINUTES LATER, A YOUNG GIRL CROSSES THE ROAD, DODGES THE TRAFFIC AND DELIVERS THE SALADS. I THOUGHT OUT LOUD, 'WHY DOESN'T SHE JUST PUSH HER SALAD CART OVER HERE, UNDER THE TREE, AND MAKE LIFE EASIER?' BUT IT WAS ONE OF THE MOST MEMORABLE EATING EXPERIENCES I HAVE HAD IN SAIGON.

Wash the liver, drain well and set aside. In a bowl, combine the curry powder, lemongrass, chillies, soy sauce, sugar and 1/2 teaspoon salt. Mix well, then add the liver and toss to coat well in the marinade. Cover and place in the fridge to marinate for 30 minutes. Drain the liver, reserving the marinade.

Heat the oil in a deep frying pan over medium–high heat, then add the liver and quickly fry both sides until brown. Remove the liver from the pan, discarding the oil left in the pan. Return the liver to the pan and add the reserved marinade, then add enough water to cover the liver. Bring to the boil, then reduce the heat and simmer for about 10 minutes, or until all the liquid has evaporated, turning the liver over constantly. Remove the 'dried' liver from the pan and cut into thin slices.

In a salad bowl, combine the liver, green papaya, mint, Vietnamese mint and Asian basil. Pour over Aunty Nine's salad dressing and toss well. Garnish with peanuts.

SERVES 4-6 AS PART OF A SHARED MEAL

- 300 g (10½ oz) beef liver
- 1 tablespoon Thai red curry powder
- 1 lemongrass stem, white part only, chopped
- 2 bird's eye chillies, sliced
- 2 teaspoons light soy sauce
- 2 teaspoons sugar
- 250 ml (9 fl oz/1 cup) vegetable oil
- 500 g (1 lb 2 oz) green papaya, peeled and finely shredded
- 1 handful mint leaves, sliced
- 1 handful Vietnamese mint leaves, sliced
- 1 handful Asian basil leaves, sliced
- 125 ml (4 fl oz/½ cup) Aunty Nine's salad dressing (page 330)
- 2 tablespoons roasted peanuts, chopped (page 328)

SAIGON CHINESE SAUSAGE AND JICAMA ROLLS
BÒ BÍA

I AM ENJOYING A SNACK OF *BO BIA* RICE PAPER ROLLS FROM A STREET STALL. I'M SITTING WITH SOME STUDENTS, WHO HAVE JUST FINISHED SCHOOL. SUDDENLY, THEY SPOT THE POLICE; THEY GRAB THEIR PLATES AND STOOLS AND RUN, AND I FOLLOW SUIT. WE HIDE BEHIND A BUILDING AND WAIT UNTIL THE POLICE ARE GONE, THEN RETURN TO OUR SEATS AND CONTINUE EATING. THE VENDOR THANKS US AND CONTINUES ROLLING. THIS SEEMS TO BE A REGULAR OCCURRENCE FOR A STREET VENDOR. WITH NO PERMIT, THEY HAVE TO CONSTANTLY KEEP AN EYE OUT, AND THE LOCALS DO WHAT THEY CAN TO HELP.

50 g (1¾ oz/½ cup) dried shrimp
2 Chinese sausages (lap cheong)
2 eggs, lightly beaten
2 tablespoons vegetable oil
500 g (1 lb 2 oz) jicama, peeled and julienned
2 garlic cloves, finely chopped
18 dried round rice paper wrappers (22 cm/8½ inch diameter)
3 tablespoons chilli paste
3 tablespoons hoisin sauce
1 bunch Asian basil, leaves picked
1 green oak lettuce or butter lettuce, leaves separated
hoisin dipping sauce (page 330)
80 g (2¾ oz/½ cup) roasted peanuts, crushed (page 328)

Put the dried shrimp in a bowl, cover with water and soak for 20 minutes, then drain. Put the sausages in a deep frying pan and cover them with water. Bring to a simmer over medium heat and cook, turning often, until all the water has evaporated, then continue to cook the sausages, turning often, until browned. Remove from the pan, cool, then thinly slice on the diagonal.

Place a non-stick frying pan over medium–low heat. Combine the eggs and ½ teaspoon of the oil in a bowl, then pour about a quarter of the beaten egg into the pan to form a thin layer over the base. Cook for 1 minute, or until the egg sheet will slide off the pan, then turn it over and cook for a further 30 seconds. Remove and place on a chopping board. Repeat this process until all the egg mixture is cooked; you should end up with three or four egg sheets. Stack the egg sheets on top of each other as they are cooked, then roll them together into a tight roll and slice thinly.

Place a heavy-based saucepan on low heat, add the jicama, then cover and cook for 30 minutes (no oil or water is needed — the jicama will cook in its own juices). Remove and set aside. Wipe out the pan and return it to the stovetop. Add the remaining oil and brown the garlic, then add the shrimp and ½ teaspoon freshly ground black pepper and stir-fry for 4 minutes. Remove from the pan.

To assemble the rolls, cut 6 sheets of rice paper in half. Fill a bowl with warm water and briefly dip one whole sheet of rice paper in the water until just softened, then lay it on a plate. Dip a half sheet of rice paper in the water and lay it vertically in the middle of the round sheet. This will strengthen the roll. In the middle of the rice paper, spread ½ teaspoon of chilli paste and hoisin sauce, followed by 3 pieces of sausage and an egg strip, placing them in a line about 4 cm (1½ inches) from the top. Add some jicama, then 3 basil leaves, some torn lettuce and sprinkle with some of the shrimp. To form each roll, fold the sides into the centre over the filling, then the bottom of the paper up and over; roll up to form a tight roll. Garnish the hoisin dipping sauce with peanuts. Serve the rolls with the dipping sauce.

MAKES 12 ROLLS

AUNTY FIVE'S RICE CAKE WITH EGG AND SOY
BÁNH BỘT CHIÊN MỢ NĂM

IT'S 6 P.M., I'M HUNGRY AND I JUST NEED A LITTLE SNACK BEFORE DINNER. I APPROACH A STREET VENDOR STANDING IN FRONT OF A BLACKENED ROUND HOTPLATE. I TAKE A STOOL AND HE PREPARES ME A SMALL SERVE — IT IS CRISP BUT CHEWY, SOFT AND TASTY, AND REMINDS ME OF AUNTY FIVE'S RICE CAKES. HE TELLS ME THE BATTER IS JUST TAPIOCA FLOUR AND WATER, BUT THIS IS THE KIND OF RECIPE THAT FAMILIES LIKE TO KEEP SECRET, SO I CALLED AUNTY FIVE AND ASKED HER.

WHEAT STARCH IS WHEAT FLOUR WITHOUT THE PROTEIN, GLUTEN; HENCE IT IS ALSO KNOWN AS NON-GLUTINOUS FLOUR. I USE WHEAT STARCH HERE AS IT GIVES A MORE BOUNCY TEXTURE TO THE CAKE. BUY WHEAT STARCH FROM YOUR ASIAN STORE, IN THE FLOUR SECTION.

To make the batter, combine the rice flour, wheat starch and 1/2 teaspoon salt in a bowl. Add 1 litre (35 fl oz/4 cups) of water, mixing until the salt has dissolved and a smooth batter forms.

Coat a 22 cm (8 1/2 inch) square, 3.5 cm (1 1/2 inch) deep baking tin with some of the garlic oil. Set aside.

Heat a saucepan over low heat and add the batter, stirring constantly until the mixture becomes glue-like in texture, then remove from the heat. Spoon the batter into the prepared tin and press firmly down onto the batter, spreading it out evenly and tightly into the tin. Transfer the tin to a large steamer and steam over high heat for 15 minutes. Remove the tin from the steamer and let it cool. Once cooled, remove the rice cake from the tin and slice into 2 cm (3/4 inch) bite-sized pieces. Set aside.

Mix the light and dark soy sauces together in a bowl. Divide the rice cakes and the beaten eggs into two batches, as you will need to cook the cakes in two lots.

Heat a large non-stick frying pan over high heat. Add 2 tablespoons of the garlic oil and half the crushed garlic to the pan, then transfer the first batch of rice cakes to the pan, spreading them out evenly. Add 2 tablespoons of the soy sauce mixture and fry for 4 minutes on each side, or until brown and slightly crisp. Add half the spring onion and pour over half of the eggs; the egg will trickle onto the base of the pan, between the cakes, and cook. Cook for 1 minute, then turn the rice cakes over, cutting through the egg to turn, and sizzle for a further minute. Remove from the pan to a warmed plate, cover loosely with foil and keep warm.

Wipe the pan clean, and return the pan to the heat again. Repeat this process with the remaining ingredients. Transfer all the cooked rice cakes to a serving platter. Garnish with 1/2 teaspoon freshly ground black pepper and crushed peanuts, and drizzle with red rice vinegar.

SERVES 4–6 AS A SNACK

BATTER
250 g (9 oz/2 cups) rice flour
125 g (4 1/2 oz/1 cup) wheat starch

125 ml (4 fl oz/1/2 cup) garlic oil (page 329)
2 tablespoons light soy sauce
2 tablespoons dark soy sauce
4 eggs, beaten
2 garlic cloves, crushed
4 tablespoons thinly sliced spring onion (scallion)
4 tablespoons roasted peanuts, crushed (page 328)
4 tablespoons Asian red rice vinegar

CHO LON'S LEMONGRASS CHILLI CHICKEN
GÀ XÀO XẢ ỚT CHỢ LỚN

WHEN I WAS TEN YEARS OLD, A TWELVE-YEAR-OLD BOY NAMED DUNG CAME TO LIVE WITH US IN SYDNEY. HE WAS MY SECOND COUSIN ON MY MOTHER'S SIDE. HE CAME FROM VIETNAM ALL ALONE, SPOKE NO ENGLISH, VERY LITTLE VIETNAMESE, BUT WAS FLUENT IN MANDARIN. DUNG AND HIS FAMILY GREW UP IN SAIGON'S CHINATOWN, 'CHO LON'. WHEN I WAS IN SAIGON, I TRACKED DOWN DUNG'S FAMILY AND WENT TO VISIT THEM. AS I ENTERED THE STREETS OF CHINATOWN — THE AIR SCENTED WITH THE RICH AROMA OF CHINESE HERBAL MEDICINE, THE LANES DOTTED WITH CHINESE-STYLE TEMPLES AND PAGODAS AND DIM SUM RESTAURANTS — I REALLY FELT AS IF I WAS IN CHINA. NO ONE SPEAKS VIETNAMESE HERE, ONLY MANDARIN. I MET DUNG'S FAMILY AND WE SHARED A CHINESE MEAL TOGETHER.

1 tablespoon fish sauce

2 teaspoons sugar

500 g (1 lb 2 oz) chicken Marylands (chicken leg quarters), chopped through the bone into 3 x 4 cm (1¼ x 1½ inch) pieces

2 tablespoons vegetable oil

1 lemongrass stem, white part only, finely chopped

2 garlic cloves, crushed

2 bird's eye chillies, thinly sliced

125 ml (4 fl oz/½ cup) young coconut water

1 small onion, cut into thin wedges

2 spring onions (scallions), thinly sliced on the diagonal

1 bird's eye chilli, sliced

In a bowl, combine the fish sauce, sugar and ½ teaspoon each of salt and freshly ground black pepper, stirring to dissolve the sugar. Add the chicken pieces and turn them to coat in the marinade. Cover the bowl and place in the fridge to marinate for 30 minutes.

Heat a saucepan over medium heat, add the oil and fry the lemongrass until brown, then add the garlic and chilli, stirring until fragrant. Now add the undrained chicken and stir-fry for 10 minutes. Pour in the coconut water and bring to the boil. Add the onion, then reduce the heat and simmer for 10 minutes, or until the liquid has reduced by half. Transfer to a serving bowl and garnish with the spring onions and chilli. Serve with jasmine rice.

SERVES 4–6 AS PART OF A SHARED MEAL

ROAST PORK
HEO QUAY

AT HOC MON MARKETS WITH MY AUNTY EIGHT, I SAW WONDERFULLY COLOURED ROASTED PORK HANGING FROM HEAVY HOOKS. ITS SKIN WAS CRACKLING, THE FAT DRIPPING WITH FLAVOUR — ALL I NEEDED WAS A CRISP BAGUETTE AND A SLIM CUCUMBER. I TURNED BEHIND ME TO FIND VENDORS SELLING JUST THAT!

Dip the skin of the pork belly briefly into boiled, hot water, taking care to keep the flesh out of the water. Clean the skin by scraping the surface with a knife to remove the outer layer; the skin should be a consistent white colour. Wash the skin, then, using a large sharp knife, score the skin in either parallel lines or a crosshatch pattern.

Combine 1/2 teaspoon of the five-spice, 1 tablespoon of the annatto oil, 1 teaspoon salt, the bicarbonate of soda and cornflour in a bowl, and mix well. Rub the mixture evenly over the pork skin.

In a separate bowl, combine the remaining five-spice, annatto oil and 1 teaspoon salt. Mix well, then coat the pork meat with the mixture, massaging it in well. Place the pork in a dish, cover with plastic wrap and place in the fridge to marinate for at least 6 hours, or overnight.

Preheat the oven to 250°C (500°F/Gas 9). Put the pork in a roasting tin, skin side up, and roast for 20 minutes, then reduce the heat to 150°C (300°F/Gas 2) and roast for a further 10 minutes. Brush the skin with the sesame oil and roast for a further 20–30 minutes, or until the pork is cooked through.

Using a cleaver or large heavy knife, chop the pork belly into 2 cm (3/4 inch) pieces. Serve with jasmine rice, and a small bowl of sliced chilli and soy sauce for dipping.

SERVES 4-6 AS PART OF A SHARED MEAL

NOTE Annatto seeds, also known as achiote, are used to add a golden colour to foods such as pork, chicken or rice. Annatto seeds and oil are sold in Asian and Indian markets. If you can only find the seeds, these can be used to make the oil. Heat 1 tablespoon of annatto seeds in a saucepan over low heat with 125 ml (4 fl oz/1/2 cup) of oil. Heat just until the oil begins to simmer; don't overheat or the seeds will turn black. Remove from the heat and set aside to cool, then strain the oil into a jar.

1 kg (2 lb 4 oz) pork belly, on the bone
1 teaspoon five-spice
2 tablespoons annatto oil (see note)
1 teaspoon bicarbonate of soda (baking soda)
2 teaspoons cornflour (cornstarch)
2 teaspoons sesame oil
1 bird's eye chilli, thinly sliced
light soy sauce, for dipping

WOK-TOSSED BEEF WITH KOHLRABI
BÒ XÀO SU HÀO

KOHLRABI MEANS 'CABBAGE TURNIP'; IT IS IN THE SAME FAMILY AS THE CABBAGE AND BROCCOLI, ITS TEXTURE AS CRISP AS ITS COUSINS. THERE ARE TWO TYPES OF KOHLRABI — PURPLE AND LIGHT GREEN — BUT GO FOR THE GREEN ONES, AS THEY DON'T SEEM TO BE AS TOUGH IN TEXTURE. WHEN BUYING IT AT THE MARKET, LOOK FOR A VEGETABLE THAT RESEMBLES A ROUND SPUTNIK SATELLITE.

1 kohlrabi, peeled and sliced into 3 cm (1¼ inch) long pieces, about 3 mm (⅛ inch) thick
2 tablespoons vegetable oil
1 tablespoon finely chopped garlic
1 small onion, thinly sliced
300 g (10½ oz) beef sirloin, trimmed and sliced into 3 mm (⅛ inch) thick strips
1 tablespoon fish sauce
2 teaspoons light soy sauce
2 teaspoons oyster sauce
2 teaspoons sugar

Bring 1 litre (35 fl oz/4 cups) of water to the boil in a large saucepan. Add the kohlrabi and blanch for 2 minutes. Drain, then submerge in ice-cold water for 2 minutes, then drain again.

Heat 1 tablespoon of the oil in a wok over high heat and fry half the garlic and half the onion for 1 minute until fragrant. Add the beef and stir-fry for 1 minute, then remove the beef and onion and set aside.

Add the remaining oil to the wok over high heat and stir-fry the kohlrabi with the remaining garlic and onion for 2 minutes. Return the beef to the wok, add the fish sauce, soy sauce, oyster sauce, sugar and 1 teaspoon freshly ground black pepper, and stir-fry for a further 2 minutes. Transfer to a serving bowl and serve with jasmine rice.

SERVES 4–6 AS PART OF A SHARED MEAL

CHICKEN COOKED IN GINGER
GÀ NẤU GỪNG

WE SIT ON COOL GREEN TILES IN MY AUNTY NINE'S LIVING ROOM; A HUGE SHRINE IS ABOVE ME, ALONG WITH A FRAMED PICTURE OF MY UNCLE. NEXT TO HIS PICTURE THERE IS AN OFFERING OF A PLATE OF CHICKEN COOKED IN GINGER, PILED HIGH AND LOOKING DELICIOUS. I FEEL LIKE A CHILD AGAIN; I LICK MY LIPS SECRETLY BUT I KNOW THE RULES — I HAVE TO WAIT UNTIL THE INCENSE BURNS OUT, WHICH SYMBOLISES THAT UNCLE HAS FINISHED, AND ONLY THEN AM I ALLOWED TO EAT.

Finely chop 50 g (1¾ oz) of the ginger, then combine in a bowl with the rice wine, oyster sauce, soy sauce and 1 teaspoon salt. Mix well, then add the chicken, massaging the marinade into the flesh. Cover and place in the fridge to marinate for 20 minutes.

Soak the preserved white radish in water for 20 minutes, then drain. Cut the radish and remaining ginger into thin slices and set aside.

Put the chicken in a large saucepan, then place the ginger slices and preserved radish on top. Pour the stock over the chicken and bring to the boil, skimming the impurities off the surface until the stock is clear. Cover the pan, reduce the heat and simmer for 5 minutes, then remove the lid and cook for another 5 minutes. Transfer to a serving bowl and garnish with the chilli and spring onions. Serve with jasmine rice.

SERVES 4-6 AS PART OF A SHARED MEAL

200 g (7 oz) ginger, peeled
2 tablespoons shaoxing rice wine
1 teaspoon oyster sauce
1 teaspoon dark soy sauce
500 g (1 lb 2 oz) boneless, skinless chicken thighs, cut into 2 x 3 cm (¾ x 1¼ inch) pieces
20 g (¾ oz) preserved white radish
250 ml (9 fl oz/1 cup) chicken stock (page 328)
1 bird's eye chilli, sliced
2 spring onions (scallions), thinly sliced on the diagonal

AUNTY EIGHT'S SWEET CORN PUDDING
CHÈ BẮP DÌ TÁM

AUNTY EIGHT, AUNTY NINE, MUM AND DAD ARE ALL COOKING IN THE SAME ROOM — THIS IS A VERY BAD IDEA. WE ARE IN AUNTY EIGHT'S MARKET PLACE, USING HER CORN AND MAKING HER SWEET CORN PUDDING WHEN AN ARGUMENT BREAKS OUT AS TO WHETHER OR NOT SHE SHOULD BE USING STICKY RICE AND PANDAN LEAVES. ALL PARTIES INVOLVED HAVE THEIR OWN IDEAS AND, OF COURSE, THEIR IDEAS WERE BETTER THAN ANYONE ELSE'S. SO BEGAN THE SWEET CORN COOK OFF — FOUR VERSIONS OF SWEET CORN PUDDING, WHICH WE THEN HAD TO EAT FOR THE NEXT THREE DAYS. MY VOTE IS FOR AUNTY EIGHT'S RECIPE, AS IT IS THE MOST AUTHENTIC.

100 g (3½ oz/½ cup) white sticky (glutinous) long-grain rice
2 pandan leaves, each tied in a knot
6 corn cobs, kernels removed using a large sharp knife
150 g (5½ oz/⅔ cup) sugar
150 ml (5 fl oz) coconut milk
250 ml (9 fl oz/1 cup) sweet coconut milk (page 337)
toasted sesame seeds, to serve

Wash the sticky rice in cold water and strain. Repeat this process again. Put the sticky rice in a heavy-based saucepan along with the pandan leaves and 625 ml (21 fl oz/2½ cups) of water. Bring to the boil, then reduce the heat to low, stirring constantly for 5 minutes, or until the rice expands and the water has absorbed.

Now add the corn kernels and sugar and cook, stirring, for a further 5 minutes, then add the coconut milk and continue to stir for 2 minutes. Discard the pandan leaves. Serve in small bowls and top with the sweet coconut milk and toasted sesame seeds.

SERVES 4–6

MY
MEKONG

9

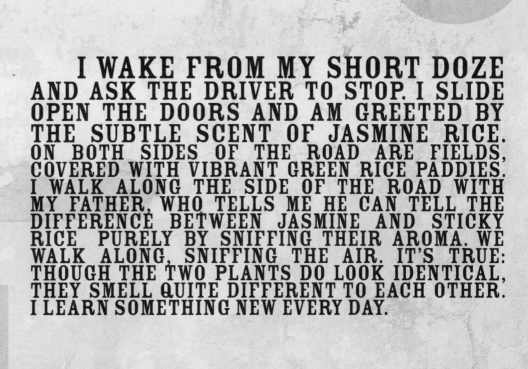

I WAKE FROM MY SHORT DOZE AND ASK THE DRIVER TO STOP. I SLIDE OPEN THE DOORS AND AM GREETED BY THE SUBTLE SCENT OF JASMINE RICE. ON BOTH SIDES OF THE ROAD ARE FIELDS, COVERED WITH VIBRANT GREEN RICE PADDIES. I WALK ALONG THE SIDE OF THE ROAD WITH MY FATHER, WHO TELLS ME HE CAN TELL THE DIFFERENCE BETWEEN JASMINE AND STICKY RICE PURELY BY SNIFFING THEIR AROMA. WE WALK ALONG, SNIFFING THE AIR. IT'S TRUE: THOUGH THE TWO PLANTS DO LOOK IDENTICAL, THEY SMELL QUITE DIFFERENT TO EACH OTHER. I LEARN SOMETHING NEW EVERY DAY.

We see a group of ducks feeding on rice seeds, moving from one paddy to the next. They cross the busy highway; all bikes, cars and trucks stop to let them cross, then they waddle slowly to the next feeding ground.

Looking around, I can't believe we are in the twenty-first century; farmers still cast rice seeds, replant and irrigate the fields by hand. They use buffaloes to plough seedbeds, using the same centuries-old techniques, walking in ankle-deep water for most of the day in the scorching sun, protected only by their conical hats, and yet Vietnam manages to export 5 million tonnes of rice a year. The majority is cultivated here in the Mekong Delta, one of the world's largest deltas; the river itself runs from Tibet through China, Myanmar, Thailand, Laos and Cambodia down to Vietnam, through to the South China Sea.

We arrive at a small village along the Mekong River. We are here to meet family on my mother's side, many of whom I have never met. The driver takes us as far as he can, carefully manoeuvring the car along the thin, bumpy track, then he pulls up beside some guys on motorbikes, who have come to meet us. We abandon the car, hop on the back of the bikes and ride down a winding footpath, swerving local people along the way.

" THEN HE CUTS THE SNAKE'S HEART OUT AND, WITH IT STILL BEATING IN HIS HAND, SWALLOWS IT WHOLE. THIS IS THE FIRST TIME THAT I HAVE SEEN THIS RITUAL. WHEN IT'S MY TURN, I PUT THE STILL-BEATING HEART IN A SHOT GLASS OF RICE WINE; IT CONTINUES TO BEAT, MAKING THE GLASS VIBRATE, THEN I SWALLOW IT WHOLE. "

We arrive at a house right on the river's edge, surrounded by dense jungle, with more than thirty people waiting outside, the youngest standing towards the front and the eldest standing behind. I get off the motorbike and am introduced to each and every one of them.

Many of the children are my distant cousins, and the elders are my grandmother's sisters. Some of the men, much older than me, fold their arms and bow their heads to me in respect and address me as uncle. Even though I am at least twenty years younger, it is the Vietnamese custom that I address them as my nephews. This is because their mother is my mother's distant niece, so it is customary for them to address me as an elder, regardless of their age or mine.

There is much excitement in the air. One of my young cousins climbs up a coconut tree and chops several young ones down for us to drink. I drink the juice and then I am directed to go to the backyard to the rice paddy, to pay respects to my grandmother's parents.

Most deceased relatives are buried in the backyard or in rice paddies. For decades, my grandmother's parents were at rest in the family's rice paddy, but recently the government decided to take the land from my family and ordered them to remove the gravestones. My mother and her brothers had the tombs dug up and reburied next door at my nephew's rice paddy, where I stand now.

I light some incense and pay my respects, then I'm whisked away with the men to go hunting for snakes and bush rats. They catch the rats simply by setting up cage traps, and as for the snakes … well, I decide to leave that to the more experienced. Within an hour we have caught four snakes, two eels and eight rats. The rats look like mice really, and even I was thinking twice about eating them; I thought bush rats were supposed to be big, furry and meaty.

At home we let the snakes out onto the wet concrete floor. The kids play with them for a while until my forty-five-year-old nephew is bitten. The bite draws blood, but luckily the snake is not venomous.

My nephew cleans up his wound, then slices the snake's throat and draws all of its warm blood into shot glasses of rice wine for the men to shoot down (not pleasant). He then slices the bile duct and squeezes the green liquid into the shot glasses; we drink that too. Then he cuts the snake's heart out and, with it still beating in his hand, swallows it whole. This is the first time that I have seen this ritual. When it's my turn, I put the still-beating heart in a shot glass of rice wine; it continues to beat, making the glass vibrate, then I swallow it whole. I can still feel it beating, tickling my stomach! They tell me that snake hearts make men very 'strong' in bed.

The snakes are then blanched in hot water, scaled and butterflied and rolled intricately into a coil and boiled. Once partly cooked, the bone tears away from the flesh in one motion. The snakes are cooked in ten different ways, from stir-fried with lemongrass, to a dish of crispy crackling snake skin. The bush rats are simply marinated and chargrilled. The snake tastes like a cross between an eel and calamari, and the rat like a cross between quail and frog.

We enjoy the most magnificent feast, our large family spread out over three round tables overlooking the Mekong River, with each family group cooking their favourite dishes: turmeric eel, chicken in shrimp paste, beef-tossed with glass noodles, and fried elephant fish with a beer sauce, to name a few. To my surprise, my mother refuses to eat the rat.

'Come on mum, just have a little taste, they caught it especially for us.'

'I won't eat it, OK!' she says, with a horrified look. 'When I was sixteen years old we had a rat problem at our fruit market; they were everywhere. One day I picked up a basket of mangosteens and a rat ran out from behind. I jumped high into the air in fright, then landed right on top of the rat and squashed it to death with my bare foot; its eyeballs squished between my toes! I thought I was going to pass out. I still have vivid images of it today; rats scare the hell out of me, and I've had nightmares about it for years.'

After dinner, my nephews and nieces ask me if I'd like to go for a walk to look at the abundant fruit trees that line the Mekong River. I had forgotten how fantastic it was to hang out with so many family members; we had never met before but we had instantly bonded with each other.

We walk along the river until we come across a rice mill. Inside, tall machines, covered in dust and spider webs, vibrate and roar in the large shed. Men lug huge sacks of rice from the small boats, they are given a blue wooden peg for every sack, then the pegs are counted at the end of the day and the men are paid 4 cents for each peg.

The rice grain is poured out onto the ground into large mounds, and then vacuumed up through a massive pipe that feeds into the machine. The machine removes the husks from the rice, dividing the broken rice from the wholegrain rice. Nothing is wasted: the husks are sold to fuel fire, the rice powder is fed to fish and ducks, and the broken rice is sold as broken rice. When the rice is separated, it is polished, bagged, weighed, sealed with red thread and sold.

It's hard to believe that half the Vietnamese population is involved in rice production. Vietnam is such a hard-working nation, and I now see where my parents get their work ethic from. After seeing the labour-intensive work that goes into producing rice, I now appreciate every grain that I put into my mouth.

Rice is something that I eat almost every day and I tend to forget how important it is in my diet. I eat rice soup when I'm unwell, rice noodles in delicate broths, rice paper with raw ingredients, toasted rice powder in salads, rice flour in crispy crepes, sticky rice in puddings and, of course, hot jasmine rice to balance out the salty, sweet and sour flavours of Vietnamese dishes.

When we first arrived in Australia, our dinner was often steamed jasmine rice served with fish sauce and cucumber. This simple meal remains a regular dish for me today.

We wake at dawn to visit the floating markets in Can Tho. The family boat is waiting for us; I can literally step out of the house and straight onto the boat. We arrive at the markets; it's early but already it's rush hour. Small boats paddle past — one sells hot baguettes filled with pork, another sells coffee and fresh juice, and another arrives selling tapioca noodles with a boiling coconut broth poured over them. We place our order and bowls are passed over from boat to boat, the whole family enjoying a bowl for breakfast. We eat fast for we need to keep moving, as the traffic on the river is getting heavier.

However, not all the boats move freely about the river. The larger boats are anchored and their goods for sale are placed on top of tall poles at the front of the boat. It's a novelty for my aunty to have someone new to show around, and she enthusiastically points out to me what each boat sells: some have a watermelon spiked on top of the pole, others have jackfruit, durian, papaya, pineapple, custard apples, coconuts, pomelo or bunches of lychees. Most of the fruit vendors seem to live on their boats; they brush their teeth beside their clothes, which hang on the top deck, kitchens are built towards the back and hammocks sway beside open windows.

It's not only fruit and vegetables on sale: boats float past selling pots, pans, flowers and dry goods, and mum points out a small boat coming our way with a lottery ticket tied to the bow.

There is so much colour, life and energy here. I feel so fortunate that I have been able to meet and spend time with my family here, and to have experienced the Mekong Delta in such an authentic way.

On our drive back to Saigon, my father reaches over and taps the driver on the shoulder and asks him to stop. Without saying a word, dad slides the door open and goes for a walk. Ten minutes later, just as we were beginning to worry about him, he returns. I can see by the look on his face that there is something wrong. Do I dare ask?

He points to an area dense with overgrown jungle set behind the rice paddies. He takes a big breath.

'This was where I escaped death. It had been raining heavily all day; my platoon and I were walking through the heavily booby-trapped jungle. Then I heard a click and knew I had stepped on a land mine. I froze and made sure I didn't lift my foot. My men quickly came to my assistance and stuck their bayonet into the device to weigh it down. I carefully took my foot off and walked slowly backwards. Minutes later the landmine exploded; we dived for cover. Just as we were getting to our feet and brushing ourselves off, we were suddenly fired upon from all directions. I was shot and fell to the ground. I was bleeding but I couldn't feel any pain; thankfully I was only shot in the arm and I was so very lucky to be alive.'

We listen in stunned silence as my father speaks. This was the first time that I had ever heard him talk openly about his time during the war. When I was a child, I had always wondered how he got the scars on his arm and back, but I never asked him and he never told me.

I can sense his relief at finally being able to share this with us. I want to hear more but I don't press him further; I know he'll tell me when he is ready.

MỘT MIẾNG KHI ĐÓI BẰNG MỘT GÓI KHI NO

A SMALL PIECE OF FOOD WHEN YOU'RE HUNGRY WEIGHS AS MUCH AS A BIG BOX OF FOOD WHEN YOU'RE FULL.

ALWAYS GIVE TO PEOPLE IN NEED — EVEN THE SMALLEST GESTURE MEANS A LOT.

BEEF AND WATER DROPWORT SALAD
GỎI BÒ CẦN NƯỚC

DON'T BE ALARMED, THIS VARIETY OF WATER DROPWORT IS THE EDIBLE KIND, NOT THE POISONOUS KIND. IT IS ALSO KNOWN AS WATER CELERY, AS THE PLANT'S LEAVES HAVE A SIMILAR SHAPE TO CELERY. THE FLAVOUR CAN BE COMPARED TO THAT OF WATERCRESS AND PARSLEY COMBINED. YOU CAN BUY WATER DROPWORT FROM ASIAN MARKETS.

1 bunch water dropwort, washed and cut into 5 cm (2 inch) lengths
1 onion, thinly sliced
250 ml (9 fl oz/1 cup) Mum's vinaigrette dressing (page 330)
2 tablespoons vegetable oil
2 garlic cloves, finely chopped
350 g (12 oz) beef eye fillet, trimmed and sliced into strips
4 tablespoons Aunty Nine's salad dressing (page 330)
½ teaspoon roasted sesame seeds

Bring a saucepan of water to the boil and blanch the water dropwort for 1 minute, then refresh in iced water and drain. Transfer to a bowl and add the onion, then pour over Mum's vinaigrette dressing, tossing the salad every few minutes for 10 minutes. Drain, then transfer to a large salad bowl.

Place a frying pan over high heat. Add the oil and fry the garlic until fragrant, then add the beef, season with ½ teaspoon freshly ground black pepper, and stir-fry for no more than 3 minutes. Remove the beef from the pan and add to the salad bowl with the water dropwort, pour over Aunty Nine's salad dressing and toss well. Garnish with sesame seeds.

SERVES 4-6 AS PART OF A SHARED MEAL

MEKONG'S PRAWN AND NOODLE SOUP COOKED IN COCONUT MILK
BÁNH CANH TÔM NƯỚC DỪA

TRAVELLING THROUGH THE MEKONG, I NOTICED THE LARGE INFLUENCE THAT CAMBODIA HAS HAD ON THIS PART OF VIETNAM. THIS NOODLE SOUP IS A CLASSIC CAMBODIAN-STYLE SOUP. WHEN I ORDERED IT FOR THE FIRST TIME, I WAS A LITTLE HESITANT AS I THOUGHT IT WAS GOING TO BE FAR TOO HEAVY, BUT I FOUND THE SOUP TO BE QUITE LIGHT AND VERY WELL BALANCED.

I USE UDON NOODLES IN THIS RECIPE AS THEY ARE READILY AVAILABLE, BUT IF YOU HAPPEN TO BE AT A SPECIALISED VIETNAMESE MARKET, ASK FOR TAPIOCA NOODLES AND GO FOR THOSE INSTEAD.

In a saucepan, combine 500 ml (17 fl oz/2 cups) of water, the milk, sugar and fish sauce. Stir well and bring to the boil. Add the coconut milk and bring back to the boil, then add the prawns and simmer for a further 2 minutes, or until the prawns are just cooked.

Meanwhile, fill a large saucepan with water and bring to the boil. Blanch the udon noodles for 2 minutes and drain, then divide the noodles evenly among the soup bowls.

Remove the prawns out of the coconut milk broth with a slotted spoon and divide them among the bowls, placing them on top of the noodles. Ladle over the coconut broth to cover the noodles. Garnish each soup with some spring onion and a few coriander sprigs, and sprinkle with a pinch of freshly ground black pepper.

SERVES 6

100 ml (3½ fl oz) milk
2 tablespoons sugar
2 tablespoons fish sauce
350 ml (12 fl oz) coconut milk
300 g (10½ oz) raw tiger prawns (shrimp), peeled and deveined, then chopped
500 g (1 lb 2 oz) packaged preboiled udon noodles
2 spring onions (scallions), green part only, thinly sliced
coriander (cilantro) sprigs, to garnish

CARAMELISED PORK WITH SWEET PINEAPPLE
THỊT KHO KHÓM

I REALLY ENJOY EATING ANYTHING CARAMELISED IN VIETNAMESE CUISINE — THE SALTY BALANCED WITH THE SWEET. BE SURE TO DRIZZLE ALL THE DELICIOUS SAUCE OVER YOUR RICE AND USE ONLY FRESH PINEAPPLE.

2 tablespoons fish sauce
1 teaspoon oyster sauce
½ teaspoon dark soy sauce
1 tablespoon finely chopped garlic
2 tablespoons sugar
500 g (1 lb 2 oz) boneless pork leg, skin on, cut into 3 x 5 cm (1¼ x 2 inch) pieces
1 tablespoon vegetable oil
5 spring onions (scallions), white part only, trimmed and halved crossways
½ sweet pineapple, peeled, trimmed and cored, cut into 3 cm (1¼ inch) pieces
2 bird's eye chillies, sliced

In a bowl, combine 1 tablespoon of the fish sauce, the oyster sauce, soy sauce, half the garlic, the sugar, 1 teaspoon salt and 1 teaspoon freshly ground black pepper. Mix well, then add the pork, turning to coat in the marinade. Cover and place in the fridge to marinate for 30 minutes.

Heat the oil in a large saucepan over medium–high heat, add the pork and cook for 3 minutes, turning, until golden all over. Add the remaining garlic and the spring onions and stir well.

Add the pineapple, the remaining 1 tablespoon of fish sauce and 125 ml (4 fl oz/½ cup) of water. Reduce the heat to medium–low and simmer for 15 minutes, or until the pork is cooked. Transfer to a serving bowl and garnish with chilli, and serve with jasmine rice.

SERVES 4-6 AS PART OF A SHARED MEAL

PORK SPARERIB AND SALTED RADISH SOUP
CANH SƯỜN CẢI MUỐI

SALTED RADISH CAN BE FOUND AT YOUR ASIAN MARKET. THEY ARE SOLD DRIED, WHOLE, FLATTENED AND ELONGATED, AROUND 15-25 CM (6-10 INCHES) IN LENGTH, AND YOU CAN BUY THEM INDIVIDUALLY BY WEIGHT. THE USE OF SALTED RADISH IN THIS RECIPE GIVES THE SOUP A GOOD BALANCE OF SOUR, SWEET AND SALTINESS. IT ALSO BRINGS A CRISP, CRUNCHY TEXTURE TO THE SOUP.

Soak the salted radish in 500 ml (17 fl oz/2 cups) of water for 1 hour, then drain, reserving the soaking water. Slice the radish into thin pieces on the diagonal.

Bring 2 litres (70 fl oz/8 cups) of water to the boil in a large saucepan. Add the pork ribs and cook for 5 minutes, skimming any impurities off the surface. Pour in the reserved radish water, then add the salted radish, fish sauce and 1/2 teaspoon freshly ground black pepper. Bring back to the boil, then reduce to a low simmer for 30 minutes.

Transfer to large soup bowls, garnish with the spring onion and coriander, and serve with jasmine rice.

SERVES 4-6 AS PART OF A SHARED MEAL

100 g (3½ oz) salted radish
300 g (10½ oz) pork spareribs, chopped into 2 x 3 cm (¾ x 1¼ inch) pieces
2 teaspoons fish sauce
2 spring onions (scallions), green part only, thinly sliced
1 handful coriander (cilantro) leaves

BEEF WOK-TOSSED WITH GLASS NOODLES AND CURRY POWDER
BÒ XÀO LĂN

I HAVE ALWAYS LOVED THIS DISH. MY FATHER WOULD COOK THIS EVERY TIME HE HAD HIS MATES OVER — IT WAS THE PERFECT DRINKING FOOD. YOU CAN USE EITHER THAI OR MALAY CURRY POWDER IN THIS RECIPE, AS LONG AS THE COLOUR IS RED AND THE FLAVOUR IS HOT. THE BEEF CAN BE SUBSTITUTED WITH EEL OR MAKE IT SIMPLY WITH VEGETABLES ALONE.

50 g (1¾ oz) dried bean thread (glass) vermicelli noodles
3 dried wood ear mushrooms
½ teaspoon hot Thai red curry powder
½ teaspoon ground turmeric
½ teaspoon chilli flakes
2 tablespoons fish sauce
1 tablespoon sugar
2 tablespoons vegetable oil
2 garlic cloves, finely chopped
1 onion, cut in half (then ½ diced, ½ cut into wedges)
1 lemongrass stem, white part only, finely chopped
350 g (12 oz) beef eye fillet, trimmed and thinly sliced
3 tablespoons coconut milk
2 tablespoons roasted peanuts, crushed (page 328)
1 bunch rice paddy herb, leaves roughly sliced
1 bunch sawtooth herb, leaves roughly sliced
1 bird's eye chilli, thinly sliced
light soy sauce, for dipping

Put the bean thread vermicelli in a bowl, cover with water and soak for 20 minutes, then drain. Use kitchen scissors to cut the vermicelli into 10 cm (4 inch) lengths. Put the mushrooms in a bowl, cover with water and soak for 20 minutes, then drain and thinly slice.

Combine the curry powder, turmeric and chilli flakes in a small bowl and set aside. In another small bowl, combine the fish sauce and sugar with 2 tablespoons of water. Stir well to dissolve the sugar, then set aside.

Heat a wok over medium heat. Add the oil, garlic, diced onion and lemongrass and stir-fry until fragrant. Increase the heat to high, then add the beef and stir-fry for 2 minutes. Add the curry powder mixture and stir-fry for 1 minute, then add the vermicelli, mushrooms, onion wedges and fish sauce mixture. Toss well, then pour in the coconut milk and stir-fry for 2 minutes.

Garnish with peanuts, rice paddy herb and sawtooth herb. Serve with jasmine rice, and a small bowl of sliced chilli and soy sauce for dipping.

SERVES 4-6 AS PART OF A SHARED MEAL

DUCK BREAST PAN-FRIED WITH PRESERVED BEAN CURD
VỊT NƯỚNG CHAO

IF YOU ARE ONE OF THOSE PEOPLE WHO AREN'T KEEN ON TOFU AND THINK IT'S BLAND, THEN YOU MUST TRY PRESERVED BEAN CURD. ALSO KNOWN AS FERMENTED BEAN CURD OR 'VIETNAMESE CHEESE', THESE CUBES OF BEAN CURD HAVE BEEN FERMENTED IN RICE WINE. THERE ARE DIFFERENT VARIETIES AVAILABLE, SUCH AS WHITE OR RED BEAN CURD MARINATED IN SESAME OIL OR CHILLI, ALTHOUGH THE CHILLI FLAVOUR IS MY PICK. THESE CAN BE FOUND IN YOUR ASIAN MARKET IN GLASS JARS. YOU CAN KEEP THE JARS REFRIGERATED FOR 3 MONTHS.

40 g (1½ oz) preserved red
  bean curd
1 tablespoon sugar
2 garlic cloves, finely chopped
4 slices ginger, finely chopped
1 tablespoon finely chopped
  red Asian shallots
4 tablespoons vegetable oil
2 duck breast fillets, skin on
  (600 g/1 lb 5 oz in total)
200 g (7 oz) okra, trimmed and
  halved lengthways
1 tablespoon Dad's spicy saté
  sauce (page 337)
1 small handful coriander (cilantro)
  leaves
preserved bean curd dipping sauce
  (page 332), to serve

Place the preserved bean curd in a large bowl and mash using a fork. Add the sugar, garlic, ginger, shallots and 2 tablespoons of the oil, and stir to combine. Add the duck breasts, turning to coat them in the marinade. Cover and set aside at cool room temperature for 20 minutes.

Combine the okra with Dad's spicy saté sauce in a bowl, tossing to coat the okra, then cover and set aside for 15 minutes. Preheat the oven to 180°C (350°F/Gas 4).

Heat a frying pan over medium heat. Add the remaining 2 tablespoons of oil, then add the duck breasts to the pan and brown for 3 minutes on each side. Put the duck, skin side up, in a baking tin and place in the oven. Cook for 5–8 minutes, or until the duck is cooked but still a little pink in the middle. Remove from the oven, cover loosely with foil and set aside to rest in a warm place for 10 minutes.

Heat a frying pan over medium heat and stir-fry the undrained okra for 3 minutes, or until just tender, then set aside.

Slice the duck, skin side up, into thick strips widthways, place on a serving plate and garnish with the stir-fried okra and the coriander. Serve with jasmine rice, and a small bowl of preserved bean curd dipping sauce.

SERVES 4–6 AS PART OF A SHARED MEAL

CHARGRILLED CHICKEN IN SHRIMP PASTE
GÀ NƯỚNG MẮM RUỐC

DON'T BE AFRAID OF SHRIMP PASTE, IT'S JUST FERMENTED DRIED SHRIMP. YES, ITS AROMA IS MUCH MORE PUNGENT THAN FISH SAUCE, BUT ONCE COMBINED WITH HERBS AND SPICES ITS INTENSE SMELL DISSIPATES AND IT ADDS DEPTH OF FLAVOUR AND FRAGRANCE TO A DISH. BE ADVENTUROUS AND GO TO THE ASIAN MARKET AND BUY A JAR BUT CHOOSE THE SOFT VARIETY, NOT THE HARD ONE. AFTER USE, SEAL THE JAR WELL AND REFRIGERATE FOR UP TO 3 MONTHS.

Soak 12 bamboo skewers in cold water for 30 minutes to prevent them from burning.

In a bowl, combine the shrimp paste, lemon juice, sugar, lemongrass, paprika and garlic, stirring well to dissolve the sugar. Add the chicken, stir to coat in the marinade, then add the oil and stir again. Cover the bowl and place in the fridge to marinate for at least 2 hours, or overnight for a better flavour.

Thread the chicken onto the skewers evenly. Heat a barbecue grill or chargrill pan to medium–high. Add the chicken skewers and chargrill for 4 minutes on each side, or until cooked through. Serve with jasmine rice.

MAKES 12 SKEWERS

3 teaspoons shrimp paste
3 teaspoons lemon juice
3 teaspoons sugar
½ lemongrass stem, white part only, finely chopped
½ teaspoon hot paprika
1 garlic clove, finely chopped
500 g (1 lb 2 oz) boneless, skinless chicken thighs, cut into 3 x 5 cm (1¼ x 2 inch) pieces
2 teaspoons vegetable oil

CRISP SNAPPER WITH '333' BEER SAUCE
CÁ CHẼM HẤP BIA

WHEN DINING IN VIETNAMESE RESTAURANTS, YOUR TABLE IS GIVEN A LARGE TUB FILLED WITH ICE AND BEER. WHEN YOU WANT ANOTHER BEER, YOU JUST HELP YOURSELF, AND THEN THROW YOUR EMPTIES INTO ANOTHER TUB BESIDE IT. THIS IS QUITE DANGEROUS, AS YOU FIND YOU DRINK A LOT MORE THAN YOU USUALLY WOULD. AT THE END OF THE DINNER, THE WAITER TALLIES UP HOW MANY EMPTY BOTTLES YOU HAVE AND ADDS IT TO YOUR BILL — PURE GENIUS. THERE ARE TWO VIETNAMESE BEERS AVAILABLE IN AUSTRALIA, '333' AND 'HUDA' BEER.

Using a sharp knife, make two diagonal incisions into both sides of the fish. Dust the fish with the potato starch, shaking off any excess starch.

Pour the oil into a large wok and heat to 200°C (400°F), or until a cube of bread dropped into the oil browns in 5 seconds. Carefully place the fish in the oil and deep-fry on each side for 3 minutes. Remove and place the fish on paper towel to drain.

In a frying pan, heat the 2 tablespoons of oil, then add the garlic and onion and stir-fry for 1–2 minutes until fragrant. Add the tomatoes, Asian celery and brown sugar and stir-fry for 1 minute, or until caramelised. Add the fish sauce, oyster sauce, chilli sauce and beer, and simmer for 2 minutes.

Transfer the fish to a serving plate, pour over the vegetables and sauce and garnish with coriander sprigs, sesame seeds and chilli, if using. Serve with jasmine rice.

SERVES 4-6 AS PART OF A SHARED MEAL

1 whole snapper (600 g/1 lb 5 oz), cleaned
potato starch, for dusting
1 litre (35 fl oz/4 cups) vegetable oil, for deep-frying, plus 2 tablespoons extra
1 garlic clove, finely chopped
1 small onion, cut into wedges
4 cherry tomatoes, halved
6 Asian celery stems, cut into 5 cm (2 inch) lengths
3 tablespoons soft brown sugar
1 tablespoon fish sauce
1 tablespoon oyster sauce
1 tablespoon chilli sauce
185 ml (6 fl oz/¾ cup) '333' Vietnamese beer (or any lager)
coriander (cilantro) sprigs, to garnish
½ teaspoon toasted sesame seeds
2 long red chillies, thinly sliced on the diagonal (optional)

WOK-TOSSED CRAB IN SATE SAUCE
CUA SỐT SA-TẾ

OUR TIME SPENT WITH FAMILY IN THE MEKONG DELTA WAS ALL ABOUT EATING LOCAL DISHES AND COOKING WITH LOCAL PRODUCE. MY FATHER CREATED THE SPICY SATE SAUCE RECIPE, USED HERE AND IN OTHER RECIPES, WHILE ATTEMPTING TO MAKE THE TRADITIONAL VERSION. VIETNAMESE SATE SAUCE IS NOT LIKE THE MALAY-STYLE PEANUT SATAY SAUCE — THE VIETNAMESE VERSION IS CHILLI-BASED AND IS USED IN STIR-FRIES AND ADDED TO BROTHS.

2 live crabs, blue swimmer or mud crab, 400 g (14 oz) each
vegetable oil, for deep-frying
potato starch, for dusting
½ green capsicum (pepper), thinly sliced
3 red Asian shallots, finely chopped
2 garlic cloves, finely chopped
4 tablespoons Dad's spicy saté sauce (page 337)
3 spring onions (scallions), cut into 5 cm (2 inch) lengths
2 long red chillies, thinly sliced on the diagonal

To prepare your crabs humanely, place them in the freezer for 1 hour to put them to sleep. Remove the upper shell of the crab, pick off the gills, which look like little fingers, and discard them. Clean the crab under running water and drain. Place the crab on its stomach and chop the crab in half lengthways with a heavy cleaver, then chop each half into 4 pieces. With the back of the cleaver, gently crack each claw — this makes it easier to extract the meat.

Pour the oil into a wok and heat to 200°C (400°F), or until a cube of bread dropped into the oil browns in 5 seconds. Dust the crab pieces with potato starch, shaking off the excess. Deep-fry the crab in batches for 3 minutes, turning once, until golden brown. Remove the crab from the wok and drain on paper towel. Remove the oil, reserving 2 tablespoons, and clean the wok.

Heat the reserved oil in the wok, then add the capsicum and stir-fry for 1 minute, then add the shallots and garlic and fry until fragrant. Add the saté sauce and stir for 1 minute. Return the crab to the wok with the spring onions and toss, making sure to coat the crab well. Transfer to a serving platter and garnish with chilli. Serve with jasmine rice and finger bowls.

SERVES 4-6 AS PART OF A SHARED MEAL

WOK-FRIED RICE WITH CHICKEN AND SALTED FISH POWDER
CƠM CHIÊN GÀ CÁ MẶN

MY PARENTS SERVED THIS DISH AT THEIR VERY FIRST RESTAURANT, PHO CAY DU, IN CABRAMATTA, SYDNEY. I REMEMBER A CUSTOMER TELLING ME THAT THIS DISH REMINDED HIM OF HIS HOME IN THE MEKONG. THIS ISN'T YOUR REGULAR CHINESE FRIED RICE; THIS FRIED RICE IS MEKONG-STYLE AND HAS MANY LAYERS TO IT. I WAS VERY EXCITED WHEN I SAW IT BEING SERVED IN THE MEKONG DELTA. THE SUBTLE SALTINESS OF THE FISH POWDER REALLY MAKES THIS RICE DISH UNIQUE. YOU CAN FIND SALTED MACKEREL STEAK PACKAGED IN SINGLE PORTIONS AT YOUR ASIAN MARKET.

2 tablespoons vegetable oil
80 g (2¾ oz) salted mackerel steak
100 g (3½ oz) boneless, skinless
    chicken breast, thinly sliced
2 eggs, beaten
1 tablespoon finely chopped garlic
370 g (13 oz/2 cups) cooked
    jasmine rice, refrigerated
a pinch of sugar
90 g (3¼ oz/1 cup) bean sprouts
4 spring onions (scallions), sliced
¼ teaspoon sesame oil
coriander (cilantro) sprigs,
    to garnish
1 long red chilli, julienned

Place a frying pan over medium–high heat. Add 1 teaspoon of the oil and pan-fry the salted mackerel on both sides for 2 minutes, or until brown. Allow to cool, then remove the flesh, discarding the skin and bones. Using the back of a fork, crush the flesh as finely as you can.

Wipe the pan clean, then place on the stovetop over low heat. Add the crushed mackerel and dry-roast for 10 minutes, or until it becomes dry. Allow to cool, then place the mackerel in a spice grinder or in a small food processor and pulse until it becomes a fine powder. Set aside.

Bring a saucepan of water to the boil, then reduce the heat to a simmer. Add the chicken and blanch for 2 minutes, then drain and set aside.

Place a wok over medium–high heat, add the remaining oil and stir-fry the egg for 30 seconds. Now add the garlic and rice and wok-toss over high heat for 3 minutes. Add a pinch of sugar and a pinch of salt and freshly ground black pepper, then add the chicken and 3 tablespoons of the salted fish powder. Toss for a further 3 minutes, then add the bean sprouts, spring onions and sesame oil. Toss for another minute and then transfer to a serving bowl. Serve garnished with coriander sprigs and chilli.

SERVES 4–6 AS PART OF A SHARED MEAL

EEL CHARGRILLED WITH LEMONGRASS AND TURMERIC
LƯƠN NƯỚNG XẢ

IN THE BACK LANES OF CAN THO IN THE MEKONG DELTA, I CAME ACROSS AN EATERY THAT HAD A BANQUET MENU SERVING ONLY EEL. I STARTED WITH AN EEL BROTH, FOLLOWED BY SALT AND PEPPER EEL, THEN WOK-TOSSED EEL IN SEAWEED, EEL WITH CASSAVA AND GLASS NOODLES, AND THEN THIS CHARGRILLED EEL, WHICH WAS MY FAVOURITE. EELS ARE VERY POPULAR IN VIETNAM, ENJOYED FOR THEIR FIRM FATTY FLESH AND THEIR OWN RICH DISTINCTIVE TASTE. IF YOU HAVE THE CHOICE, BUY A LIVE ONE. EELS ARE READILY AVAILABLE AT YOUR LOCAL ASIAN FISHMONGER.

Combine all the marinade ingredients in a large bowl, add 1 teaspoon each of salt and freshly ground black pepper, and mix. Add the eel, stirring to coat well. Cover and set aside at cool room temperature for 20 minutes. Drain the eel well, reserving the marinade.

Heat a barbecue grill or chargrill pan to medium and cook the eel for 3 minutes on each side, brushing with the reserved marinade as it cooks. Remove to a bowl and garnish with coriander. Serve with jasmine rice.

SERVES 4-6 AS PART OF A SHARED MEAL

500 g (1 lb 2 oz) eel fillets, boned, with skin on, cut into 5 cm (2 inch) pieces (or ask your fishmonger to do this for you)
1 small handful coriander (cilantro) leaves

MARINADE
1 teaspoon Thai red curry powder
1 teaspoon ground turmeric
2 lemongrass stems, white part only, finely chopped
2 garlic cloves, finely chopped
1 bird's eye chilli, finely chopped
1 teaspoon sugar
2 teaspoons fish sauce
2 tablespoons vegetable oil

FAMILY IN PHAN THIET

10

I CAN'T SEEM TO FALL ASLEEP. I'M A LITTLE NERVOUS ABOUT MEETING MY HALF SIBLINGS TOMORROW: TWO OLDER SISTERS AND AN OLDER BROTHER. I DON'T EVEN KNOW THEIR NAMES, SO I GUESS I'LL CALL THEM BROTHER TWO, SISTER THREE AND SISTER FOUR.

I'm meeting them only because my father asked me when we were in Saigon if I wanted to meet them, but I really wasn't that interested then. He hinted at it again a few days ago, so I agreed.

When I first learned that my father had another family, I was angry and upset and I didn't speak to him for nearly half a year. I couldn't understand how he could have two wives, and how he could have kept his other wife and their three children a secret for so long. But the more time I spend in Vietnam, discovering more about my culture and family, the more I have come to understand how things operate here. I was raised in Australia and I have a different set of values, but in Vietnam I have found it is common for men to have two or three wives. The first wife is known as the 'big' wife and the second is the 'small' wife, and both parties seem to accept each other.

This custom is still practised today. I have met numerous men in Vietnam who speak freely about their big and small wives, and I've met small wives talking about the big wife. At first I couldn't really get my head around it, so I asked my mother how she can be so apparently cool and calm about it.

'Your father and I were introduced by our parents; we had an arranged marriage. Destiny has carved our life out for us, Luke; even if we try to change it, we can't. If I go through some hardships in this current life, it means I have done some bad things in the past life. It all balances out; you just have to accept it and get on with it.'

Lying there in my bed, thinking about what she had said, didn't really make me feel any better, but I suppose that if she has accepted it, then

I should too. But as I lie in the darkness, I can't get images out of my head, of meeting my brother and seeing someone who looks exactly like me.

Our three-hour drive to Phan Thiet takes more than four hours as I deliberately take ten bathroom stops in an attempt to delay the fearful family reunion.

It's a typical Vietnamese family welcome, with the whole family waiting at the front of the house, all grouped together, standing up straight, smiling and waving in unison. When my father steps out of the van, his children come running towards him, giving him big hugs and kisses, rubbing his belly. They are in awe of him and so excited to see him again, showing him the kind of affection that I've rarely seen in our family.

Dad introduces me to my half siblings, addressing them as older brother Two, and older sisters Three and Four. I shake their hands and feel totally lost for words. I am sweating, nervous and very uncomfortable.

'We don't even look like each other,' I blurt out, then make a hasty retreat to the bathroom again.

When I venture outside, my sister Four waves me over. Their backyard is filled with hundreds of climbing green cactus trees, flowering with vibrant red dragon fruit. She picks a dragon fruit from the tree and slices it in half, exposing its translucent white flesh and tiny black seeds; its flavour is deliciously sweet and subtle. We spend the next hour walking through the dragon fruit plantation, talking about the work that goes into growing the fruit and how different regions in Vietnam grow different varieties of dragon fruit, each differing in colour and sweetness.

We fill a basket with ripe fruit and go back to the house. The kitchen is filled with chaos as the family prepares lunch. They shout and bicker at each other as if in a fight, but it's actually only recipes they are arguing about, and who has the better one. Sister Three grabs my arm and we escape for a peaceful drive to the beach.

On secluded Mui Ne beach we see hundreds of fishing boats, painted red and yellow, bringing their catch to shore. Waiting on the sand are women with conical hats and wet sandals. They carry small scales and rush to the boats as they near the shore. The women push and shove each other; the battle is on to get the best catch at the best price. They yell, shout and bargain, as hundreds of crates filled with fish are sorted, weighed and sold.

My sister tells me that this is what she does every morning: she wakes up early, waits for the boats of anchovy to arrive, then fights for the best price, picking through the lot, separating the good fish from the bad, then sells them to fish sauce manufacturers.

I love learning how things are made, from the raw ingredient to the finished product, so we drive to the fish sauce factory where she sells her fresh anchovies. Fishing is Phan Thiet's largest industry and over 75,000 tonnes of fish are caught each year, most of it being used to produce the premium fish sauce for which Phan Thiet is famous.

We then drive to an area where many fish sauce manufacturers are based. The air is heavy with the pungent odour of fermenting fish, dried seafood and purple anchovy and shrimp paste   If you don't like the smell of fish sauce, you would most likely kill yourself here.

> **❝ WE DRIP SOME FISH SAUCE INTO OUR GLASS, LOOK AT ITS AMBER COLOUR, THEN WE SWIRL, WE SMELL, WE DIP OUR FINGER INTO THE LIQUID AND TASTE. ❞**

I meet a fish sauce maker, who is excited to have a visitor. He grabs his hat, gives us each a small glass, and leads us through his distillery.

Rows of giant wooden vats stand high, with ladders built up the side of each vat; if it wasn't for the smell, I would have thought I was in a winery. Each vat holds 8000 kilograms of anchovies, made up of three parts fish to one part salt. It is weighed down, then left to ferment for 18 months, allowing the fish to release all of its water. He explains that his sauce is of very high quality, because once he filters the fish water he doesn't add any more liquid or salt, which makes his sauce pure and free of preservatives. It is rare to find this grade of sauce in Australia, as most of the fish sauce that Australia imports has been diluted or has additives.

As you would in a winery, we move around to different vats and taste different vintages. We drip some fish sauce into our glasses, look at its amber colour, then we swirl, we smell, we dip our finger into the liquid and taste. To my surprise, it isn't that salty and actually has a nice sweet finish; the saltiness it does have is subtle and clean, not in the slightest overpowering. This is definitely the extra virgin olive oil of fish sauces.

I ask the fish sauce maker if I could return one day and be his apprentice for a few months. He laughs and says I would need to commit ten years of my life to him, for this is how long it takes to perfect the art of fish sauce making.

At home, we find brother Two preparing a decadent steamboat for our first course. We set up a table outside and fill it with an array of seafood, herbs, vegetables and noodles. We all sit around the table, dunking fish, prawns, cuttlefish, scallops and vegetables into the simmering broth, drinking beer and talking. We don't talk about personal things or how we feel about meeting one another; instead we talk about the speciality dishes and exotic sea creatures of Phan Thiet. We get to know each other through the one thing we all have in common — our passion and love for food. All of my family in Vietnam, be it on my mother's or father's side, are all connected to or work in some way with food. It is part of who were are, and it is something that I am very proud of.

Brother Two wakes me up early and takes me to visit his friend Hiep, whose family runs a small noodle-making business that makes and supplies rice noodles to *pho* restaurants around town.

'Why do you want to know how to make rice noodles?' Hiep asks me. 'Do you want to set up your own noodle factory, perhaps? Who do you work for?'

Brother Two jumps to my defence. 'Hiep, calm down, I told you on the phone, he's my brother. He owns a restaurant in Sydney and is very interested in food production. He's just curious about what foods we have in Phan Thiet, and I brought him here to show him!'

Hiep wipes the serious look off his face and grins. 'Luke, I was just checking. It's a small town and business is competitive. I had to make sure that you weren't here to steal my secret recipe and start up your own company.'

I completely understand Hiep's concerns; my parents had been just as protective with their secret family recipes. When I first opened Red Lantern, I had to wait until the kitchen staff finished for the night before I could prepare my secret broths and marinades. I was exhausted, but I had to respect my parents' wishes. It was only after they sold their restaurant in Cabramatta that they were comfortable with me sharing these recipes with my staff.

Hiep kindly explains the whole process of noodle making. His wife, Thang, comes out and they both take turns talking through the various steps. Hiep points at large tubs filled with rice and water. The rice is soaked for two days, then turned into a liquid batter. The batter is left overnight, allowing it to separate. Hiep's wife discards the liquid on the top and pours the remaining thick batter into a bucket — this batter is used to make the rice noodles.

She takes the bucket to another room, where their son works alone in a room filled with steam, lit with only thin rays of natural sunlight. He pours a thin layer of batter onto large circular trays and pushes them through a steam oven, fuelled by burning rice husk; they take only minutes to cook. He removes the transparent sheets and places them on top of each other in high piles. They come out steaming hot; I could eat them just as they are.

Hiep collect the rice sheets and takes them to his wife, who turns an old large wheel, feeding each sheet through the cutting machine. The blades slice through the sheets and they slowly drop into a heaped pile as soft, thin, delicate rice noodles. The noodles are bagged, weighed and delivered directly to the restaurants, the noodles still hot when they arrive. How I admire and envy the freshness of produce in Vietnam.

That evening, we all drive to the headland and look out at the ocean. As darkness falls, hundreds of fishing boats turn on their spotlights to attract cuttlefish, turning the sea into a beautiful, bright floating city.

I think about all the different experiences I have had on my Vietnam trip, from travelling with Suzanna, travelling alone, and then travelling with my parents. I have met the most incredible people, made very dear friends and, along the way, have discovered some really wonderful traditional recipes.

I've visited Vietnam many times now, but this trip has been by far the most rewarding. Each time I return to this picturesque country I grow a little more from the unique experiences I have. I have not only learned about wonderful ingredients and recipes, I have discovered so much more about who I am, and who my parents are. I feel I have learned more about them in these last three weeks than I have in the previous thirty years. They have finally dropped their barriers and let me in and I feel very privileged that I have heard their stories, and had the chance to meet my new family — some of whom I had never met before, and others that I didn't even know existed.

On my next trip to Vietnam, I won't feel like I'm visiting — I'll be coming home — and I'm looking forward to spending time with my large extended family, to discover more about this beautiful country and her culture and, naturally, food and cooking will play a huge part of that.

STEAMED PORK AND CRAB TERRINE
CHẢ CUA BIỂN

THIS CRAB TERRINE IS TRADITIONALLY EATEN WITH *COM SUON*, A BROKEN RICE DISH SERVED WITH PORK CUTLETS AND FRIED EGG. I PREFER TO EAT IT ON ITS OWN AS A STARTER OR SNACK, SERVED WITH A CRISP BAGUETTE AND DRIZZLED WITH DIPPING FISH SAUCE.

3 dried wood ear mushrooms

20 g (³/4 oz) dried bean thread (glass) vermicelli noodles

4 eggs

300 g (10½ oz) blue swimmer crabmeat (bought ready-picked from your fishmonger)

200 g (7 oz) minced pork

2 garlic cloves, crushed

2 teaspoons vegetable oil

1 tablespoon sugar

1 bird's eye chilli, sliced on the diagonal

2 tablespoons spring onion oil (page 329)

2 tablespoons dipping fish sauce (page 331)

Put the mushrooms in a bowl, cover with water and soak for 20 minutes, then drain and thinly slice. Put the bean thread vermicelli in a bowl, cover with water and soak for 20 minutes, then drain. Use kitchen scissors to cut the vermicelli into 3 cm (1¼ inch) lengths.

In a bowl, put 2 whole eggs and 2 egg whites, then beat well. (Beat the 2 remaining egg yolks in a separate bowl and set aside for later use.) Add the mushrooms, vermicelli, crabmeat, pork, garlic, vegetable oil, sugar and 1 teaspoon each of salt and freshly ground black pepper. Knead all the ingredients together for 3 minutes.

Divide the mixture among 6 small, shallow heatproof bowls, then firmly press the mixture flat and cover with plastic wrap. Working in batches if necessary, place the bowls in a steamer over a wok or saucepan of boiling water, cover and steam over high heat for 20 minutes. Remove and discard the plastic wrap and pour the reserved egg yolks over the top of the mixture, dividing it evenly among the bowls. Steam for a further 10 minutes with the lid off.

Remove the bowls from the steamer and cool. Turn the crab terrines out of their moulds onto a chopping board and slice into 2 cm (³/4 inch) wide strips. Garnish with chilli and spring onion oil, and dress with dipping fish sauce. Serve with jasmine rice or a crisp baguette.

SERVES 6 AS A STARTER OR SNACK

LILY FLOWER AND PORK SOUP
CANH KIM CHÂM THỊT HEO

DRIED LILY FLOWERS ARE ALSO KNOWN AS GOLDEN NEEDLES, AND CAN BE FOUND AT MOST ASIAN MARKETS. WHEN FRESH, THESE DAYLILIES ARE A STUNNING ORANGE COLOUR, BUT AS A DRIED FLOWER THEY ARE AN UNASSUMING BROWN. PICKING OFF THE STEMS AND TYING THE FLOWERS IN A KNOT MAY BE A LITTLE TIME-CONSUMING, BUT IT'S WORTH IT FOR THE EARTHY SWEET FLAVOUR THEY RELEASE.

Season the pork with 1/2 teaspoon each of salt and freshly ground black pepper, and set aside for 20 minutes. Soak the bean thread vermicelli in water for 20 minutes, then drain and use kitchen scissors to cut into 4 cm (1 1/2 inch) lengths. Soak the dried lily flowers in water for 20 minutes, then drain. Pick off the hard stem ends, then tie each flower into a knot.

Bring 1.5 litres (52 fl oz/6 cups) of water to the boil in a saucepan. Add the pork, fish sauce and sugar. Bring to the boil, then reduce the heat and simmer for 15 minutes, skimming any impurities off the surface. Now add the lily flowers and simmer for a further 15 minutes. Turn the heat to high and add the vermicelli and mushrooms, and bring back to the boil, then turn the heat off.

Transfer to soup bowls and garnish with the spring onions and coriander sprigs. Serve with jasmine rice, and a small bowl of sliced chilli and fish sauce for dipping.

SERVES 4-6 AS PART OF A SHARED MEAL

300 g (10 1/2 oz) lean, boneless
    pork belly, thinly sliced
40 g (1 1/2 oz) dried bean thread
    (glass) vermicelli noodles
50 g (1 3/4 oz) dried lily flowers
2 tablespoons fish sauce
1 teaspoon sugar
100 g (3 1/2 oz) button mushrooms,
    stems removed and halved
2 spring onions (scallions),
    green part only, thinly sliced
coriander (cilantro) sprigs,
    to garnish
1 bird's eye chilli, thinly sliced
fish sauce, for dipping

RAZOR CLAM SALAD
GỎI SÒ MÓNG TAY

THE TIDE IS LOW, THE SKY SPECTACULAR. WE ROLL OUR PANTS UP TO OUR KNEES, GRAB A BUCKET EACH AND START OUR HUNT FOR RAZOR CLAMS ON THE SHORES OF MUI NE BEACH. I SPOT PERFECT ROUND HOLES AND DIG IN THE SAND WITH MY BAMBOO STICK. THEY ARE SURPRISINGLY FAST, MANY GET AWAY, BUT I AM ABLE TO CATCH MY SHARE. RAZOR CLAMS CAN BE FOUND AT ASIAN FISH MARKETS, OR USE PIPIS AS A SUBSTITUTE.

500 g (1 lb 2 oz) razor clams, shells cleaned
1 tomato, slightly underripe
½ sweet pineapple, peeled, trimmed and cored, sliced into batons
1 Lebanese (short) cucumber, seeded and sliced into batons
1 tablespoon sliced spring onion (scallion), white part only
½ bunch sawtooth herb, leaves sliced
1 large handful Vietnamese mint leaves
2 teaspoons fried garlic (page 329)
½ teaspoon sesame oil
4 tablespoons Aunty Nine's salad dressing (page 330)
½ bunch rice paddy herb, leaves torn
1 bird's eye chilli, thinly sliced

Fill a wok with water and bring to a rapid boil. Add the clams in batches and cook for 2–3 minutes, or until they just begin to open. Remove the clams from the wok and transfer to iced water to soak for 2 minutes. Drain the clams and remove the flesh from the shells.

To seed the tomato, cut it in half horizontally and squeeze out the seeds or scoop them out with a teaspoon. Thinly slice the tomato flesh.

Put the clam flesh in a bowl. Add the tomato, pineapple, cucumber, spring onion, sawtooth herb, Vietnamese mint, fried garlic, sesame oil and ½ teaspoon freshly ground black pepper. Dress with Aunty Nine's salad dressing and toss well. Transfer to a serving bowl and garnish with rice paddy herb and sliced chilli.

SERVES 4–6 AS PART OF A SHARED MEAL

CUTTLEFISH AND BANANA BLOSSOM SALAD
GỎI MỰC BẮP CHUỐI

WHEN I WAS TWELVE, I ASKED MY MOTHER WHAT WAS THE DIFFERENCE BETWEEN A SQUID AND A CUTTLEFISH. SHE LOOKED AT ME LIKE I WAS A FOOL BEFORE EXPLAINING THAT CUTTLEFISH HAVE AN INTERNAL SHELL — ITS SPINE — WHICH IS CALLED THE CUTTLEBONE. IT IS ALSO ROUNDER IN SHAPE AND IS PREFERRED OVER SQUID AS IT HAS MORE TEXTURE. FOR SOME REASON I'VE ALWAYS REMEMBERED THIS QUESTION I ASKED MY MOTHER; MAYBE IT WAS BECAUSE I WAS EMBARRASSED THAT I DIDN'T KNOW THE ANSWER, OR MAYBE IT WAS BECAUSE I JUST COULDN'T BELIEVE THAT SHE EXPECTED A YOUNG BOY TO KNOW THAT KIND OF THING. ANYHOW, THIS SALAD IS ALL ABOUT TEXTURE, AND WITH EVERY MOUTHFUL YOU WILL EXPERIENCE FIVE DIFFERENT ONES.

Peel off the outer purple leaves of the banana blossom until you reach the inner, pale yellow core, reserving one of the purple leaves for garnish. Thinly slice the yellow core of the blossom, then transfer it to a bowl, pour in enough cold water to cover, and add the vinegar. This stops it from discolouring. Soak for 10 minutes, then drain. Put the reserved purple leaf in the serving bowl or plate, for garnish.

Place a frying pan over high heat. Add the oil, ginger, half the chilli and the cuttlefish. Stir-fry for 3 minutes, then remove and set aside.

In a bowl, combine the banana blossom, cuttlefish, fried garlic, sesame oil and all the herbs. Dress with the dipping fish sauce and toss well. Transfer to the serving bowl and garnish with the remaining chilli.

SERVES 4-6 AS PART OF A SHARED MEAL

300 g (10½ oz) banana blossom
1 tablespoon white vinegar
2 tablespoons vegetable oil
4 cm (1½ inch) piece of ginger, peeled and julienned
2 bird's eye chillies, sliced
500 g (1 lb 2 oz) cuttlefish, cleaned, tubes scored on the inside and sliced into 2 x 3 cm (¾ x 1¼ inch) pieces
1 teaspoon fried garlic (page 329)
1 teaspoon sesame oil
1 handful Vietnamese mint leaves, roughly sliced
1 handful perilla leaves, roughly sliced
1 handful mint leaves, roughly sliced
4 tablespoons dipping fish sauce (page 331)

STREETSIDE SAVOURY PORK RICE FLOUR CAKE
BÁNH MẶN

WHEN TRAVELLING IN VIETNAM, I OFTEN EAT THIS STREETSIDE DISH. *BANH MAN* **IS A VERY TRADITIONAL SNACK THAT YOU ONLY SEE LOCALS EAT. IT HAS UNUSUAL FLAVOURS AND TEXTURES, AND IS A DISH THAT I'D LIKE TO INTRODUCE YOU TO.**

300 g (10½ oz/2¼ cups) rice flour

50 g (1¾ oz/⅓ cup) plain (all-purpose) flour

550 ml (19 fl oz) coconut milk

2 tablespoons sugar

100 g (3½ oz/1 cup) dried shrimp

100 ml (3½ fl oz) vegetable oil

6 red Asian shallots, diced

100 g (3½ oz) minced pork

2 spring onions (scallions), sliced

500 g (1 lb 2 oz) jicama, peeled and cut into 1 cm (½ inch) dice

1 small handful coriander (cilantro) leaves

125 ml (4 fl oz/½ cup) dipping fish sauce (page 331)

In a bowl, combine the rice flour, flour, coconut milk, sugar, 2 teaspoons salt and 450 ml (16 fl oz) of water. Whisk well and set aside. Put the dried shrimp in a bowl, cover with water and soak for 20 minutes, then drain.

Place a frying pan over medium heat. Add 2 tablespoons of the oil, the shallots and shrimp and stir-fry for 4 minutes. Remove from the pan and set aside in a large bowl.

Wipe the pan clean and add 1 tablespoon oil, the pork, spring onions and a pinch of salt and freshly ground black pepper. Stir-fry for 3 minutes, then remove to the bowl with the shrimp. Wipe out the pan again and place over medium heat. Add the remaining 2 tablespoons of oil and the jicama and stir-fry for 5 minutes, or until all the juices evaporate and the jicama is lightly golden and beginning to soften. Remove the jicama from the pan and add to the bowl with the pork and shrimp, and mix well.

Place a large steamer over a saucepan of boiling water. Grease a 20 cm (8 inch) square, 6 cm (2½ inch) deep baking tin. Heat the tin in the steamer for 5 minutes.

Pour about one-quarter of the batter into the tin to a depth of 1 cm (½ inch). Place the tin in the steamer, cover and steam over high heat for 5 minutes. Remove the lid and puncture the surface of the batter 20 times with a skewer. Now pour another quarter of the batter into the tin, again about 1 cm (½ inch) deep, then cover and steam for 5 minutes. Remove the lid and puncture the surface with a skewer. Repeat this process until all the batter has been steamed, 5 minutes each time, making sure you puncture each layer with holes.

With a large spoon, evenly spread the pork mixture on top of the batter and steam for a further 10 minutes. Remove the cake from the tin and allow to cool. Once cooled, cut into 4 cm (1½ inch) squares. Garnish with coriander and serve on individual plates. Dress with dipping fish sauce.

MAKES 25 PIECES

LEMONGRASS CRUSTED TOFU
TÀU HŨ XẢ ỚT

FIRM TOFU GOES THROUGH THE SAME PROCESS AS SILKEN TOFU; THE ONLY DIFFERENCE IS THAT FIRM TOFU IS PRESSED FOR LONGER, WHICH DRAWS MORE LIQUID OUT OF IT. FIRM TOFU IS IDEAL FOR THIS RECIPE BECAUSE IT CAN BE CRUSTED AND HANDLED WITHOUT BREAKING APART, IT RETAINS ITS MOISTURE AND HAS QUITE A 'BOUNCY' TEXTURE.

Drain the tofu and slice into 5 x 10 cm (2 x 4 inch) pieces, then pat dry with paper towel. Leave the tofu on the chopping board or transfer to a tray. In a bowl, combine the lemongrass, chilli, garlic, sugar, 1 teaspoon salt and ½ teaspoon freshly ground black pepper. Mix all the ingredients together, then coat both sides of the tofu with the mixture.

Heat a large frying pan over medium–high heat. Add the oil and pan-fry each side of the tofu for 3 minutes, or until browned and crisp. Garnish with coriander sprigs and serve with jasmine rice.

SERVES 4-6 AS PART OF A SHARED MEAL

450 g (1 lb) firm tofu
1 lemongrass stem, white part only, finely chopped
1 bird's eye chilli, finely chopped
1 tablespoon finely chopped garlic
1 teaspoon sugar
2 tablespoons vegetable oil
3 coriander (cilantro) sprigs

CITRUS-CURED TIGER PRAWNS ROLLED IN TAMARIND
GỎI TÔM THẤU ME

THIS DISH WAS INTRODUCED TO ME BY MY HALF-SISTER THREE. WHEN WE MET FOR THE FIRST TIME ONLY RECENTLY, ALL WE TALKED ABOUT WAS FOOD AND RECIPES. THIS RECIPE USES VIETNAMESE FISH MINT, *RAU DIEP CA*, AND I'VE ONLY SEEN IT IN VIETNAMESE MARKETS; THE GREEN LEAVES ARE HEART-SHAPED. WITH ITS BOLD FISHY FLAVOURS, IT'S AN ACQUIRED TASTE FOR SOME PALATES, SO EAT A LEAF BEFORE YOU BUY IT.

500 g (1 lb 2 oz) raw tiger prawns (shrimp)
125 ml (4 fl oz/½ cup) lemon juice
10 long red chillies, chopped
4 garlic cloves, chopped
50 g (1¾ oz) seedless tamarind pulp
4 tablespoons sugar
2 tablespoons fish sauce
4 tablespoons roasted peanuts, finely crushed (page 328)
16 dried round rice paper wrappers (22 cm/8½ inch diameter)
1 bunch perilla, leaves picked
1 bunch mint, leaves picked
1 bunch Vietnamese fish mint, leaves picked
1 Lebanese (short) cucumber, halved crossways, then sliced into matchsticks
1 star fruit, halved, then thinly sliced
90 g (3¼ oz/1 cup) bean sprouts

Peel, devein and butterfly the prawns. Put the prawns and lemon juice in a non-metallic bowl and set the prawns aside to cure in the juice for 10 minutes.

In a food processor, put the chillies, garlic, tamarind, 3 tablespoons of the sugar and 1 tablespoon salt, and pulse until the ingredients are mixed well and a smooth paste forms.

In a bowl, combine the remaining sugar with 3 tablespoons of hot water, stirring until the sugar has dissolved. Add 1 tablespoon of the tamarind and chilli paste, the fish sauce and 2 tablespoons of the crushed peanuts, and mix well. Transfer to 4–6 small dipping bowls and set aside.

Gently squeeze out the excess lemon juice from the prawns; the prawns will have 'cooked' in the acid in the lemon juice. Add the prawns to the remaining tamarind and chilli paste, coating the prawns well.

Transfer the prawns to a serving platter and garnish them with the remaining crushed peanuts.

To assemble the rolls, fill a large bowl with warm water and dip one sheet of rice paper in the water until just softened, then lay it flat on a plate. Lay one prawn horizontally on the rice paper, approximately 4 cm (1½ inches) from the top. On top of the prawn, add some perilla, mint, Vietnamese mint, cucumber, star fruit and bean sprouts. To form the roll, fold the sides into the centre over the filling, then the bottom of the paper up and over. Roll from the bottom to top to form a tight roll. Serve the rolls with the dipping sauce.

MAKES 16 ROLLS

FAMILY SEAFOOD STEAMBOAT
LẨU HẢI SẢN

WE ALL SQUEEZE AROUND A SMALL WOODEN TABLE OUTSIDE MY FAMILY'S HOME. THE TABLE BELONGS TO A SOUP VENDER, AND WE WAIT PATIENTLY FOR HER TO SELL OUT OF HER SOUP BEFORE WE TAKE OVER. THE TABLE HAS A HOLE CUT OUT IN THE MIDDLE TO ALLOW THE COAL TO BURN. WE PLACE OUR STEAMBOAT POT ON TOP AND SURROUND IT WITH AN ARRAY OF FRESH SEAFOOD, VEGETABLES AND HERBS. THE STEAMBOAT BEGINS TO BOIL AND IN WE GO — CHOPSTICKS FLYING HERE AND THERE, EVERYONE DUNKING, DIPPING AND DEVOURING.

You'll need a portable gas stove for cooking at the table and a special steamboat hotpot or a large saucepan.

Put the rice vermicelli in a saucepan of boiling water and bring back to the boil. Cook for 5 minutes, then turn off the heat and leave in the water for 5 minutes. Drain the noodles, rinse under cold water, and set aside.

In a large saucepan, combine the chicken stock, 1 tablespoon salt, the sugar and fish sauce. Mix well and bring to the boil.

Place the gas stove and the steamboat hotpot or large saucepan in the middle of the dinner table. Transfer 2 litres (70 fl oz/8 cups) of the chicken stock mixture to the steamboat. On three separate platters, arrange the vegetables and herbs, seafood, and vermicelli. In small dipping bowls, add some sliced chilli and soy sauce for dipping.

When the stock starts to simmer, each person dips some greens and seafood into the stock until cooked. They then retrieve their cooked ingredients with their chopsticks, and ladle some stock into their bowls. As the greens and seafood cook, the more flavoursome the stock becomes. When the stock starts to boil down, replenish the pot with more stock.

SERVES 4-6

225 g (8 oz) dried rice vermicelli noodles
3 litres (105 fl oz/12 cups) chicken stock (page 328)
2 tablespoons sugar
2 tablespoons fish sauce
½ Chinese cabbage (wong bok), washed and sliced into 4 cm (1½ inch) pieces
1 bunch mustard greens, washed and sliced into 4 cm (1½ inch) pieces
1 bunch chrysanthemum leaves, washed and torn into 10 cm (4 inch) pieces
500 g (1 lb 2 oz) raw tiger prawns (shrimp), peeled and deveined
500 g (1 lb 2 oz) barramundi fillets, sliced into 5 mm (¼ inch) pieces
500 g (1 lb 2 oz) mussels
500 g (1 lb 2 oz) calamari
12 scallops, on the half-shell
4 bird's eye chillies, thinly sliced
125 ml (4 fl oz/½ cup) light soy sauce

CARAMELISED WHITEBAIT AND PORK BELLY HOTPOT
CÁ CƠM KHO TỘ

PUT SIMPLY, WHITEBAIT ARE YOUNG FISH. THEY ARE ONLY 2-5 CM (1-2 INCHES) IN LENGTH AND THE ENTIRE FISH IS EATEN — HEAD AND TAIL — AND THEY ARE NOT GUTTED. WHITEBAIT ARE TENDER WITH A SLIGHT CRUNCH, AND ARE VERY TASTY.

2 garlic cloves, finely chopped
2 tablespoons sugar
2 tablespoons fish sauce
1 teaspoon oyster sauce
½ teaspoon dark soy sauce
200 g (7 oz) small whitebait, rinsed and drained
100 g (3½ oz) boneless pork belly, cut into thin 2 x 3 cm (¾ x 1¼ inch) pieces
100 ml (3½ fl oz) chicken stock (page 328) or water
1 tablespoon garlic oil (page 329)
2 spring onions (scallions), sliced on the diagonal
2 bird's eye chillies, sliced

In a bowl, combine half the garlic, ½ teaspoon salt, the sugar, fish sauce, oyster sauce and dark soy sauce, stirring to dissolve the sugar. Add the whitebait, stir to coat, then set aside to marinate for 15 minutes.

Lay the pork belly pieces in the bottom of a clay pot or heavy-based saucepan, add the whitebait, then pour in the marinating liquid. Place the clay pot on the stovetop over high heat and bring to the boil. Add the chicken stock or water and return to the boil, skimming any impurities off the surface. Reduce the heat to low and simmer for 5 minutes, then add the remaining garlic and the garlic oil. Stir, then take off the heat.

Garnish with the spring onions and chilli and sprinkle with some freshly ground black pepper. Serve with jasmine rice.

SERVES 4-6 AS PART OF A SHARED MEAL

CRISP PRAWNS ROLLED IN YOUNG GREEN RICE FLAKES
TÔM CHIÊN CỐM

I WAS INTRODUCED TO GREEN RICE FLAKES FOR THE FIRST TIME IN PHAN THIET, WHEN WE ASKED A COOK FROM A LOCAL RESTAURANT TO MAKE SOMETHING UNUSUAL. HE COATED PIECES OF CUTTLEFISH WITH GREEN RICE FLAKES AND FLASH-FRIED THEM. GREEN RICE FLAKES ARE HARVESTED AS A YOUNG GRAIN, THEY ARE ROASTED AND THEN POUNDED WITH A HUGE WOODEN MORTAR, FLATTENING THE GRAIN AND REMOVING THE HUSKS. YOU CAN FIND THEM IN YOUR ASIAN MARKET. I BOUGHT A BAG OF THEM FROM THE MARKETS AND ASKED LOCALS WHAT OTHER DISHES I COULD USE THEM IN. THIS WAS MY FAVOURITE RECIPE.

Soak 18 bamboo skewers in cold water for 30 minutes to prevent them burning. Peel only the body of the prawns, leaving the heads and tails intact, then devein them. Insert a skewer under the tail of the prawn, through the body and into the head, making the prawn straight on the skewer. Repeat with all the prawns and skewers, using one skewer for each prawn, and positioning the prawn on the end of the skewer.

Dust the body of the prawns with the flour, shaking off the excess. Oil your hands and take a heaped tablespoon of fish paste; shape the paste around the body of the prawns (leaving the head and tail uncovered), pressing it tightly to coat the prawns evenly. Repeat this process with all the paste and prawns. Sprinkle the rice flakes on a flat tray and roll the prawns in the flakes, creating a thick coating of flakes around the fish paste.

Pour the oil into a wok or saucepan and heat to 180°C (350°F), or until a cube of bread dropped into the oil browns in 15 seconds. Add the prawns in batches and deep-fry for 2 minutes, or until crisp. Serve with the salt, pepper and lemon dipping sauce.

MAKES 18

18 raw large tiger prawns (shrimp)
75 g (2½ oz/½ cup) plain (all-purpose) flour
300 g (10½ oz) fish paste (page 334)
150 g (5½ oz) young green rice flakes
vegetable oil, for deep-frying
salt, pepper and lemon sauce (page 332), to serve

WHOLE FISH CHARGRILLED IN LOTUS LEAF
CÁ NƯỚNG LÁ SEN

THE LOTUS PLANT IS MY MAGICAL PLANT; IT CAPTURES MY ATTENTION AND ADMIRATION EVERY TIME I SEE IT POKING OUT OF ITS POND, WITH SUCH A VIBRANT DISPLAY OF COLOUR AND BEAUTY. WHILE I'M TAKEN BY ITS APPEARANCE, I'M ALSO AMAZED BY THE MANY WAYS IT IS USED IN VIETNAMESE COOKING: FROM PLUCKING ITS SEEDS FOR DESSERTS, TOSSING ITS ROOTS AND STEMS IN STIR-FRIES AND SALADS, TO USING ITS LEAVES FOR WRAPPING AND STEAMING. YOU CAN FIND DRIED LOTUS LEAVES AT YOUR ASIAN MARKET, OR YOU CAN USE BANANA LEAVES AS A SUBSTITUTE.

1–2 dried lotus leaves
1 whole fish (600 g/1 lb 5 oz), such as snapper or barramundi, cleaned
4 tablespoons Phu Quoc seafood sauce (page 334)
2 spring onions (scallions)
1 lime, thinly sliced

Soak the dried lotus leaves in hot water for 15 minutes to soften, then drain. Coat the fish with 2 tablespoons of the seafood sauce, and set aside to marinate for 10 minutes. Thinly slice the spring onions on the diagonal and put them in a bowl of water to soak.

Drain the fish well. Place the lime slices down each side of the fish, then place the fish in the centre of the lotus leaf. Wrap the fish up in the lotus leaf to cover completely, then seal both ends with toothpicks. (If the lotus leaf tears, use the second leaf as a backup.)

Heat a barbecue grill to high and chargrill the fish parcel on each side for 15 minutes, or until the fish is cooked through. Transfer the fish to a platter. Using kitchen scissors, cut through the lotus leaf down the middle, then open out the leaves like a parcel. Garnish with the spring onions and dress with the remaining seafood sauce. Serve with jasmine rice.

SERVES 4-6 AS PART OF A SHARED MEAL

SAUTEED KING PRAWNS IN COCONUT MILK
TÔM KHO NƯỚC DỪA

I AM IN MY HALF BROTHER'S FISHING BOAT, CHUGGING THROUGH THE WATERS OF PHAN THIET. WE ANCHOR UNDER A BRIDGE FOR SOME SHADE AND COOL BREEZE. HE FIRES UP SOME COAL AND SAUTES SOME PRAWNS IN COCONUT MILK IN AN OLD WARPED PAN, ON THE EDGE OF HIS BOAT. WE SHARE HALF A DOZEN BEERS TOGETHER, MAKING SMALL TALK AND ENJOYING THE CALMING SEA.

Peel only the body of the prawns, leaving the heads and tails intact, then devein them. In a small bowl, combine the fish sauce and sugar and stir until the sugar has dissolved. Divide the fish sauce mixture into two halves, and use one half of the mixture to marinate the prawns for 10 minutes.

Place a large frying pan over medium–high heat, add 1 tablespoon of the oil, then seal the prawns for 1 minute on each side. Remove the prawns and set aside.

Wipe the frying pan clean, return the pan to medium–high heat and add the remaining oil, the garlic and shallots and fry for 1 minute, or until fragrant. Add the coconut milk and remaining fish sauce mixture, and stir. Return the prawns to the pan, tossing them to coat in the sauce. When the liquid begins to boil, take the pan off the heat. Garnish with freshly ground black pepper, spring onion and chilli, and serve with jasmine rice.

SERVES 4-6 AS PART OF A SHARED MEAL

500 g (1 lb 2 oz) raw large tiger prawns (shrimp)
2 tablespoons fish sauce
1 tablespoon caster (superfine) sugar
2 tablespoons vegetable oil
1 tablespoon finely chopped garlic
2 red Asian shallots, finely chopped
250 ml (9 fl oz/1 cup) coconut milk
1 spring onion (scallion), sliced on the diagonal
1 long red chilli, julienned

BASIC RECIPES

CHICKEN STOCK
NƯỚC LÈO GÀ

6 garlic cloves
8 spring onions (scallions), white
    part only
1 whole chicken (1.6 kg/3 lb 8 oz)
4 cm (1½ inch) piece of ginger,
    sliced

Crush the garlic and spring onions into a paste using a mortar and pestle. Wash the chicken thoroughly under cold running water, making sure to remove all traces of blood, guts and fat from the cavity.

Put the chicken in a large saucepan or stockpot with 6 litres (210 fl oz/ 24 cups) of water and bring to the boil. Reduce the heat to a slow simmer and skim the surface for 10 minutes until you have removed most of the fat, then add the ginger and the garlic and spring onion paste. Cook for a further 2 hours, then strain and allow the stock to cool. Refrigerate for up to 3 days, or freeze until required.

MAKES ABOUT 5 LITRES (175 FL OZ/20 CUPS)

ROASTED PEANUTS
ĐẬU PHỌNG RANG

250 g (9 oz) unsalted raw, peeled
    peanuts

In a dry wok, stir-fry the peanuts over medium heat until the peanuts are cooked to a light brown colour. If the recipe asks for crushed roasted peanuts, this can be done using a mortar and pestle until coarsely ground. Store the roasted nuts in an airtight container for up to 2 weeks.

MAKES 250 G (9 OZ)

FRIED RED ASIAN SHALLOTS
HÀNH PHI

Peel and thinly slice the shallots and wash under cold water. Dry the shallots with a cloth, then set them aside on paper towel until completely dry.

Pour the oil into a wok and heat to 180°C (350°F), or until a cube of bread dropped into the oil browns in 15 seconds. Fry the shallots in small batches for 30–60 seconds, or until they turn golden brown and crisp, then remove with a slotted spoon. Drain on paper towel. The fried shallots are best eaten freshly fried, but will keep for up to 2 days in an airtight container.

MAKES 100 G (3½ OZ/1 CUP)

200 g (7 oz) red Asian shallots
1 litre (35 fl oz/4 cups) vegetable oil

FRIED GARLIC AND GARLIC OIL
TỎI PHI VÀ MỠ TỎI

Pour the oil into a wok and heat to 180°C (350°F), or until a cube of bread dropped into the oil browns in 15 seconds. Add the garlic to the oil and fry for 45–60 seconds, or until the garlic is golden, then strain through a metal sieve and place on paper towel to dry. Be careful not to overcook the garlic in the oil, as it continues to cook once it is removed from the wok. Reserve the garlic oil. Store the fried garlic in an airtight container for up to 4 days. The garlic oil will keep for up to 1 week in the fridge.

MAKES 2 TABLESPOONS FRIED GARLIC; 250 ML (9 FL OZ/1 CUP) GARLIC OIL

250 ml (9 fl oz/1 cup) vegetable oil
6 garlic cloves, finely chopped

SPRING ONION OIL
MỠ HÀNH

Put the oil and spring onions in a saucepan over medium heat. Cook the spring onions for about 2 minutes, or until the oil just starts to simmer, then remove the pan from the heat and allow to cool. Strain the oil into a jar. The spring onion oil will keep for up to 1 week in the fridge.

MAKES 250 ML (9 FL OZ/1 CUP)

250 ml (9 fl oz/1 cup) vegetable oil
6–8 spring onions (scallions), green part only, thinly sliced

MUM'S VINAIGRETTE DRESSING
DẦU DẤM

100 ml (3½ fl oz) white vinegar
2 teaspoons garlic oil (page 329)
75 g (2½ oz/⅓ cup) caster
   (superfine) sugar

Combine the vinegar, garlic oil, sugar and 2 tablespoons water in a bowl, and stir to dissolve the sugar. Season with a pinch of salt and freshly ground black pepper and stir to combine. Store in a jar in the fridge for up to 2 days.

MAKES ABOUT 250 ML (9 FL OZ/1 CUP)

AUNTY NINE'S SALAD DRESSING
DẦU DẤM DÌ CHÍN

4 tablespoons lemon juice
2 tablespoons caster (superfine)
   sugar
1 tablespoon fish sauce
2 garlic cloves, crushed
1 bird's eye chilli, finely chopped

Combine all the ingredients and ½ teaspoon freshly ground black pepper in a bowl and mix well. Store in a jar in the fridge for up to 2 days.

MAKES ABOUT 125 ML (4 FL OZ/½ CUP)

HOISIN DIPPING SAUCE
TƯƠNG NGỌT

125 ml (4 fl oz/½ cup) hoisin sauce
1½ tablespoons white vinegar
125 ml (4 fl oz/½ cup) milk
3 teaspoons roasted peanuts,
   crushed (page 328)
1 bird's eye chilli, thinly sliced

In a saucepan, combine the hoisin sauce and vinegar. Place the pan over medium heat and stir in the milk. Continue to stir until just before boiling point is reached, then remove from the heat and allow to cool. To serve, garnish with the peanuts and chilli. Store in a jar in the fridge for up to 1 week.

MAKES ABOUT 250 ML (9 FL OZ/1 CUP)

DIPPING FISH SAUCE
NƯỚC MẮM CHẤM

Combine the fish sauce, rice vinegar, sugar and 125 ml (4 fl oz/½ cup) of water in a saucepan and place over medium heat. Stir well and cook until just before boiling point is reached, then remove from the heat and allow to cool. To serve, add the garlic and chilli, then stir in the lime juice. Store, tightly sealed in a jar in the fridge, for up to 5 days.

MAKES ABOUT 250 ML (9 FL OZ/1 CUP)

3 tablespoons fish sauce
3 tablespoons rice vinegar
2 tablespoons sugar
2 garlic cloves, chopped
1 bird's eye chilli, thinly sliced
2 tablespoons lime juice

STICKY SOYA BEAN AND PORK DIPPING SAUCE
SỐT TƯƠNG CHẤM

Put the rice in a large bowl and cover with water. Set aside to soak for a few hours at room temperature, then drain. Line a bamboo or metal steamer with a piece of muslin and place over a saucepan of boiling water. Spread the rice onto the muslin, cover with the lid and steam over high heat for 20 minutes. Remove the steamer from the heat and set the rice aside, covered, for 10 minutes. Remove the lid and leave the rice to cool.

Heat the oil in a saucepan over medium–high heat. Add the garlic and cook, stirring, for 1 minute, or until fragrant, then add the pork and cook for another minute. Add the fermented soya beans, sesame seeds, peanuts, chilli, 125 ml (4 fl oz/½ cup) of water and the steamed rice. Bring to the boil, then reduce the heat to a low simmer for 5 minutes, stirring. Take off the heat and cool.

Once cooled, pour the sauce into a food processor and pulse until smooth. The sauce should be warmed before serving. Store any leftover sauce, covered and refrigerated, for up to 2 days.

MAKES 375 G (13 OZ/1½ CUPS)

50 g (1¾ oz/¼ cup) white sticky (glutinous) long-grain rice
2 tablespoons vegetable oil
1 garlic clove, finely chopped
100 g (3½ oz) minced pork
100 g (3½ oz) fermented soya beans, crushed
1 tablespoon toasted sesame seeds, crushed
2 tablespoons roasted peanuts, crushed (page 328)
1 bird's eye chilli, finely chopped

PRESERVED BEAN CURD DIPPING SAUCE
NƯỚC CHẤM CHAO

200 g (7 oz) preserved white
   bean curd
2 tablespoons preserved bean
   curd liquid
2 tablespoons lemon juice
4 tablespoons caster (superfine)
   sugar
1 lemongrass stem, white part only,
   finely chopped
2 bird's eye chillies, finely chopped

Put the bean curd in a bowl and mash with a fork. Add the remaining ingredients and stir well to dissolve the sugar. Store in an airtight container in the fridge for up to 1 week.

MAKES 375 ML (13 FL OZ/1½ CUPS)

SALT, PEPPER AND LEMON SAUCE
MUỐI TIÊU CHANH

1 tablespoon sea salt
2 tablespoons white peppercorns
2 lemons, juiced

Heat a small frying pan over medium heat, add the sea salt and peppercorns and dry-roast until fragrant. Remove and cool. Using a mortar and pestle, finely grind the sea salt and peppercorns or use an electric spice grinder. Mix the salt and pepper with the lemon juice. Use immediately as a dipping sauce for steamed crabs or grilled lobster or prawns.

MAKES ABOUT 80 ML (2½ FL OZ/⅓ CUP)

TAMARIND WATER
NƯỚC ME

250 g (9 oz) seedless tamarind
   pulp
750 ml (26 fl oz/3 cups) boiling
   water

Put the tamarind pulp in a heatproof container and pour over the boiling water. Once it is cool enough to handle, break the pulp up with your hands, then pass the mixture through a sieve, to make a smooth paste.
   Tamarind water will keep, in an airtight container in the fridge, for up to 1 month. Add to soups, curries, sauces or stir-fries.

MAKES 750 ML (26 FL OZ/3 CUPS)

LEMON-FISH DIPPING SAUCE
NƯỚC MẮM CHẤM CHANH ỚT

In a bowl, combine the sugar and fish sauce, stirring until the sugar has dissolved. Add the lemon juice, garlic and chilli and stir to combine. Store in a jar in the fridge for up to 3 days.

MAKES 250 ML (9 FL OZ/1 CUP)

5 tablespoons caster (superfine) sugar
4 tablespoons fish sauce
3 tablespoons lemon juice
4 garlic cloves, crushed
2 bird's eye chillies

ANCHOVY AND PINEAPPLE SAUCE
MẮM NÊM

Put the sugar in a bowl with the boiling water and stir until dissolved. Allow to cool, then combine with the rest of the ingredients and mix well. Store in a jar in the fridge for up to 3 days.

MAKES 125 ML (4 FL OZ/½ CUP)

1 tablespoon sugar
2 tablespoons boiling water
1 tablespoon fermented anchovy sauce
2 tablespoons unsweetened pineapple juice
1 tablespoon crushed fresh pineapple
1 teaspoon finely sliced lemongrass, white part only
1 garlic clove, crushed
1 bird's eye chilli, finely sliced

PHU QUOC SEAFOOD SAUCE
SỐT ĐỒ BIỂN PHÚ QUỐC

3 tablespoons olive oil
1 garlic clove, finely chopped
2 cm (¾ inch) piece of ginger,
    peeled and finely chopped
½ lemongrass stem, white part
    only, finely chopped
2 spring onions (scallions),
    thinly sliced
4 red Asian shallots, finely chopped
2 teaspoons fish sauce
1 teaspoon sugar
1 bird's eye chilli, finely chopped
¼ teaspoon ground turmeric
juice of ½ lime
2 tablespoons chopped dill

Heat the olive oil in a saucepan over medium heat. Add the garlic, ginger, lemongrass, spring onions and shallots and fry until fragrant. Reduce the heat to low and add the fish sauce, sugar, chilli and turmeric and stir for 1 minute, then add the lime juice and dill. Remove from the heat and set aside to cool. Store in a jar in the fridge for up to 1 week.

MAKES ABOUT 125 ML (4 FL OZ/½ CUP)

FISH PASTE
CHẢ CÁ

1 middle-cut Spanish mackerel
    cutlet (300 g/10½ oz)
1 garlic clove, finely chopped
2 spring onions (scallions), white
    part only, thinly sliced
2 teaspoons fish sauce

Clean any blood from the cutlet, then remove the skin and bones. Cut the flesh into small pieces and transfer to a mortar along with the garlic, spring onions and ½ teaspoon each of salt and freshly ground black pepper.

Pour the fish sauce into a small bowl. Dip the pestle into the fish sauce and pound the fish, returning the pestle to the fish sauce when the fish begins to stick to it. Repeat this process until you have used all the fish sauce and the fish has formed a fine paste and the texture is very elastic; this process takes about 10 minutes.

Use the paste to make about 16–20 fish balls, which can be used in noodle soups or to make fried fish cakes. To make fish balls, use two oiled teaspoons to shape the paste into small oval-shaped mounds (called quenelles), or simply use your hands to mould the fish into small balls (lightly oil your hands first to prevent the fish paste sticking to them).

MAKES 300 G (10½ OZ), OR 16-20 FISH BALLS

NOTE You can use a small food processor to make the fish paste if you prefer, however you will get a better texture if you make the paste using a mortar and pestle.

PICKLED VEGETABLES
ĐỒ CHUA

In a saucepan, combine the rice vinegar, sugar and 1 tablespoon salt, stir well and bring to the boil. Remove from the heat and set aside to cool.

Cut the cucumbers in half lengthways and scrape out the seeds with a spoon. Cut the cucumber, carrot, daikon and celery into 5 cm x 5 mm (2 x ¼ inch) batons. Combine the lemon wedges with the vegetables and place in a 1 litre (35 fl oz/4 cup) plastic or glass container. Pour the cooled pickling liquid over the vegetables to completely submerge them. Cover with a lid, place in the fridge and allow to pickle for 3 days before use. Store any leftover pickled vegetables in the fridge for up to 1 week.

MAKES 800 G (1 LB 12 OZ)

625 ml (21 ½ fl oz/2½ cups) rice vinegar
440 g (15½ oz/2 cups) sugar
2 Lebanese (short) cucumbers
1 carrot
1 small daikon
1 celery stalk
½ lemon, cut into thin wedges

PICKLED MUSTARD GREENS
DƯA CẢI CHUA

Cut the mustard greens in half lengthways, then cut into 5 cm (2 inch) long pieces and wash thoroughly. Blanch in boiling water for 30 seconds, then refresh in iced water and place in a colander to drain.

In a saucepan, combine 1.5 litres (52 fl oz/6 cups) of water, the sugar and 2½ tablespoons salt, and stir until boiling, then turn off the heat and allow to cool.

Clean and cut the spring onions into 5 cm (2 inch) long pieces, then mix evenly with the mustard greens and place in a 2 litre (70 fl oz/8 cup) storage container. Pour the cooled pickling liquid over the vegetables, making sure they are completely submerged. Cover with a lid, place in the fridge and allow to pickle for at least 1 week before use. Store any leftover pickled mustard greens in the fridge for up to 1 week.

MAKES 1 KG (2 LB 4 OZ)

1 kg (2 lb 4 oz) mustard greens
1 tablespoon sugar
8 spring onions (scallions)

SAPA SESAME SALT
MUỐI VỪNG SAPA

1 tablespoon sea salt
1 teaspoon ground white pepper
3 tablespoons toasted sesame
  seeds
2 tablespoons roasted peanuts,
  crushed (page 328)
2 teaspoons galangal powder
2 teaspoons sugar

Combine all the ingredients in a small bowl, mixing well. Transfer to an airtight jar and use for dipping grilled meats or to season jasmine rice. Store in a container in the pantry for 2 weeks.

MAKES ABOUT 100 G (3½ OZ)

PORK TERRINE
CHẢ LỤA

1 tablespoon sea salt
1 kg (2 lb 4 oz) pork leg, minced
  (ask your butcher to mince the
  pork finely)
2½ tablespoons fish sauce
1 large banana leaf

Dry-roast the sea salt in a dry wok for a few minutes over medium heat until aromatic. Place the pork, salt and fish sauce in a food processor and pulse until it forms a very fine paste.

Soak the banana leaf in hot water for 5 minutes, dry and lay it flat on the work surface. Cut the leaf in half and cross one piece over the other. Place the pork paste in the centre and draw up all sides to form a tight parcel. Secure with string and cook in a large saucepan of simmering salted water for 1 hour. Remove from the pan, allow to cool, then remove the banana leaf and slice the pork when needed. Refrigerate for up to 1 week.

MAKES 1 KG (2 LB 4 OZ)

NOTE You can freeze leftover pork terrine in small portions to use for next time, or use as a filling for Vietnamese baguettes.

DAD'S SPICY SATE SAUCE
SỐT SA-TẾ

Put the dried shrimp in a bowl, cover with water and soak for 20 minutes, then drain. Pound the shrimp using a mortar and pestle until crushed, then set aside.

Heat the oil in a wok over medium heat, add the garlic and spring onions and fry until fragrant. Now add the crushed shrimp, crabmeat, brown sugar, oyster sauce, fish sauce, chilli flakes and 1 teaspoon salt. Stir to combine, then reduce the heat to a low simmer for 30 minutes, stirring every 5 minutes. Add the chilli oil, stir and simmer for a further 5 minutes.

Use this spicy saté sauce as a dipping sauce for noodle soups or add it to stir-fries. The sauce will keep, refrigerated, for up to 2 weeks. Bring to room temperature before using.

MAKES 625 ML (21 FL OZ/2½ CUPS)

100 g (3½ oz/1 cup) dried shrimp
500 ml (17 fl oz/2 cups) vegetable oil
4 garlic cloves, finely chopped
10 spring onions (scallions), white part only, sliced
200 g (7 oz) crabmeat (bought ready-picked from your fishmonger)
2 teaspoons soft brown sugar
1 tablespoon oyster sauce
2 teaspoons fish sauce
25 g (1 oz) chilli flakes
100 ml (3½ fl oz) chilli oil

SWEET COCONUT MILK
NƯỚC CỐT DỪA

Combine the tapioca flour with 2½ tablespoons of water in a small bowl. Stir to form a smooth paste, then set aside.

In a small saucepan over low heat, add the coconut milk, sugar, pandan leaf and ¼ teaspoon salt. Stir in the flour mixture, and continue to stir until the coconut milk begins to thicken and is heated through, then take off the heat, discarding the pandan leaf.

Use the sweet coconut milk to pour on top of any sweet pudding. Store in the fridge for up to 2 days.

MAKES ABOUT 375 ML (13 FL OZ/1½ CUPS)

1 tablespoon tapioca flour or potato starch
300 ml (10½ fl oz) coconut milk
50 g (1¾ oz) sugar
1 pandan leaf, knotted

GLOSSARY

AMARANTH
These are known as *rau den* in Vietnamese but also called Chinese spinach, African spinach or Indian spinach. There are many varieties, but go for the thick-stemmed ones with red and green leaves.

ASIAN CELERY
Also called Chinese celery, these have thin, hollow stalks and a stronger taste and smell than ordinary celery. Use in stir-fries and soups or blanch and use in salads. Buy bunches with firm stems.

BAMBOO SHOOTS
These are the young edible shoots of the bamboo tree. They are sold whole or sliced in tins or in sealed bags sitting in water. Rinse well and drain before use.

BITTER MELON
Similar to a pale green cucumber but covered in a bumpy skin. Blanch the flesh in boiling water or degorge before use to reduce bitterness.

CASSAVA
Cassava is a starchy root vegetable with brown skin and white flesh. Fresh cassava is available in most Asian markets. If it is out of season, buy frozen cassava; this has already been peeled.

COCONUT WATER
Young coconut water is the liquid found in young green coconuts. This is sold as a liquid in tins from Asian markets and is sometimes labelled as coconut juice.

DRIED MUNG BEANS
Dried green mung beans with the skins removed are yellow. Buy peeled mung beans from Asian markets. They need to be soaked, then are boiled or steamed.

DRIED SHRIMP
Dried shrimp are shrimp that have been sun-dried for 2–3 days until they shrink to the size of your fingernail. There are many dried shrimp varieties, which you can use as flavourings in soups, salads, stir-fries and sauces. The flavour is strong, and they should be soaked for at least 20 minutes before use. Buy dried shrimp at your Asian market, in the dry goods section.

FISH SAUCE
A pungent, salty liquid used widely in Vietnamese cooking as a condiment and flavouring. When using fish sauce as a dipping sauce, use a good-quality fish sauce such as the Viet Huong brand. When using fish sauce in stocks and marinades, use a brand such as Squid.

GALANGAL
Similar in appearance and preparation to its close relative ginger, galangal is slightly pinker in colour and has a distinctive peppery flavour. It tends to be a bit woodier than ginger, so you need to grate or chop it finely before use. Choose galangal with the pinker stems, as these are fresher than the browner ones.

HAIRY MELON
Also known as hairy gourd, fuzzy gourd or hairy cucumber. It is light green in colour and is covered with small downy hairs. Scrub the melon to remove the hairs, then use as directed in the recipe.

HERBS
Vietnamese cooking is renowned for its use of fresh herbs. Look for them in your local Vietnamese or Asian market, as there is really no substitute for their unique flavour and aroma.

Asian basil (*rau que* or *hung que*): Also known as Thai basil or Asian sweet basil, this has purplish stems, green leaves and a sweet aniseed aroma and flavour.

Perilla (*tia to*): This broad-leafed herb is related to mint, and can be red or purplish green in colour. It is similar to Japanese shiso.

Rice paddy herb (*ngo om*): This aromatic small-leafed herb grows in rice fields. It has a citrusy aroma and flavour, and is used in soups or seafood dishes.

Sawtooth herb (*ngo gai*): Also known as sawtooth coriander or long coriander, this herb has slender, long green leaves with serrated edges. It has a strong coriander-like flavour, and is often used as a garnish for soups.

Vietnamese fish mint (*rau diep ca*): This is only available in Vietnamese markets; the leaves are heart-shaped, and it has a bold fishy flavour.

Vietnamese mint (*rau ram*): This herb has narrow pointed and pungent-tasting leaves.

JICAMA

Pronounced hee-kam-mah, this bulb-like root vegetable has crisp white flesh and a dusty brown skin, which is peeled before use. Unlike its relative the potato, it can be eaten raw, and can be used in salads, stir-fries and to make chips.

KAFFIR LIME LEAVES

These fragrant uniquely double-shaped leaves are added to soups and salads to give them a wonderful aroma and tangy flavour. Kaffir leaves, also called makrut leaves, are sold fresh and dried from Asian markets. I use fresh leaves in my recipes.

PALM SUGAR

A dark, unrefined sugar, palm sugar (jaggery) is widely used in Southeast Asian cooking, not only in sweet dishes but to balance the flavours in savoury dishes. Buy in blocks or jars from the Asian market. The easiest way to use it is to shave the sugar from the cake with a sharp knife, or to grate it. I prefer the light yellow or pale brown sugar from Vietnam or Thailand.

PANDAN LEAVES

Also called pandanus leaves, these long, flat emerald-green leaves are used for the wonderful fragrance they give to dishes, both sweet and savoury. Tie the leaves into a knot so they easily fit into the pot, and remove before serving. The fresh leaves are sold in bundles from your Asian market.

PEANUTS

An important ingredient in Vietnamese cooking, used in sauces, salads or as a garnish. The peanuts I use in my recipes are shelled and skinned raw peanuts. These are then roasted (page 328). Once opened, store in the fridge and use within 3 months.

PRESERVED BEAN CURD

Also called fermented bean curd, these are cubes of bean curd (tofu) that have been preserved in rice wine, and you can find different varieties such as white or red bean curd marinated in sesame oil or chilli. Buy in jars from your Asian market.

RICE FLOUR

Ground from long-grain rice, these flours are used to make noodles, rice cakes and food wrappers. Don't confuse ordinary rice flour with glutinous rice flour, as they are different. Glutinous rice flour is sweeter and is made from glutinous short-grain rice; the flour turns firm and sticky when cooked.

SHAOXING RICE WINE

Also called Chinese rice wine, this is made from rice, millet and Shaoxing's local water. Aged wines are served warm as a drink in China, and the younger wines are used in cooking.

SHRIMP PASTE

Made from fermented shrimp that are ground, salted and dried, then bottled or compressed into a hard block. While it does have a very strong aroma, shrimp paste adds depth of flavour and fragrance to your dish. Buy shrimp paste from your Asian market. I prefer the soft variety, not the hard one, and I like to use Lee Kum Kee brand.

SOY SAUCE

Soy sauce is a naturally brewed liquid made from fermented soya beans mixed with wheat, water and salt. Dark soy sauce is less salty, thicker and darker than light soy sauce, because it has been fermented for longer. Light soy sauce has a light, delicate flavour, but is saltier than dark soy, and is often used as a dipping sauce. It may be labelled as superior soy sauce or simply as soy sauce.

TAMARIND

This is used as a souring agent, adding tartness to dishes. Buy tamarind pulp from Asian markets packaged as a wet block. Cut off a little from the block and mix it with hot water. Use your hands to mash the pulp up, as mashing it with a fork won't do the job very effectively.

TAPIOCA FLOUR

This may also be labelled as tapioca starch. Tapioca flour is made from the cassava plant and is used as a thickening agent or to dust food before frying. Use the leftover flour in baked goods: it will give a crisp, chewy texture to the end result.

WATER DROPWORT

The variety I use here is the edible kind, not the poisonous kind. It is also known as water celery, as their leaves have a similar shape to celery; they taste similar to watercress and parsley combined. Buy water dropwort from Asian markets.

INDEX

Published in 2009 by Murdoch Books Pty Limited

Murdoch Books Australia
Pier 8/9, 23 Hickson Road
Millers Point NSW 2000
Phone: +61 (0) 2 8220 2000
Fax: +61 (0) 2 8220 2558
www.murdochbooks.com.au

Murdoch Books UK Limited
Erico House, 6th Floor
93–99 Upper Richmond Road
Putney, London SW15 2TG
Phone: +44 (0) 20 8785 5995
Fax: +44 (0) 20 8785 5985
www.murdochbooks.co.uk

Publisher: Jane Lawson
Designer: Sarah Odgers
Editor: Kim Rowney
Photographers: Alan Benson; front cover, all recipes and location shots, except for pages specified.
  Suzanna Boyd; 1, 2, 3, 6, 8–9, 10–11, 16–17, 21, 22–23, 36–37, 48–49, 100–101, 102,
  109, 160–161, 194–195, 301, inside front cover, inside back cover, back cover.
Food stylist: Luke Nguyen
Food Editor: Leanne Kitchen
Production: Kita George

National Library of Australia Cataloguing-in-Publication entry
Author: Nguyen, Luke
Title: The songs of Sapa: stories and recipes from Vietnam/Luke Nguyen.
ISBN: 9781741964653 (hbk.)
Subjects: Cookery.
Notes: Includes index.
Subjects: Cookery, Vietnamese.
  Vietnam–Description and travel.
Dewey Number: 641.59597
A catalogue record for this book is available from the British Library.

Vietnamese translation and typesetting: All Language Typesetters and Printers Pty Ltd.
Colour separation by Splitting Image Colour Studio, Melbourne, Australia.
Printed in 2009 in China.

OVEN GUIDE: You may find cooking times vary depending on the oven you are using. For fan-forced
ovens, as a general rule, set the oven temperature to 20°C (35°F) lower than indicated in the recipe.